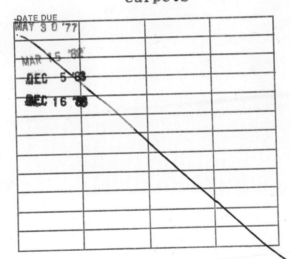

ORIENTAL RUGS
AND
CARPETS

PLATE I.   Medallion Rug of Silk, First Half Sixteenth Century.   Probably woven
at Kashan, Persia

Joseph E. Widener Collection, National Gallery, Washington, D.C.

ORIENTAL RUGS

AND
CARPETS

A COMPREHENSIVE STUDY

by

ARTHUR URBANE DILLEY

REVISED BY MAURICE S. DIMAND
Curator of Near Eastern Art, Metropolitan Museum of Art

J. B. LIPPINCOTT COMPANY
PHILADELPHIA   NEW YORK

Fourth Printing

Copyright © 1959 by Maurice S. Dimand

Copyright 1931 by Charles Scribner's Sons

Renewal Copyright 1959 by Arthur Urbane Dilley

Revised Edition

Printed in the United States of America

Library of Congress Catalog Card Number 59-13247

ISBN–0–397–00110–X

TO THE CLASS OF 1897

HARVARD COLLEGE

INTRODUCTION

JUST as each summer sunset, notable for beauty, is indubitably, we are told, the work of a famous Chinese painter gone to his reward of immortality, so this narrative of oriental rugs is just another painting of a beautiful subject, limitless as a sunset, done to grace perchance a fleeting moment of attention.

Beauty of rugs, as of sunsets, is seen usually with no depth of comprehension and registered in the memory, if at all, only by the faintest imprint. Forever we catch glimpses of beauty, lose the grandeur we dimly discern, and retain the sediment of our experience. Obviously we are mortals, and attain to the summits of understanding and recollection which the gods once enjoyed, only after arduous ascent of steep and difficult slopes.

Knowledge of oriental rugs is said to be particularly difficult of attainment because of the abstract character of expression which, except for the rugs of China and mediæval India, the art indulges. If this is true, the elusive and superior spirit that permeates it is all the more worthy of a vain attempt at capture. Herein is such an attempt. Herein is an interpretation,—the first to be undertaken,—of the spirit of rugs as revealed by the record of national personality.

The historical Asiatic scene depicted is an augmented adaptation of the colorful materials compounded with rarest skill and vast labor by Edward Granville Browne, in his superb *Literary History of Persia*, and by Stanley Lane-Poole, in *Mediæval India* and the *Story of Turkey*. Equally this writing owes unpayable but acknowledged debt to the scholarly books of Riegl, Martin, Bode, Kendrick and Tattersall,

INTRODUCTION

Sarre and Trenkwald, Jacoby, Mumford, Hawley and Hartley Clark, whose primacy as expositors of the art can never be contested; and to the catalogues and monographs of Valentiner, Breck and Morris, Pope, Riefstahl and Dimand.

Keen appreciation for valuable assistance is gratefully acknowledged to Mr. Frederick Moore, for data used in the chapter on Chinese Rugs; to Professor Nicholas Martinovitch of Columbia University, for classical allusions in "Rugs Have a Beginning"; and to a host of persistently helpful friends of long oriental experience, whose names are omitted only because they are too numerous to inscribe. "Of everything that is done in his town, the oriental has an inkling." My indebtedness to him is incalculable. Acknowledgment and thanks are tendered the Metropolitan Museum of Art, Mr. Joseph E. Widener, Mr. Henry F. Du Pont, Mr. James W. Barney, and Mr. Mitchell Samuels for permission and assistance to record, in color, intimation of the beauty of important rugs; to the American Art Association, for some helpful rug plates; and to the Near East Foundation, for some interesting pictures. Treasured most, as the source of the will to undertake and complete a strenuous task, is the subsidy of affection and encouragement provided by the family circle.

From the reader the author begs indulgence for errors of knowledge and judgment unavoidable in so extensive an exploration of so human a subject.

ARTHUR URBANE DILLEY.

New York City,
September 22, 1931.

ACKNOWLEDGMENT

For courteous permission to quote from the following works the author makes grateful acknowledgment to their respective publishers: Joseph Arthur, Comte de Gobineau, *Five Oriental Tales*, The Viking Press; E. G. Browne, *A Year Among the Persians*, The Macmillan Co.; Harold Lamb, *Genghis Khan, Emperor of All Men*, Robert McBride & Co.; Arthur Waley, *170 Chinese Poems*, Alfred A. Knopf; Ella C. and P. M. Sykes, *Through Deserts and Oases of Central Asia*, The Macmillan Co.; C. M. Doughty, *Travels in Arabia Deserta*, Horace Liveright; C. P. Skrine, *Chinese Central Asia*, The Houghton Mifflin Co.; Stanley Lane-Poole, *Mediæval India*, also his *The Story of Turkey*, G. P. Putnam's Sons; V. Sackville-West, *Passenger to Teheran*, Doubleday, Doran & Co.

CONTENTS

CONTENTS

ILLUSTRATIONS

In Color and Black and White

ILLUSTRATIONS

ILLUSTRATIONS

ILLUSTRATIONS

ILLUSTRATIONS

ILLUSTRATIONS

ILLUSTRATIONS

ILLUSTRATIONS

ILLUSTRATIONS

MAPS

xxi

ORIENTAL RUGS
AND
CARPETS

CHAPTER I

RUGS HAVE A BEGINNING

LONG before men built cities and empires, human beings rising from the soil of Asia devised the essential paraphernalia of existence. Among the many things they did was to rub one material against another. Rubbing flint against wood they made fire, fibre against fibre yarn, and plants against yarn stain, the first process of dye. Interlocking and knotting, the next stages of putting two and two together, produced for floors, walls, couches, doorways and animals textile coverings which originally were all one and the same fabric. The large reed mats decorated with design of dyed woollen thread, used to-day by the Pamir Kirghiz tribes, are an interesting survival of one of the early stages of composition.

Oriental rugs are the invention of shepherd tribes, whose descendants created villages and cities, monarchies and empires, which were made resplendent by natural growth and refinement of the art learned on hills and plains. The people of the later Stone Age, congregated along the Tigris, Euphrates and Nile Rivers, used rugs. The problem as to which of these settlements used them first, or whether they were concurrently conceived, is purely archæological. Expert opinion now favors the Mesopotamian civilization, and lay opinion heartily concurs because of proximity of the materials which are indispensable to the art.

The historical period of oriental rugs begins with the Assyrian and Babylonian Empires. Wall reliefs found in the excavations at Quyun-

I

djik and Khorsabad, site of the city of Sargon II, King of Assyria 722-705 B.C., perpetuate the forms of rugs elaborately designed in native geometric and floral manner. Similar rugs depicted on the enamelled wall tiles from the palace of Rameses II, Egyptian monarch 1300 B.C., indicate importation from Assyria; and discoveries made in the tombs of the fifth dynasty at Sakkara, near Memphis, show clearly the influence of Assyrian rugs on native Egyptian rug weaving, practised probably in Memphis and Thebes.

Ancient reputation for rugs rests exclusively with Babylon. All the classic world knew and admired Babylonian carpets. Pliny in his *Natural History* praised them, and Metellus Scipio wrote that Babylonian rugs, used for table coverings, were sold for the equivalent of thirty-two thousand dollars, and that "in our days Nero paid for them four million sesterces," or one hundred and sixty thousand dollars. Babylonian weaving, transported to Tyre and Sidon, became the source of the famous Hebrew tabernacle embellishments recorded in the Book of Exodus:

"Moreover, thou [Moses] shalt make ten curtains; with cherabim of cunning work shalt thou make them. . . . And thou shalt make curtains of goats' hair to be a covering upon the tabernacle. . . . And thou shalt make a hanging for the door of the tent of blue and purple and scarlet, wrought with needle work. . . . And for the gate of the court shall be a hanging of twenty cubits, and beneath upon the hem of it thou shalt make pomegranates of blue and of purple and of scarlet." These were elaborate weavings, and in the all-inclusive oriental meaning, they were rugs.

Persia under Cyrus the Great conquered Babylon in the year 538 B.C. and appropriated the arts of the city. "The sepulchre of Cyrus, in the centre of the royal gardens at Pasargadæ, was covered with the richest artistic textiles of Babylon, and purple carpets." Thereafter Persia was the textile dictator of the world, acknowledged by Egypt as the successor of Assyria, and Persian designs of animals the new style of ornamentation employed by the rug weavers of Alexandria.

Reference to Persian-Alexandrian "belluata tapetia" is made by Athenæus, the Greek philosopher, who records "carpets embroidered with figures of animals" as part of the procession of Ptolemy Philadelphus in the year 250 B.C. Equally interesting is the reference in a play by Plautus (184 B.C.), in which the comedian says: "I'll make your sides to be right thoroughly marked with thongs, so much so that not even Campanian coverlets are colored as well, nor yet Alexandrian tapestry of purple embroidered with beasts all over."

About one hundred and forty years after Persia had conquered Babylon, Xenophon records in the *Anabasis* an interesting item of Persian rugs in the experience of Timasion, one of his fellow generals, who possessed Persian carpets salvaged from the expedition. Seuthes, a rich Thracian, wishing to obtain the fabrics, invited Timasion to dine with him. Timasion accepted the invitation, knowing fully the obligation of making a gift to his host, and, drinking to Seuthes, "made him a present of a silver cup and a carpet worth ten minæ" (one hundred and eighty dollars).

The peoples of Asia Minor derived the art of rugs either from Babylon or from the common nomad source, or from both. Miletus, famous city of Ionia, owes an immortality in rugs to Aristophanes, 400 B.C., who in the *Frogs* has Dionysus say:

> "Truly an exquisite joke 'twould be,
> Him with a dancing-girl to see,
> Lolling at ease on Milesian rugs."

The rugs of Sardis, capital of Lydia, have their historian in Athenæus, who mentions both "a certain young man who used out of his preposterous luxury to lie on a couch covered with a smooth Sardian carpet," and a Persian king "who used to go on foot through the hall of the Melophori, very fine Sardian carpets being spread in his road, on which no one but the king ever trod." Caparisons for horses and covers for divans and tables are mentioned in the Edict of Diocletian, 300 A.D., as being woven in Cappadocia and Pontus; and rug designs on the façade of the tombs in Phrygia indicate that the art was there practised.

Throughout the ages the Orient has indulged the luxury of rugs. Homer's hardy heroes seemingly used plain rugs, dyed in a single hue. The bed of Priam was adorned with "fair, purple coverlets." "Divine Achilles (and his friends) upon chairs repose their limbs, their feet on purple carpets." The modern practice of plain carpeting has both ancient and honorable antecedent, regardless of the sentiments of artists.

Rugs greatly under oriental influence through close commercial relations were made in Corinth, Syracuse and Carthage. Silius Italicus compares the textiles of Syracuse with those of Babylon and asserts them equally "famous and celebrated." Ten African rugs, meaning Carthaginian, are tabulated in the *Historia Augusta Vitæ Aureliani* with ten male mantles.

The method of rug weaving in early times, depicted on ancient vases, is described by Ovid (43 B.C.-18 A.D.) in the *Metamorphoses*. Minerva engages Arachne in a contest of weaving skill:

> "Each her station straight assumes,
> Tightens each web; each slender thread prepares.
> Firm to beam the fabric is fixed; the reed
> The warp divides, with pointed shuttle swift
> Gliding between; which quick their fingers throw,
> Quick extricate, and with the toothy comb
> Firm pressed between the warp, the threads unite.
> In slender threads they twist
> The pliant gold and in the web display,
> Each as she works, an ancient story fair."

Theoretically, the product of this weaving was flat-surfaced, and would be classified by us as khilim or tapestry. Of the classic writers only Herodotus drops a remark that suggests the fabrication of knotted carpets. "The Egyptians," says he, "have adopted customs and usages in almost every respect different from the rest of mankind. Among them the women attend markets and traffic, but the men stay at home and weave. Other nations in weaving throw the wool upwards; the Egyptians downwards." That the male Egyptian labored prodigiously upon the loom is recorded by an unknown poet: "The weaver inside the house is more wretched than a woman. His knees are at the place of his heart. He has not tasted the air. Should he have done but a little in a day of his weaving, he is dragged as a lily in a pool. He gives bread to the porter at the door, that he may be allowed to see the light."

In the use of rugs the early East was infinitely more prodigal than the West. Xenophon in his romance *Cyropædia* says: "Of Persian luxury I wish to give you some illustrations. In the first place it is not sufficient for them to have soft couches spread for them, but they place the feet of their couches upon carpets, that the floor may offer no hard resistance, but that the carpets may yield."

Greek practice, as represented by Æschylus (500 B.C.) in the tragedy of *Agamemnon*, was hardier and more considerate of the prerogatives of the gods:

Clytemnestra: "But now I pray thee, my dear lord, descend from this chariot, not placing on the ground, O King, thy foot which laid Ilion low. Let the way of entrance be instantly covered with purple."

Agamemnon: "We ought to honor the gods with such gifts. I bid you honor me as a man, not as a god. Without tapestry for the feet or the embroidered woof, Fame proclaims my glory."

Only after the Macedonian conquest of Asia did the Persian custom of dining upon carpets become the practice of the Hellenic world; and only after the Roman conquest of Greece was the art carried to Rome. "The men of the army (returning from Greece) first brought

to Rome rich tapestry, with hangings and other works of the loom."
Later, Roman soldiers returned from Asia Minor burdened with oriental loot. But in Rome, as in America some decades ago, followers
of the old manners disdained the barbarian rugs. According to Plu-
tarch: "Cato himself informs us that having gotten among some goods,
to which he was heir, a piece of Babylonian tapestry, he immediately
sold it." In a brief time, however, oriental tapestries decorated the
coffins of Roman emperors.

The Romans used both geometric and floral forms interchangeably
for rugs and mosaic floors; animal forms rarely were employed. The
famous mosaic floor of Palestrina, near Rome, depicting the camel,
hippopotamus and crocodile of the Nile, and a few minor works of
similar character, are simulated in classical Western weaving only by
fragments of early Greek textiles, portraying ducks and the heads of
deer, unearthed from the sandy tumulus of southern Russia by recent
archæologists. The early Orient seemingly made no similar discrimi-
nation, and the later Orient executed figure subjects in silks, brocades
and rugs as well as in the wall paintings and enamelled tiles of palaces.
Achievements and amusements of rulers, and the events of war, were
the popular subjects.

Of great importance to us are fragments of pre-Islamic rugs exca-
vated in Syria and Egypt. A fragment of a pile rug in the Metropolitan
Museum of Art, found in Antinoë in Upper Egypt, has a geometrical
and floral design inspired by Roman and early Christian mosaic pavements. The rug had a field with several rectangles and a double
border. The vine scroll of the border recalls the polychrome Coptic
tapestries of the V and VI centuries. The technique of this rug is different from the true knotted rugs. It was developed from the well-
known Coptic technique of loop weaving. The pile was produced by
cutting each row of loops.

Le Coq, on his expedition into Chinese Turkestan, discovered in

6

ruins of the fifth or sixth century a fragment of a rug constructed with knots each tied upon a single warp. This method was employed in weaving the early rugs of Spain, intact examples of which come down to us from the thirteenth or fourteenth century. One of five fragments of early Egyptian rugs disinterred in old Cairo, now exhibited by the Metropolitan Museum of Art and assigned to the twelfth century, is constructed in similar manner. The inference that knotting was begun on a single warp is not without justification; and the belief that the art originated in central Asia is supported by the discoveries made by Sir Aurel Stein in Chinese Turkestan and by Colonel Kozloff in upper Mongolia of very ancient fragments of rugs ornamented with primitive patterns of simple color scheme. Eventually the story of early rugs will be compiled from data of archæologists. In the meantime known facts of rugs are a legion of dazzling magnificence, and acquaintance with them, like knowledge of all abstract arts, an elixir of spirit and release from human problems.

Zoroaster created the first religion of the Persians, and fire-altar rugs and symbols of the faith still bear it witness. Cyrus the Great took possession of Babylon and appropriated for Persia the pre-eminent rug art of antiquity. Alexander the Great, dying in the attempt to annex Persia to Macedonia, bequeathed to the art of rugs features of the art of Greece. Chosroes I, in his palace at Ctesiphon, delighted in a jewel-studded garden carpet that soldiers of the Mohammedan army cut into fragments for its treasure. Mohammedanism climaxed in the courts of the caliphs, whose rug possessions would make all but our few greatest rugs appear the mats of paupers.

Jenghis Khan created the cataclysm that resulted in the use of Chinese art motives by Persian rug weavers; and Tamerlane, barbarian art patron, inspired the grandeur observed in the rugs of succeeding Persian monarchs. Tahmasp, God-King of Persia and contemporary of Queen Elizabeth of England, probably ordered the creation of the famous tomb carpets of Ardabil; and Akbar, Emperor of India, directed that Persian rug weaving be surpassed on his personal looms. Shah Abbas at Ispahan impressed his splendor upon Russian, Polish and Venetian monarchs by gifts of rugs of silk, and so dominated the thought of Persia that the most costly of existing rugs bear the name of his capital.

Only through mastery of the amazing plots and personalities of this vast drama, whose every thread is woven into the art of rugs, is knowledge worthy of the art to be attained. The mastery is no hardship or painful pursuit, but a diversion and aftermath of the legend of King Solomon's carpet recorded in rabbinical literature.

"When God appointed Solomon king over every created thing, He gave him a carpet sixty miles long and sixty miles wide, made of green silk interwoven with pure gold and ornamented with figured decorations. Surrounded by his four princes—prince of men, prince of demons, a lion, prince of beasts, and an eagle, prince of birds— when Solomon sat upon the carpet he was caught up by the wind and sailed through the air so quickly that he breakfasted at Damascus and supped in Media. One day Solomon was filled with pride at his greatness and wisdom. As a punishment the wind shook the carpet, throwing down forty thousand men. Solomon chided the wind for the mischief it had done, but the latter rejoined that the king would do well to turn toward God and cease to be proud; whereupon Solomon felt greatly ashamed."

Flying farther, Solomon noticed a magnificent palace, its entrance hidden by sand, drifted by the wind; its door, eventually disinterred, covered with inscriptions; and within— But why continue the tale, when now, after a circuitous trial flight, we ourselves have arrived at a door opening upon a greater mystery?

CHAPTER II

RUGS OF KINGS, CALIPHS AND SHAHS

ORIENTAL rugs are flying sparks and glowing embers from the forge and anvil that is Asia. Whoever would know them must sit beside the ancient hearth and see the blacksmith forge the lives of weavers. For out of the lives of weavers, who in Asia are the vast multitude of many peoples, comes the spirit of life in rugs, which is their high distinction and just claim upon attention. The hearth of our reverie is Persia, which ever was the centre of the life of weaving.

The Persian, like the western European, is an Aryan, or Irani as he calls himself. In consequence his words for father, mother and daughter—*pader, mader, dokhtar*—have a familiar sound. His utmost forebears tended flocks somewhere in the heart of Asia until tiring of plains they sprang to horse, and climbing the high plateau on the west drove a diagonal course to Persia or Pars, now called Fars, and, dismounting, obtained among Europeans the country's name.

The idols, or "vulgar gods," that rode with the early Persians grew old after a thousand years and "galloped down the lessening hill." Worship of them was terminated by worship of the "aristocratic abstractions" of Zoroaster, first of seers, who observed two primeval spirits, the Good and the Evil in thought, word and deed battling over the world. "When these two spirits first came together," he said,

9

"they established life and destruction, and ordained the worst world, Hell, for the wicked, but the Best Thought, Heaven, for the righteous. The wicked one, Ahriman, chose to do evil. The Holiest Spirit, Ormuzd, who wears the solid heavens as a robe, chose Righteousness."

Immediately priests created a ritual, kindled sacred fires upon holy altars, and forbade pollution of the hallowed earth. In consequence of the injunction, bodies of the dead were laid in Towers of Silence, in continuation of the nomad practice of abandoning them upon the plains. The winds were wise and victorious: "When the wind blows from behind them and brings their breath unto men, then men know where blows the breath of victory." Upon the Goddess of Waters was bestowed "a golden crown with a hundred stars, with eight rays, a fine well-made crown, with fillets streaming down." At least six hundred and possibly ten hundred years before the rise of Christianity, the Persian attained to religious thought close to the stars of his highlands, so rich was it in imaginative beauty. This thought became the religion of the first Persian state and source of the first religious rug symbols, flame and serpent.

ACHÆMENIAN KINGS AND BABYLONIAN-PERSIAN RUGS

On a barren plain in southwestern Persia is a dilapidated stone mausoleum, vainly inviting veneration. "In this house," asserts the historian, "the body of Cyrus was laid in a golden coffin upon a couch, the feet of which were of hammered gold. Underneath, carpets of royal purple were spread, over it a covering of Babylonian tapestry, and around rich vestments, costly jewels and precious stones." Above the entrance, in former years, was an inscription: "O Man, I am Cyrus, son of Cambyses, who founded the Persian Empire and was King of Asia. Grudge me not therefore this monument."

Cyrus the Great (558-530 B.C.) amalgamated the Aryan tribes, proved his mastery of the art of war against Crœsus, King of Lydia, whom he magnanimously made counsellor of the Persian state; conquered Babylon, which was his vast exploit; and left to his successors not a state but an empire, and to his weaving subjects the art of Persian rugs established upon the acclaimed achievements of Babylonian tapestry.

Magnificent Cyrus was succeeded by contemptible Cambyses, who added Egypt to Persia; and then by Darius, merger of Persia and Asia, who correctly designated himself "The Great King, King of Kings, King of Persia, King of the Provinces, Son of Vishtasp, Grandson of Arshama, the Achæmenian." Then succeeded theatrical Xerxes, who from marble and silver thrones reviewed "the iron storm that poured in vain its arrowy shower on sacred Greece." For finale came four lesser kings to murdered ends, and Alexander the Macedonian to terminate the agony of this first and greatest Persian dynasty.

In the art of Persian rugs, which doubtless as crude matting came into being with crude idols on the plains of central Asia, the Achæmenian Dynasty represents the acquisition of religious symbols and attainment to the dais of Babylon.

ALEXANDER THE GREAT, 334-323 B.C.

Alexander, encouraged by the experience of Xenophon and the immortal Ten Thousand, undertook and accomplished the revenge of Greece with an army of only thirty-five thousand men. In retaliation for the burning of Athens, "the eye of Greece," he destroyed Persepolis, "city of the Persians," which contained the Hall of One Hundred Columns, the Palace of Darius, the pillared halls of Xerxes, the throne-room of Artaxerxes, the deserted mansion of fugitive Darius Codomannus, and the royal library preserving the scriptures and records of ancient Iran.

Dryden's poem, "Alexander's Feast," recounts the holocaust:

> "And the king seized a flambeau with zeal to destroy;
>   Thais led the way,
>   To light him to his prey,
> And, like another Helen, fired another Troy."

The historian condemns the act in equally memorable words: "He who wars against the arts, wars not against nations, but against all mankind." For compensation we have the second Gordian knot in the skein of life, and in rugs the increment of Greek art in Persian art. The value of the latter is to be computed from such articles as the silver bowl from Eastern Persia, approximately of the first century B.C., now in the collection of Count Stroganoff in Rome, on which is portrayed a Persian carpet decorated in the Greek manner.

Alexander and his Macedonians enjoyed "a little rule, a little sway," and left to the crafty cavalry of Parthia the task of driving back invading Rome. Five hundred and fifty years elapsed before Persia, under monarchs called the Sasanids, descendants of Sasan, who claimed descent from the Achæmenian kings, produced a second line of remarkable rulers, a second era of great earthly possessions, and a second period of the religion of Zoroaster.

Sasanian Kings and Greco-Persian Rugs, 226-641 A.D.

Ardashir, the dynasty founder, who overthrew Parthia and assembled under the crown the vast lumbering region of Old Persia and forty thousand Zoroastrian priests to re-establish the national faith, which had been supplanted by idolatry, has no recognized position in the art of rugs; but his successor, Shapur I, who defeated, captured and flayed the Roman Emperor Valerian, created a court of infinite grandeur in the great city of Shapur, whose ruins are close to the ruins of Persepolis.

The belief that the decoration of the rugs and other textiles of this court and its immediate successors constituted a blending of Greek and Persian art is supported by the statement of Yakut, Arab geographer of the thirteenth century: "They tell that the King Sabur Zul Aktaf (Shapur), after the conquest of countries belonging to the Greeks, transferred his prisoners into Khuzistan (southwestern Persia), where they were settled. Thus from that old time, in the cities of Tustar (Shustar), Bacinna and Menuth, they—the Greeks—made brocades and other valuable textiles, as well as carpets."

Chosroes I, 531-579 A.D.

Then Chosroes I, in the palace at Ctesiphon, "sat in his audience hall where was his crown, like unto a mighty cask, set with rubies, emeralds and pearls, with gold and silver, suspended by a chain of gold from the top of the arch; and his neck could not support the crown, but he was veiled by draperies till he had taken his seat and had introduced his head within his crown; and no one who had not previously seen him looked upon him without kneeling in reverence." The great lord of Rome, Emperor Justinian, assisted to defray the expense of this grandeur by an annual tribute of four hundred and forty thousand pieces of gold.

"Victorious and respected among the princes of Asia, Chosroes gave audience in his palace at Ctesiphon to the ambassadors of the world. Their gifts or tributes, arms, rich garments, gems, slaves and aromatics were humbly presented at the foot of the throne; and he condescended to accept from the King of India a maid seven cubits (ten feet) in height, and a carpet softer than silk, the skin, as it was reported, of an extraordinary serpent." The palace, whose central arch is still standing, contained the famous "Spring of Chosroes" carpet, the story of which, to be recounted later, constitutes one of the few fine tragedies of this narrative. The throne was covered with "four carpets of woven gold brocade embroidered with pearls and rubies, the pictorial subjects representing the four seasons."

CHOSROES II, 589-628 A.D.

With Chosroes II, or Parvis, meaning Generous, the dynasty attained a climax of luxury and indulgence that probably never has been surpassed. "The spacious halls and salons, the winter and summer apartments, the bowers and pavilions of his palace, contained the spoils of empires. Artists from all lands had wrought on choice objects, carvings, embroideries, mosaics and paintings, which lent voluptuous comfort and splendor to walls, ceilings and floors. Artisans of Greece had assisted Persian sculptors to decorate the marble pillars and to emblazon the achievements of the Great King on the rocks of the everlasting hills. Carpets woven of soft wool and silk, embroidered with pearls and gems, covered the vast floors, sometimes over four hundred feet long in one piece."

Heaven, too, was paved with rugs, if truth reposes in the *Book of Arda Viraf*, precursor of Dante in the realms of heaven and hell: "On the star track I saw the pious on thrones and carpets made of gold. I saw also the souls of good rulers and monarchs, who ever increase their greatness, goodness, power and triumph when they walk in splendor in their golden trousers; and it seemed to me sublime. I saw also the souls of artisans, who in the world served their masters, as they sat on thrones which were well carpeted; and it seemed to me sublime."

When Chosroes II was defeated in 628 by the Byzantine army, his favorite residence, Dastagerd (north of Bagdad), was looted of all its many valuable treasures. The Byzantine Emperor Heraclius I (*c* 575-641) found in the palace silks, soft rugs—that is, pile rugs—and smooth-faced rugs embroidered with a needle.

Mohammed, 570-632 A.D.

Mohammed was an Arab of the tribe of Koraish, ruling class of Mecca and guardian of the sacred Kaaba, ancient shrine of Arabian idolatry, of the Black Stone and of the Sacred Well of Zem Zem. Within the compound of the shrine were some three hundred and sixty stone and wooden images of "Ozza," "Lat," "Manif" and other gods whom the Arabs worshipped and propitiated with costly gifts. Against this stupidity and the exactions of his tribe Mohammed raised the cry: "There is no God but Allah, and Mohammed is the Prophet of Allah." This treason occasioned the threatening of his life and his flight to Medina, a journey of two hundred and fifty miles, June, 622 A.D.

Thereafter for eight years Mohammed preached, converted, raided Meccan caravans, fought Meccan armies, and eventually, in the year 630 A.D., took Mecca and destroyed its idols. Later, with his wives around him in litters, and an escort of eighty thousand men, driving before them many camels adorned with festive garlands, ready for the sacrifice, he made the final pilgrimage to the sanctuary of his people. "Behold me, O Allah," he cried. "To thee belong all honors, all praises, all power! Thou art One."

The service which Mohammed rendered the benighted Arab and millions of other Asiatics is best summarized by Ibu Hisham, who wrote in 828 A.D.: "We were barbarous folk, worshipping idols, eating carrion, committing shameful deeds, violating the ties of consanguinity, evilly treating our neighbors, the strong among us consuming the weak. And thus we continued until God sent unto us an Apostle from our midst, whose pedigree, integrity, faithfulness and purity of life we know, to summon us to God, that we should declare his unity and worship him, and put away the stones and idols which we and our

15

Fathers used to worship in his stead; and he bade us be truthful in speech, and faithful in the fulfilment of our trusts, and observing of the ties of consanguinity and the duties of neighbors, and to refrain from forbidden things and from blood; and he forbade us from immoral acts and deceitful words, and from consuming the property of orphans; and from slandering virtuous women; and he commanded us to worship God, and to associate naught else with him, and to pray and give alms and fast."

ARAB CONQUEST OF PERSIA, 636-642 A.D.

Tradition reports that on the night of Mohammed's birth, in the "Year of the Elephant," fourteen battlements of the palace of the Persian king were shaken to the ground by an earthquake; and that the chief priest of the Zoroastrians, whose sacred fire of a thousand years had been extinguished by the tremor, saw in a dream Persia overrun by Arabian camels and horses. The fulfilment of this dream, which took place during the sovereignty of Omar, Mohammed's second successor, is recorded imperishably by Al-Fakhri.*

"During the time of 'Umar, al-Muthanna wrote to him informing him of the troubled state of Persian affairs, and of the accession of Yazdigird to the throne, and of his youth, for he was but twenty-one years of age. Then 'Umar called the people to public prayer, and urged them to attack the Persians; and they all consented willingly. Then he summoned Sa'd, and conferred on him the chief command in 'Iraq. So Sa'd marched forth with the people.

"Now when the news of Sa'd's advance with his army reached the Persians, they despatched against him Rustam at the head of thirty thousand warriors, the Arab army consisting of only some seven or eight thousand men. And when the two armies met, the Persians laughed at the spears of the Arabs, which they compared to spindles.

* Quotation from *Literary History of Persia*, by E. G. Browne. Charles Scribner's Sons.

"Then ambassadors passed between Rustam and Sa'd; and the Arab of the desert would come to Rustam's door as he sat on a throne of gold, supported by gold-embroidered cushions in a room carpeted with gold-embroidered carpets, the Persians wearing crowns and displaying their ornaments, and the elephants of war standing on the outskirts of the assembly. So the Arab would approach with his spear

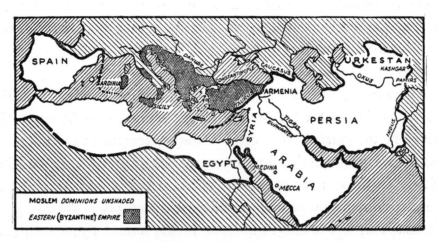

The Moslem Empire, 750 A.D.

in his hand, pressing therewith on the carpet and cushions and tearing them with its spike.

"Then they fought for several days, on the last of which happened the veering of the wind against the Persians, so that the dust blinded them; and Rustam was slain, and his army was routed, and their possessions plundered. At Kufa, Sa'd traced out the plan of a mosque, and made the capital of the province. And thus he obtained control over Ctesiphon, the Persian capital, and got possession of its treasures and stores.

"One of the apartments of the palace was decorated with a carpet of silk called the 'Spring of Chosroes,' sixty cubits [one hundred feet] in length, and as many in breadth; a paradise or garden was depicted

17

on the ground; the flowers, fruits and shrubs were imitated by figures of gold embroidery, and the colors by precious stones. Sa'd persuaded his soldiers to relinquish their claim, in the reasonable hope that the eyes of the Caliph would be delighted with the splendid workmanship of nature and industry. Regardless of the merit of art and the pomp of royalty, the rigid Omar divided the prize among his brethren of Medina. The rug was destroyed, but such was the value of the materials that the share of Ali alone was sold for twenty thousand dirhems" (one thousand eight hundred dollars). The period of this rug is also the period of the first Anglo-Saxon poetry.

A hundred years later (750 A.D.) Arab traders appeared in China and settled in several towns; and almost immediately Chinese ships arrived in the Persian Gulf. From Chinese accounts of the latter adventure we gain another impression of Sasanian rugs. I Wu Chih writes: "In the country of Tatsin [southern Persia and Arabia] they weave rugs by means of wool of different colors, taken from all kinds of beasts; they weave into them birds, beasts, human figures and dead objects, grass, trees, clouds and numerous astonishing tricks." Ko Chih Ching says: "On these rugs they represent cockatoos flying gaily at a distance." These references are of importance because the rugs to which they refer are a connecting link between the animal rugs of early Persia, copied by the weavers of Alexandria, and the hunting and animal rugs later to be described.

During the Sasanian period the art of rugs attained with the court to utmost magnificence. The rulers possessed carpets of value equal to treasuries through the practice of creating pattern out of precious stones. In consequence of the conquest of Persia by Alexander the Great and the employment of Greek weavers by Shapur I, native rug designs of gardens, flowers, trees, human, animal and bird forms were supplemented by elements of the classic art of Greece. These foreign features exercised "a little rule, a little sway," and gave way to the

18

art of Paradise brought into Persia by the religio-military force that took possession. Comparison of the influence of the two foreign arts, Greek and Arab, is well summarized in the following statement: "Hellenism never touched more than the surface of Persian life, but Iran was penetrated to the core by Arabian religion and Arabian ways."

CONTEST OVER THE SUCCESSION

If the blacksmith, at whose forge we sit in reverie, sometimes, during the foregoing years, tempered with mercy the heat of the flames in which he forged the lives of weavers, he repented his kindness upon the death of Mohammed. As if intent upon transporting the entire body of the faith to Paradise with the prophet, he filled the forge with flames that for a thousand years made western Asia a seething blast-furnace.

Mohammed, thinking only of God and Paradise, neglected to designate his successor. The result was the most sanguinary contest over successional rights that history records. Of his four immediate successors, three died at the hands of murderers; and in civil war his grandsons, scores of his friends and thousands of his adherents went to their rewards.

During the years immediately preceding Mohammed's death, the Prophet's family, the Hashemites, assumed that Ali, Mohammed's cousin, husband of Fatima, Mohammed's daughter, and father of Mohammed's treasured grandsons, Hassan and Husein, would succeed to the leadership. Ali was in his own right the head of the family of Hashem, and consequently ruler of the tribe of Koraish and governor of Mecca. But on the Prophet's death, Omar, most influential of the followers, nominated Abu-Bekr, Mohammed's closest friend, for the office of successor, and so importuned and threatened that his election was achieved.

ORIENTAL RUGS AND CARPETS

ABU BEKR, OMAR, OTHMAN, ALI, 632–661 A.D.

FOUR ORTHODOX CALIPHS—CAPITALS MEDINA AND KUFA

Abu Bekr was Mohammed's fourth disciple, his rich patron during the early years, the sole companion of his desperate Hegira, the friend without whom "no one would wish to live, even if he were in possession of every other good." Out of the chest where had been thrown the dictation of the Prophet, written by secretaries on palm-leaves and the shoulder-blades of mutton, Abu Bekr gathered the materials of the Koran, and had them published.

After two short years, Abu Bekr, on his death-bed, bequeathed the succession to Omar, whose genius in military strategy resulted in the conquest of Syria, Egypt and Persia. Upon Omar's death by assassination at the hands of a Christian, Othman, once secretary to Mohammed and member of the Omayyad family that had defended the worship of idols and opposed Mohammed's teaching, was elected the successor. Democratic election of rulers was a long-established Arab custom. Succession by primogeniture was the equally deep-rooted custom of the Persians. In consequence the cause of Ali became a Persian fetish, and the opposition to him the object of deepest hatred.

Persian detestation of Abu Bekr and Omar is forcibly illustrated by an amusing story. A Persian, observing the names of the caliphs on the wall of a mosque, spit at the first two, only to hit, to his chagrin, the sacred name of Ali. "Well, that's only what you deserve for keeping such company," was his recovering commentary.

ALI, HASSAN AND HUSEIN

Ali became caliph only after the murder of Othman by a group of malcontents. He was innocent of association with the conspirators, but numerous enemies, headed by Moawia, Governor of Syria and member of the rival Omayyad family, charged him with the deed. When, five years later, he was slain while at prayer in the mosque at Kufa, Moawia succeeded, unopposed by "pensive Hassan," Ali's oldest son. Subsequently, when Husein, Ali's second son, dared to contest the succession with Moawia's son and heir, Yazid, he and his family, attended by a little band of thirty-two horse and forty foot, were trapped on the barren plain of Kerbela by an army of five thousand soldiers under the command of the Governor of Kufa. The Governor, after promising support, had made an alliance with the enemy.

"On the morning of the fatal day he [Husein] mounted on horseback, his sword in one hand and the Koran in the other—and the battle at length expired with the death of the last of his gallant companions. Alone, weary and wounded, he seated himself at the door of his tent. As he tasted a drop of water, he was pierced in the mouth by a dart, and his son and his nephew, two beautiful youths, were killed in his arms. He lifted his arms to heaven and was slain with thirty-three strokes of lances and swords."

Re-enactment of the incidents of the martyrdom of Husein, the Christ of the Shia or Persian division of Islam, each year in Persia, in every city, town and village during seven to twelve days of Muharram, the month of mourning, is a passion-play comparable to the portrayal of a similar tragedy by the villagers of Oberammergau. The pertinence of its facts to the subject of rugs is that the causes which led to the division of Islam into rival sects occasioned war, which always in Asia was the great solvent and recreating force of art. War meant for the arts contact, amalgamation and renaissance; peace predicated isolation and decay. The Persian character of the finest rugs of Turkey is one of the numerous consequences which this tale will unfold. Of immediate importance is only the noble character of the early caliphs, who disdained rugs and all other accoutrements of kings, only to be succeeded by self-indulgent monarchs whose rugs almost rivalled the stars in number and brilliance.

Rugs of the Worldly Caliphs—Fourteen Omayyad Caliphs, 661-749 A.D.

ARABIAN IMPERIALISM—CAPITAL DAMASCUS

"The world, the flesh and the devil possessed, heart and soul," the silk-robed descendants of the champions of idolatry and persecutors of Mohammed who came to rule, through the murder of the Prophet's family, the vast Mohammedan world from the magnificent dais at Damascus. The world that possessed and overwhelmed them was not only Arabia, Syria, Asia Minor, Armenia, Persia and Central Asia, but also Egypt, North Africa and Spain—a territory far larger and infinitely richer than the domain of any Persian or Roman monarchy.

A mere incident of this wealth was a carpet specially mentioned by Ali al Dimishki, "which belonged to the Omayyad Caliph Hisham, the size, one hundred by fifty cubits [one hundred and fifty by seventy-five feet], woven of silk, embroidered with gold, with beautiful borders and underlayer, which later became part of the collection of carpets belonging to the Abbasids in the time of the Caliph Mutawakkil."

The "flesh" that beset them was family greed, which soon discarded succession by primogeniture for succession through harem intrigues, conspiracies and crimes. The "devil" that pursued was the fickle Arab nature that had lost enthusiasm for carrying on. Just a little time and the old proverb, "heat an Arab and he keeps hot for life," was worn out, and the vast empire with its millions of slaves had dissolved into natural units, each open to new argument.

Mohammed had an Uncle Abbas, whose descendants claimed equal heirship from the Prophet with the descendants of Ali. By keen diplomacy the Abbasids allied the two interests, rallied old Persia to the cause of the Prophet's family, and under a black banner and a competent general defeated and destroyed, near the site of ancient Ninevah, the last of the Omayyad usurpers.

Thirty-Seven Abbasid Caliphs, 749-1258 A.D.

Persian Ascendancy—Persian Court

Then at Bagdad arose the imperial city of the Abbasid caliphs, a new capital of the world only slightly less marvellous than imperial Constantinople. " 'This is Bagdad, city of security,' said the master of the vessel to Ali Nur-ed-Din and his slave girl. 'Winter with its cold hath departed from it, and the spring hath come with its roses, and its trees are in blossom, and its waters are flowing.' Then they walked a little way and destiny cast them among the gardens, and Nur-ed-Din said to the damsel, 'By Allah, this is a pleasant place!' This garden was called the Garden of Delight. It belonged to the Caliph Harun-ar-Rashid, who, when his heart was contracted, used to come to this garden and there sit."

The great Harun-ar-Rashid's annual income was possibly one hundred million dollars. Another one hundred years and the caliph's revenues had dwindled to four and a half millions, but magnificence was unrelaxed. "At court," writes Abulfeda, "his state officers and favorite slaves stood near him in glorious apparel, their belts glittering with gold and gems. Near by stood seven thousand eunuchs, whereof four thousand were white, the remainder black. The door-keepers of the imperial compound were seven hundred. Barges and boats, extraordinarily magnificent, floated on the Tigris. The palace itself was not less splendid. It was hung about with thirty-eight thousand pieces of tapestry, twelve thousand five hundred whereof were of silk embroidered with gold. Twenty-two thousand carpets adorned the floors."

Description by Masudi, Arab historian, geographer and traveller, of two rugs trod by the super-beings of this court has special merit of definiteness: "I entered into the hall of the upper story of the palace of the Chief of the Believers [caliphs] and found the floor covered with a Susandshird carpet, and with a smaller carpet. Around the Susandshird carpet were circular shields with human figures and Persian inscriptions which I was able to read. On the right side of the small carpet there was a picture of a king with a crown, as if he would speak. The inscription concerning him was: 'This is the picture of Shirue, the murderer of his father, King Parvis; he reigned six months.'

"Thereupon I looked at the portrait on the left of the small carpet with the inscription: 'Portrait of Yazid the Third, son of Walid; he reigned six months.' I said: 'How stupid is the inspector of rugs that he could spread before the Chief of the Believers the carpet with the portrait of Yazid, the murderer of his cousin, and of Shirue, the murderer of his father.' Ayyub, son of Sulaiman, was the inspector of carpets." The office of carpet inspector is more than a thousand years old.

The districts famous for carpet weaving during the caliphate were Khuzistan and Fars in southwestern Persia, and Tabriz and Amul in northern Persia. The Persians of the Sasanian era were weaving two types of rugs, soft pile rugs and smooth-faced tapestry-woven fabrics, fragments of which were found in Egypt and other provinces. On the western bank of the Tigris River a small town bearing the name Numaniyah is mentioned by two Arabian authors, Mukaddasi and Ibn Rustah, as "celebrated for its looms, where carpets like those of Hirah are manufactured." Nassiri Khusrau writes: "I have been told that four hundred looms are in Tun [eastern Persia] for making of carpets."

RUGS OF KINGS, CALIPHS AND SHAHS

FOURTEEN FATIMITE CALIPHS, 969-1171 A.D.

Once again, however, the adherents of Ali had been circumvented. As compensation for assistance in winning the succession for the descendants of Abbas, they expected rewards. Instead, such as escaped death in battle were executed or driven into rebellion, which culminated in the founding of a dynasty in Egypt, "a most agreeable country of temperate air, soil of gold, odor surpassing that of aloeswood, and women like the black-eyed virgins of Paradise." Here the caliphs reposed and paraded on "Saman" or straw carpets, according to Makrizi, Arab author of the fifteenth century: "Straw carpets embroidered with gold and silver were used for the decoration of the palace of the Fatimids in Cairo, and because of that a factory of them was established in the vicinity of Cairo."

In the year 1171 the rule of these caliphs was terminated by the famous Saladin, but not the career of the Egyptian industry of rugs, which began with the exhausting labor recorded by Herodotus, continued with the "carpets embroidered with the figures of animals" mentioned by Athenæus and Plautus, and rose to summits of gold and silver through the requirements of the successors of Mohammed. Fragments of the rugs of the period of the last caliphs or of the Ayyubid dynasty (1168-1250), established by Saladin, are now part of the collection of the Metropolitan Museum of Art and also of the Arab Museum, Cairo. With the rugs of the Mamluks (1252-1517), the dynasty overthrown by the Turks, we are just now becoming acquainted, thanks to Doctor Sarre, who demonstrates conclusively, it would seem, that the rugs of mosaic-pavement design, red, light-blue and yellow-green in color, hitherto attributed to Damascus and included among Turkish rugs, are actually Cairo weavings of the sixteenth century.

Years ago Doctor Martin observed and affirmed that the oldest

25

rugs of Spain were Coptic or native Egyptian in art, and possibly also in workmanship. That rugs were made in Egypt under the Fatimids is evident from literary sources. Yakubi praises Kermes rugs of Siut and Makrizi reports that among the rugs used in the Fatimid palace were so-called Kalimun rugs. Makrizi also mentions rugs made of reeds and embroidered in silver and gold. A fine reed mat is in the Metropolitan Museum. Such rugs were made in Tiberias, in Palestine. European and Turkish patterns dominated the weaving at the conclusion of the grand production epoch in the sixteenth century. Only during the last decade has the importance of Egypt as the source and stimulus of the rug art of Spain, North Africa and Syria, and as the influence that widened the scope of the native geometrical patterns of the weavers of Turkey come into clear perspective.

Eighty-seven years after the termination of the rule of the Egyptian caliphs, the Mongols, a wholly new force in Asia, overwhelmed with an avalanche of arms the last Abbasid caliph at Bagdad and inaugurated a new era.

Mongolians, Persians and Moguls Who Bequeathed Us Our Greatest Rug Possessions

Again our blacksmith stokes the forge and creates in Asia, during the thirteenth and fourteenth centuries, a superhuman fury that is compared to earthquakes, famines and pestilences, because only the most violent of nature's forces ever occasioned equal destruction of human life. The source of the holocaust was "Inner Asia," now known as Turkestan and Siberia; and the general name of the malefactors Turanians. On the side toward China they were called Mongolians, east of the Caspian Turks, and part way between and everywhere Tartars. All were accounted utmost barbarians, idolaters and nomads roaming with cattle.

The first of these peoples to conquer Persia was a Turkish tribe which came to be known as Seljuk. The great Khan was Tughril Beg, 1037-1063, who made Ispahan his capital and Bagdad his footstool. From the Persians, the Seljuks learned the love and practice of art, which permeated the Asia Minor branch of the race, and was by them transmitted to the Ottoman Turks. Newly converted to orthodox Islam, the Seljuks so outraged Christian pilgrims to the Holy Land as to bring about the Crusades, and to create for all Mohammedans a reputation for utmost intolerance.

But it was not the mad Seljuks, harvesting death with the Crusaders, who were destined to recognition as the world's greatest artists in demonocracy. This nadir belongs to the Mongols, whose capital city, Karakorum, attained to the eminence of two streets, one of Chinese merchants, one of Mohammedan traders, twelve temples of various idols, two mosques and one Nestorian church. More the Mongols needed not, for reasons sung by a warrior poet:

> "Profitless 'tis in this world to build
> The strong castle or palace.
> Ruins they are in the end;
> And profitless 'tis to build cities."

JENGHIS KHAN, 1206-1227

The perfect warrior or "Jenghis" celebrated his first victory by casting seventy rebels headlong into seventy caldrons of boiling water. Shortly, at the head of countless horsemen he pierced the wall of China, devastated ninety cities, and killed "more than eighteen million five hundred thousand human beings." Then galloping across Asia, he put to sword the inhabitants of the great cities of Kashgar, Samarkand, Bokhara, Merv and Herat, where alone one million six hundred thousand was the number of the slaughtered, and thirty Persian cities besides, for extra measure of liquidation.

"They came, they uprooted, they burned, they slew, they carried off, they departed"—such was the account of Mongol procedure given by a fugitive from the sack of Bokhara. When resistance was encountered, and most of all when some Mongol prince was slain in battle, "they spared neither old nor young, gentle nor simple, learned nor unlearned; they stabled their horses in the mosques, burned libraries,

The Empire of Jenghis Khan, 1227

used priceless manuscripts for fuel, often razed the conquered city to the ground, destroyed every living thing within it, and sowed the site with salt." When in Poland the hordes of horsemen, "stout and thickset, swarthy and ugly, with short broad noses and pointed projected chins," had collected in sacks two hundred and seventy thousand ears of victims, Pope Gregory IX endeavored to arouse a crusade against them.

With the directness and simplicity of his primitive nature Jenghis Khan expressed in a few words the motives of rulership for his time: "A man's greatest pleasure is to defeat his enemies, to drive them before him, to take from them that which they possessed, to see those whom they cherished in tears, to ride their horses, to hold their wives and daughters in his arms."*

The devastation wrought by Jenghis Khan was not without counterbalance of beneficent character. Within Asia, Arabs and Persians hobnobbed as never before with Tibetans and Chinese, exactly as Australians, Canadians, English, Americans and Japanese chatted and drank together during and after the World War. "Many shall run to and fro, and knowledge shall be increased," became a justified proverb. In consequence of increased knowledge, Chinese art was grafted upon the art of all western Asia. Had Jenghis Khan failed to avoid a pit beneath a rug upon which he was invited to sit in a supposedly friendly tent, the art of oriental rugs might never have acquired its extremely composite and brilliantly versatile character. The Ottoman Turks, driven out of central into western Asia, dispersed the Greeks and their learning throughout Europe, creating a new and better Europe. Finally Marco Polo discovered Asia as Columbus discovered America, and, reporting his discovery, created a new era.

Hulagu Khan, 1251-1265

PROPONENT OF CHINESE ART IN PERSIA

In the division of the provinces of the new Mongolian kingdom, which took place at a conference of the heirs of Jenghis at Karakorum in 1251, Persia was assigned to Hulagu, one of numerous grandsons. Seven years later this chance consignee captured Bagdad, slaughtered more than a million of its inhabitants, destroyed its invaluable records and treasures, dispatched to his ancestors the great caliph wrapped and clubbed to death within the folds of a carpet, put an end to the unity of the Mohammedan Empire, and inflicted a wound on Muslim civilization from which it never recovered. Instantly the

* Harold Lamb, *Genghis Khan, Emperor of All Men*. Robert McBride & Co.

court became a vast studio of native Mongolians and Chinese artists. Shortly Chinese artists were requisitioned in Persia, and Persian artists in China; as never before, the culture of the two nations exchanged compliments. Under the Mongols, Persian weavers manufactured fine rugs with geometrical patterns and Kufic inscriptions.

Upon Hulagu's death brilliant courts of upstart Persian dynasties were established at Bagdad, Tabriz, Shiraz, Ispahan, Kerman and Herat. Numerous splendid artists, including rug weavers and poets, among them Hafiz, adorned these courts, which were just about to compare their relative strengths when "murder most foul as in the best it is," quieted each house, and made a thousand gaping scenes.

TAMERLANE, 1369-1405

FOUNDER OF THE FINAL CULT OF SUPERLATIVE CARPETS

Ruy Gonzalez de Clavijo, head of the Spanish Mission which arrived at Samarkand in August, 1404, wrote an impression of his diabolic majesty, Tamerlane, "Sultan of Babylon" and Ruler of Persia. "He was seated in a portal in front of the entrance of a beautiful palace, and he was sitting on the ground. Before him was a fountain which threw the water very high, and in it were some red apples. The lord was seated cross-legged on silk-embroidered carpets, amongst round pillows. He was dressed in a robe of silk, with a high white hat on his head, on the top of which was a special ruby with pearls and precious stones."

The envoy observed further that "in the centre of the garden was a beautiful house adorned with carpets. Within it there was a silver gilt table on the top of which was a bed of silk embroidered with gold. The walls were hung with rose-colored silk cloths ornamented with plates of silver gilt, set with emeralds, pearls and other precious stones tastefully arranged." Near by, "a great and lofty pavilion was furnished with a crimson carpet beautifully ornamented and embroidered

30

with gold threads. The doors were of carpeting." "The ground of a tent was covered with rich silken carpets."

Whether Timur, meaning iron, was of common herdsman extraction and obtained his limp or "lane" while stealing sheep, or derived his murderous mind from the wolfish blood of Jenghis Khan matters little. Beginning in 1381 and continuing for twenty years, he and his several hundred thousand Tartar horsemen made almost annual campaigns from Samarkand in search of fame and plunder. He beat Persia insensible, first in the east from Herat to Sistan, then in the west through Ispahan to Shiraz, and finally gave three years to general subjugation.

In Sistan he caused two thousand prisoners to be built into a wall. At Ispahan he massacred over seventy thousand inhabitants, because spirited souls dared to resist his tax-gatherers. The skulls of the slain, by his peremptory command, were converted into pyramids and minarets, according to his custom. He accomplished the slaughter of one hundred thousand Hindus at Delhi, during his sojourn of five months, and flashing into the north buried alive four thousand innocents in Armenia. He erected twenty towers of skulls at Aleppo and Damascus, and a pyramid of ninety thousand heads at Bagdad. He placed twenty-seven pilfered crowns on his furrowed brow, professed himself a pious Shiite Mohammedan and entertained great reverence for the number nine. All this accomplishment gave no alleviation of distress to Persia, whose loss extended to her artists, rug weavers and eminent scholars, transported to Samarkand from Tabriz and Shiraz.

Shah Rukh, 1404-1447

Pre-eminent patron of Persian arts

Timur, the æsthetic Tartar savage, was succeeded by his fourth son, Shah Rukh, a monarch of noble and gentle character, who, at Herat, then the Persian capital, devoted himself to learning, the patronage of the arts and the restoration of the regions which his father had devastated. He and his successors were the "most artistic princes that ever reigned in Persia," sovereigns who made themselves famous for scholarship, poetry, book-making and collecting, and lavish patronage of miniature painters, rug weavers, armorers and ivory workers. To this exceeding culture Persia owes most of her high acclaim in the world of art, and Shah Abbas the grandeur of his inheritance. From the succeeding court came, during the sixteenth century, the "Ispahan" rugs so greatly esteemed by collectors.

Rugs represented in Timurid miniature paintings, made for Shah Rukh and his son Baisunkur, show a geometrical design consisting of octagonal diapers, interlacings and Kufic writing. Some of the rugs depicted in miniature paintings suggest the so-called Holbein rugs of Asia Minor and certain Moorish rugs of Spain. Judging from representations of rugs in miniatures of the end of the fifteenth century, particularly those by Bihzard, a change in rug design took place. Geometrical patterns were almost entirely replaced by arabesques and floral scrolls placed in compartments.

BLACK AND WHITE SHEEP DYNASTIES, 1378-1502

Despite the pacific disposition of Shah Rukh and the intellectual interests of the Herat court, war was a continuous occupation. After the death of Tamerlane the territory of Tabriz and Eastern Asia Minor was recovered by the "Black Sheep" Turkoman tribe of Asia Minor which Tamerlane had several times dispossessed. Shah Rukh defeated the last ruler of this dynasty, who built the Blue Mosque, and as a subject made him governor of the territory; but not for long. Tamerlane had made a grant of the country to the Turkoman tribe of Asia Minor that had fought for him under a banner displaying a white sheep; and the White Sheep under Uzun Hasan were not to be denied their legacy. This man, exceedingly tall, thin, merry and dangerous only "when too far gone," exterminated the Black Sheep, occupied Tabriz and made an alliance with the Signoria of Venice to fight the Turks, who were menacing the peace of both Asia and Europe. The denouement in the history of rugs is of utmost importance.

The exact source of the magnificent medallion rugs of northwestern Persia, that have been assigned to the latter part of the fifteenth century, because Persian miniature paintings shortly thereafter depict similar rugs, has been a ceaseless quest. Thanks to brilliant Josafa Barbaro, Venetian ambassador to Persia during the reign of Uzun Hasan, the source is probably found, and with it, of equal importance, the source at Brusa of the rugs of the Turkish court of Mohammed II (1451-1481); and the source at Cairo of the rugs of the Egyptian court of the Mamluks (1252-1517). The quotation to follow* is an important contribution to knowledge of old rugs.

"During the wars between our most excellent Signoria [the Venetian state] and Ottomans [Turks], in the year 1471, I, being a man used to hardship and of experience among barbarous people, and willing also to serve our aforesaid most excellent Signoria, was sent away with the Ambassador of Assambei [Uzun Hasan], King of Persia, who was come to Venice to persuade the Signoria to follow the wars against the said Ottomans.

"We departed from Venice with two light galleys, and after us came two great galleys well furnished with men and munitions, besides other presents for Assambei. There were presents of vessels of silver to the value of three thousand ducats [equal to dollars], cloth of gold and silk to the value of two thousand five hundred ducats; scarlets and other fine woollen cloths to the value of three thousand ducats.

"At Merdin [one hundred and fifty miles northwest of Mosul], which belongeth to King Assambei, I was lodged in a hospital founded

* *Travels to Tana and Persia*, by Josafa Barbaro and Ambrogio Contarini. The Hakluyt Society. Vol. 49. First Series.

by a brother of the King, in which they that resort thither are fed, and if they seem persons of any estimation they have carpets laid under their feet better worth than a hundred ducats apiece."

At Chesam, Kurds "slew the Persian Ambassador to Venice and my secretary with the others; and having hurt me and the rest, they took all that they found. I being on horseback fled out of the way all alone, and after me came they that were hurt.

"Being come to Thauris [Tabriz], we went into an inn from whence I signified to King Assambei, being then there present, that I was come, desiring to be brought to his presence. The next morning, being sent for, I presented myself unto him so ill apparelled that, I dare assure you, all that I had about me was not worth two ducats."

Uzun Hasan, 1466-1477

PROBABLE OWNER OF EXTANT MEDALLION AND SILK RUG MASTERPIECES

The audience with the King took place at a "lodge located in a green garden like a meadow full of truffles with mud walls. In the middle of the lodge was a fountain, like a little gutter always full of water, and in the entry of it the King himself sat on a cushion of cloth of gold, with another at his back, and beside him was his buckler of the Moresco fashion with his scimitar; and all the lodge was laid with carpets, his chiefest princes sitting round about. The lodge was all wrought of mosaic, not so small as we use but great and very fair, of divers colors. The first day I came to him he had divers singers and players with harps a yard long, which they hold with the sharp ends upward; and besides that lutes, rebickes, cymbals and bagpipes, all which they played agreeably."

Barbaro enjoyed a play which consisted in killing wolves that were brought into the market-place and loosed. Afterward he had dinner with the King, who received certain men sent from a prince of India with gifts of strange beasts: an ounce, lion, two elephants that were made to bow, a giraffe, three pairs of doves, three popinjays and two cattle called zibetto. Additionally one hundred men, one after another, presented each five turbans worth five or seven ducats apiece; others six pieces of silk; others little dishes of silver full of precious stones; others vessels, porcelain, wood of aloes, sandal and spices. Later the King showed him both the jewels received as presents and his personal collection, saying: "I could show thee a horseload of these."

At another time he was received in a chamber under a domed ceiling, "the walls hung with cloth of silk, embroiderie and gold, and all the floor covered with excellent good carpets, being about fourteen paces over. He caused certain cassocks to be brought forth of cloth of gold, of silk or furred with sables, telling me these be the cloth of the town of Yezd. Finally, he caused certain silk carpets to be brought forth, which were marvellous fair.

"The day following I repaired to him unto a great field within the town, where wheat had been sown, the grass whereof was mowed to make place for the triumph. In this place were many pavilions pitched, being in number about a hundred, of which I saw forty of the fairest. They all had inner chambers, and the roofs all cut with divers colors, the ground being covered with most beautiful carpets, between which carpets and those of Cairo and Broussa, in my judgment, there is as much difference as between the clothes made of English wools and those of Saint Mathewes. They caused me to enter into two pavilions which were full of silk apparel and of other sorts of clothes laid on a great heap, on one side of which I saw forty saddles trimmed with silver, all which apparel and saddles they told me should be given away by the King at the triumph."

The prizes awarded the next day consisted of about three hundred articles and fifty horses. The diversions consisted of dancing, wrestling

35

and endurance races between the King's footmen. "The town [Tabriz] was well decked and especially the shops, for every man set forth his best goods. The triumph finished, the King determined to go with all his train into the country, the way which they knew fittest to furnish them pasture and water, travelling between ten and fifteen miles the first days; and with him went three of his sons. There were of pavilions six thousand, camels thirty thousand, carriage mules five thousand, carriage horses five thousand, asses two thousand and horses of service twenty thousand. Afterward I numbered two thousand good mules, small cattle twenty thousand, great cattle two thousand, leopards to hunt one hundred, falcons two hundred, greyhounds three thousand, hounds one thousand, good horsemen three thousand, footmen twenty-five thousand, women of the best sort ten thousand, servants five thousand, children five thousand." Actually this was the Persian army.

M. Ambrogio Contarini, a Venetian who arrived at the court during the stay of Barbaro, reports, March 21, 1475: "It is the practice of the Shah to send his pavilion to the place where there is good pasturage and water, and to remain there till the grass is consumed, when they proceed to another place; the women are always the first on the ground to erect the tents and make preparation for their husbands. The tents of the Shah are very beautiful. The one in which he slept was like a chamber; it was covered with red felt and with doors which would serve for any room." It would be interesting to know whether the court at Herat also made a practice of going to the country with its herds. It is hardly likely. The eastern court was more scholarly; the western court rougher and the King dangerous "when too far gone." More virile and aggressive, the Tabriz court superseded the Herat court and became sovereign of a great part of Tamerlane's kingdom.

A nameless Italian merchant in Persia, in chapters appended to the foregoing text, adds the following items of interest concerning Uzun Hasan's palace and hospital: "The terrace of the palace has for each angle a gutter, which spouts out water, and the spout is immensely large and made in the form of a dragon. They are of bronze, and so large that they would do for cannon, and so well made as to be taken for live dragons. Within the palace, on the ceiling of the great [audience] hall, are represented in gold, silver and ultramarine all the battles that took place in Persia a long time since. On the floor of the hall is spread a magnificent carpet, apparently of silk, worked in the Persian manner with beautiful patterns, which is round, and of the exact measurement the place requires; likewise in the other rooms the floor is all covered. The hospital is large, having many buildings, and within it is even more beautifully ornamented than the mosque, having many large wards about ten yards long and four broad, each of these being fitted with a carpet to its measurement."

The Safavi Dynasty, 1502-1736

PRE-EMINENT PATRONS OF RUG ARTISTS AND WEAVERS

With the advent of the Safavi dynasty the Persian nation began the ascent of the third great summit of "ever diminishing heights of power." The ancient independence was to be rewon, and a new primacy in Asia and an enviable importance in Europe attained through the medium of the religion which seemingly had destroyed every national prospect nine hundred years before.

To secure the background of the event, conceive the time ripe for another orgy of religious war, another feast of flames. Conceive the cause of the descendants of the martyred Husein to be forcibly impersonated in the deeply venerated Safiyyud-Din, head of the Ardabil monastery, who claimed descent from Musa Kazim, the seventh *imam* or saint of the martyr's family. Conceive the local Persian attachment reinforced by the fealty of thousands of Turks, who, through the intercession of the family, had been released from captivity by Tamerlane.

Ismail, 1502-1524

Ismail was thirteen years of age when he rallied to the old cause of Ali and the Prophet's family his fanatically devoted followers, captured Baku and overwhelmed the White Sheep dynasty. Aged fifteen he was crowned Shah of Persia in Tabriz, which fell without contest.

Ismail was red-headed, handsome, pleasing in manner, left-handed and "brave as a game cock." For news of a marauding lion, which he would hunt alone and kill, he awarded a horse and saddle, and for news of a leopard, an unsaddled horse. From the age of three he himself had been hunted by the rulers of the White Sheep. In consequence he was as "cruel and bloodthirsty as Nero." One conquered opponent he covered with honey and confined in a cage to be tortured by wasps; the head, hands, feet and legs of another he sent as intimation of impending fate to the Turkish Sultan and other enemies, reserving the bones of the skull to be made into a gold-mounted drinking cup for his personal use.

His spectacular rise was the result of powerful but local adherence to the Shiia or Ali side of the ancient religious controversy. The outcome was the proclamation of the faith as the state religion of Persia, and the proscription of all other faiths. To the horror of the Turks, Sunni or orthodox Mohammedans, Ismail decreed the public cursing of Abu Bekr, Omar and Othman. In consequence the Turks massacred with utmost cruelty thousands and more thousands of non-conformists in Asia Minor; and Sultan Selim, the "Grim" Turk, destroyer of his own entire family, made war on Persia to avenge the insult to his religion, captured Tabriz and after a week of soldierly indulgence returned to Constantinople with such spoil of wealth, art and artisans as he chose to commandeer. An important group of

Reputed Tomb of Cyrus the Great at Pasargadae

Grand Staircase at Persepolis

Tomb of Darius

Bas-reliefs of Chosroes II at Tak-i Bostán
near Kermanshah

Chosroes's Famous Palace at Ctesiphon, near Bagdad.
Source of the Jewelled Garden Carpet, 641 A.D.

Sacred Kaaba, Mecca

PLATE II

Miniature Painting of Tamerlane, Ruler of Central and Western Asia, 1369-1405, Capital Samarkand

Type of Mongolian Horsemen Who Over-ran Asia and Destroyed Cities and Nations, 1206-1256; 1369-1405

Ruins of the Great Mosque, Samarkand

PLATE III

Masjid-i-Shah or King's Mosque, Ispahan

Shah Abbas the Great, 1588-1629

Palace of the Chahil Sutun or Hall of Forty Columns, Ispahan

PLATE IV

Garden Carpet, Persia, Sixteenth Century

Albert Figdor Collection, Vienna

Garden Carpet, Persia about 1600

Formerly Wagner Collection

Persian Garden Rug, Seventeenth Century

Formerly Orendi Collection

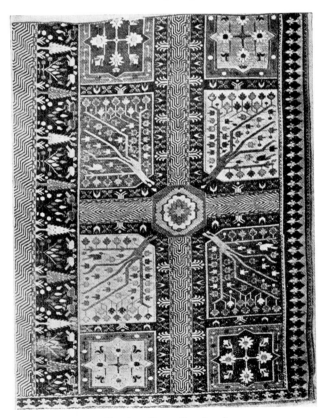

Fragment Garden Rug, Persia about 1700

Theodore M. Davis Collection, Metropolitan Museum of Art

PLATE V

PLATE VI.   Persian Medallion Rug, Late Fifteenth Century.
Possibly used in Uzun Hasan's Palace, Tabriz

James Franklin Ballard Collection, Metropolitan Museum of Art

Superlative Tree Rug, Northwest Persia about 1500

Joseph Lees Williams Memorial Collection, Philadelphia Museum

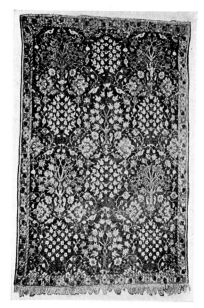

Persian Rug of Flowering Shrubs,
Sixteenth Century

Kaiser Friedrich Museum, Berlin

Persian Rug of Flowering Shrubs,
Late Sixteenth Century

James F. Ballard Collection,
Metropolitan Museum of Art

PLATE VII

Hunting Carpet, Dated 1542-1543 A.D.
Poldi Pezzoli Museum, Milan

Finest Extant Hunting Carpet, Middle Sixteenth Century
Austrian Museum for Art and Industry, Vienna

PLATE VIII

PLATE IX.   Persian Medallion-Animal Rug
Joseph E. Widener Collection, National Gallery, Washington, D.C.

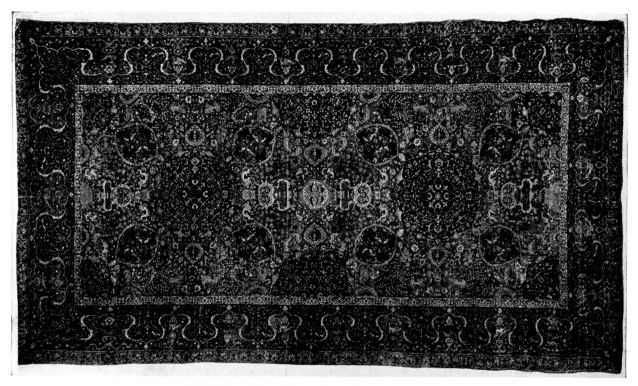

Medallion-Animal Rug, Early Sixteenth Century

Victoria and Albert Museum

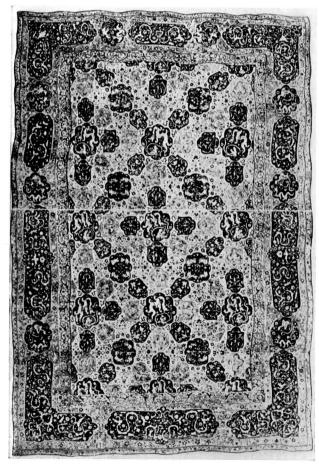

Animal Rug of Compartment Design, First Half
Sixteenth Century. Design used in other arts

Metropolitan Museum of Art

Animal Rug from Ardabil, Sixteenth
Century

Metropolitan Museum of Art

PLATE X

Vestibule of the Madrassa (college) Mader-i-Shah (Mother of Shah) Sultan Hussein (1700), Ispahan Compare ceiling motive with rug medallion

Ardabil Tomb Carpet, dated 1539. Purchased by British public subscription for the Victoria and Albert Museum

Ruins of the Blue Mosque (1450), Tabriz. Compare decoration of upper projecting arch with design of rug border

PLATE XI

PLATE XII.   Herat (Ispahan) Rug, Late Sixteenth Century

Henry F. Du Pont Collection

PLATE XIII.   Vase Rug, Persia, Sixteenth Century.   Probably woven at Joshaghan
Henry F. Du Pont Collection

PLATE XIV.   Polonaise Silk and Metal Rug, Persia, Seventeenth
Century.   Woven at Kashan, Joshaghan or Ispahan

Joseph E. Widener Collection, National Gallery, Washington, D.C.

PLATE XV. Persian Prayer Rug, Sixteenth Century. The inscriptions
are from the Koran. Shah Tahmasp period

Isaac D. Fletcher Collection, Metropolitan Museum of Art

Painting by Van Dyck (1599-1641). Children of Charles I of England
Standing upon an Herat (Ispahan) Rug

Painting by Rubens (1577-1640). "Orientale" and Herat Rug

PLATE XVI

Feraghan Rug, Mustafi Design

PLATE XVII

Tabriz, Capital of Persia, 1378-1549

Persian Village

Tomb of Esther and Mordecai, Hamadan

PLATE XVIII

Kerman Saddle Rug

Kerman, Southeast Persia (mistakenly called Kermanshah)

PLATE XIX

Afshar

Shiraz (Kashgai)

Bakhtiari

Loristan (Lor)

PLATE XX

Kurdistan, Mina Khani Design

True Kermanshah, Western Persia

Suj Bulak, Shah Abbas Design

Sehna (Senna)

PLATE XXI

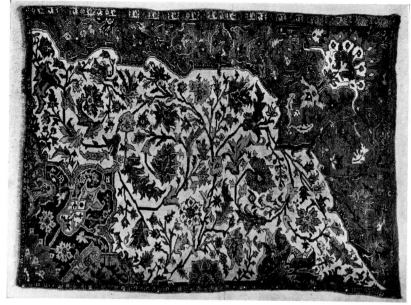

Bijar Vagireh. Rug containing a corner pattern for use as a model in the weaving of carpets

Bijar. French Rose-Panel Pattern

Bijar, Decorated with Seventeenth-Century Arabesque—Palmette Design

PLATE XXII

Karaje (Karadagh) Rug. Medallion—rosette series of local, native character

Herez Carpet. Easily identified by local border pattern commonly used in Gorevan and Serapi weaving

Tabriz Mosque Carpet. Illustrates individuality of art in a product that has no personal property patterns, and essays many varieties of Persian design

PLATE XXIII

Turkish rugs of a Persian character of art, called Ushak, is probably a by-product of this dispute.

Nothing daunted, Ismail re-established himself, extended his kingdom by vigorous wars and died at the age of thirty-eight years, to rest with the saints at Ardabil. In the journal, finished July 2, 1520, of the "Merchant in Persia," Ismail is said to have used Uzun Hasan's palace of "Eight Heavens" in Tabriz, to have built a beautiful palace at Coi and to have employed a seal resembling a large Z.

TAHMASP, 1524-1576

MONARCH OF THE PERIOD MOST PRODUCTIVE OF GREAT RUGS IN PERSIA

Tahmasp, Ismail's son and successor, was the recipient of a most felicitous letter in the year 1561: "Elizabeth, by the Grace of God, Queen of England, to the right mightie and right victorious Prince, the great Sophie, Emperor of the Persians, Medes, Parthians, Hircans, Carmenians, Margians, of the people on this side and beyond the river of Tygris, and of all men and nations between the Caspian Sea and the gulfe of Persia, greeting and most happy increase in all prosperitie. Introducing our faithful and right welbeloved servant Anthonie Jenkinson, who is determined with our license, favour and grace to passe out of this our Realme, and by God's sufferance to travel even into Persia and other your jurisdictions."

Jenkinson presented the letter and made a speech, saying he was of the "famous Citie of London." Tahmasp replied, "Oh thou unbeleeuer, we have no neede to have friendship with the unbeleeuers." Directly he ordered sand thrown on the places polluted by the Englishman, and considered his execution. Equally the Sophie made a poor impression on valiant Jenkinson, who wrote his society: "This Sophie that now reigneth, Shaw Thamas, Sonne of Ismael Sophie, is nothing valiant, and through his pusillanimitie the Turke hath much invaded

39

his countreys. His oldest son he keepeth captive in prison, for that he feareth him for his valiantnesse and activitie. He professeth a kind of holynesse, and saith hee is descended of the blood of Mahomet."

Tahmasp, recluse and melancholiac, devoted to baths, dreams and pedigree, convinced himself that he was a god. That others might entertain the same opinion he ordered the sewing up of a disrespectful poet's mouth, and the hurling of the versifier, sealed in a jar, from the top of a minaret. The weavers of his reign of fifty-three years, the second longest among Mohammedan potentates, created most of the great works of rug art. The common museum label, "Northwestern Persia, Sixteenth Century," will some day include his name, and the name of his two capitals, Tabriz and Kazvin.

Fine carpets were woven for the family tomb at Ardabil, one of which is now the chief treasure of the Victoria and Albert Museum. According to the inscription, it was ordered by Maksud of Kashan and finished in 1539. Rugs which Shah Tahmasp presented to Selim II on the latter's ascension to the throne of Turkey in 1566 are recorded by Hammer: "Among the gifts of the Ambassador to the great Vizir and other Vizirs were silken carpets of Hamadan, Dergesin and Darabdscherd. The gifts of the Shah to the Sultan were carried on forty-four camels; among them twenty large silk carpets and numerous small ones, decorated with birds, beasts, flowers and embroidered with gold, nine rugs from camel hair, masterpieces of Persian tapestries, carpets and fine textiles. From his own name the Ambassador presented to the Sultan, carpets from silk and camel hair."

SHAH ABBAS, 1588-1629

FIRST PATRON OF GOLD, SILVER AND SILK RUGS CALLED POLONAISE

Shah Abbas I, grandson of Shah Tahmasp, wrote his name in the memory book of his people, toward the end of a long list of eminent rulers, and when to-day the people open the "Book of Gold," lo! the name he wrote "leads all the rest." Reasons for his idolization are suggested in the glowing tribute to him written by Sir Anthony Sherley, who with his brother, Robert, and twenty-six followers went to Persia in the year 1599.

"His Person is such as well-understanding nature would fit for the end proposed for his being,—excellently well-shaped, of most well-proportioned stature, strong and active; his colour, somewhat inclined to a man-like blackness, is also more black by sun-burning; the furniture of his mind infinitely royal, wise, valiant, liberal, temperate, merciful; and an exceeding lover of justice, embracing royally other virtues as far from pride and vanity as from all unprincely sins or acts."

A thousand tales, like one which the Sherleys brought back to England, perpetuate his fame. "The King will go in private to the markets to see what order they keep. At Ispahan, falling into talk with a fellow that sold milk, he asked him how the governor of the place where he dwelt did behave himself. 'Why,' said the fellow, 'if I was in his place I would bring the King a dozen heads a week of villains that rob up and down the country, so that we can scarce go a stone's cast from our houses, but we shall be robbed; and the governor doth bear with them, and take money of them to let them live in that fashion.'" Out of the incident, the Governor and the villains lost their heads, and the milkman "brought the country, in one month's space, to such a quietness that a man might walk with a rod in his hand without hurt."

King at the age of sixteen, Abbas was beset on the west by the rampant Turk, to whom he lost Tabriz, Shirvan, Georgia and Luristan; and on the east by the Uzbek kingdom, to which he lost Herat, Meshed, Nishapar and Sabzawar. Forty years later, upon his death, he relinquished a powerful and influential nation, partly the result of the creation of a disciplined army, equipped with cannon, which previously the Persians had scorned as "not becoming to valiant men."

41

This innovation was an important result of the mission of the Sherleys, which contained among its members a cannon-maker. "The prevailing Persian hath learned Sherleian arts of war; and he which before knew not the use of ordnance, hath now five hundred pieces of brass and sixty thousand musketiers." Success in continuous wars recovered the old territory and added Bagdad, Baku and Merv to the Persian possessions.

To great military and administrative abilities, Abbas added rare tolerance in religious belief. He ordered the discontinuance of the Shiia practice of cursing publicly the first three caliphs, and welcomed at Ispahan, his new seat of government, men of every creed. He settled five thousand families of Armenians in a new Julfa, close to Ispahan, and coincidently, without jeopardizing the new national liberalism, consolidated the antagonistic tribes and races of his domain by stimulating a revival of devotion to the national religion and to the shrine at Meshed, which he made the Persian centre for pilgrimage.

Abbas greatly increased the revenue of the state, and expended vast treasure on imperial highways, bridges, caravanserais and general national embellishment. Not only was Ispahan made a brilliant court and metropolis, but Meshed, Ardabil, Kashan, Tabriz and Hamadan were beautified by splendid buildings, shrines and walls, to such an extent that whatever is impressive in Persia to-day is commonly attributed to Abbas the Great.

Appreciation and patronage of the fine arts was, with Shah Abbas, second nature. The manufacture of fine silk rugs, brocaded with gold and silver, continued under Shah Abbas. The looms of Kashan, and new state manufactories established at Ispahan, produced precious silk carpets, brocades and velvets. The splendid garden pavilions were equipped with silk rugs. "At our alighting at the court gate," writes Thomas Herbert, "an officer led us into a little place having a pretty marble pond or tank in the centre; the rest spread with silk carpets.

Thence we were led through a large delicate and odoriferous garden to a house of pleasure; the low room was round and spacious, the ground spread with silk carpets."

Abbas had palaces at Kashan and at Kazvin, the latter hung "in every room with gold carpets and under foot with rich arras." In Kazvin was "a place which they call the Bazar. In the middle standeth a round thing made with a seat, set up with six pillars, bravely trimmed with rich carpets, both of gold, silver and silk, and the King's chair of estate placed in the middle." Mustriffa, raised to a governorship from the humble business of milk, had in his cortège "a middle mule with his carriage covered with a carpet wrought with silk and gold."

Sir Anthony Sherley's gift of ingratiation to the Shah, on his arrival in Persia, was reciprocated with interest many times compounded. "So after the tenth day was expired the King sent twelve camels, three tents very large, with all kinds of official houses belonging to them and household stuff; sixteen mules, each mule carrying four carpets (total sixty-four), four of silk and gold, six of clean silk, the rest very fair crewel carpets." In the "Brief and True Report of Sir Anthony Shierlie, his journey into Persia reported by two Gentlemen who followed him" (printed in London in 1600), the Shah's gift is recorded as consisting of "Fortie Horse well furnished, whereof foure Saddles were Plate of Golde, set with precious Stones, and two of Silver. Fifteen Cammels and as many Mules for his Carriages. Three most faire Tents. Eighteene Carpets curiously wrought with Golde. Commanding his Messenger to tell Sir Anthony that the great Sophie would not have him to accept them as a present, but as thinges necessarie for his Journey, (being but for eight dayes,) and ever since he hath bestowed many great guiftes upon him."

For want of home training in the art of sitting upon a carpet, Sherley took to his knees at his first royal audience. "The King put me above the Turk's Ambassador, bidding me sit down there, by reason they have no stools, but sit on carpets. I could ill sit cross-legged after their manner, but kneeled on my knees; then the Ambassador told the King it was the fashion of England to sit on stools. When the King had heard these words, he presently went into the next room, and caused one of his pages to bring forth a little form, which they did use to set bottles of wine upon, and throwing a carpet of gold upon it, caused me to sit down."

That many of the King's rugs—the ones containing gold and silver, now called Polonaise—were woven at Kashan, we are constrained to infer from the following statement by Sherley. "We arrived at Cassan, [Kashan] very famous and rich. It wanteth neither Fountains, Springs, nor Gardens, but aboundeth with all the necessaries whatsoever. The best trade of all the land is there, being greatly frequented with all sorts of merchants, especially out of India. The people are very industrious and curious in all sciences, but especially in weaving Girdles and Sashes, in the making of Velvets, Sattins, Damaskes and Persian carpets of a wonderful fineness. In a word, it is the very Magazeen and Warehouse of all the Persian Cities for these stuffs."

In 1599 Shah Abbas, at the instigation of Sherley, sent the first mission of Persian ambassadors to the courts of Europe. This mission, followed by others bearing important and now historic rugs as gifts, may, in this text, be called the mission of lost rugs, because its thirty-two heavy cases of presents were stolen in Archangel, almost within the Arctic Circle, if Uruch Beg, a member of the mission, is to be believed, and later sold by English merchants in Muscovy.

The mission consisted of Sir Anthony Sherley and one Persian Ambassador, Husayn Ali Beg, jointly accredited to eight European courts, attended by four Persian secretaries, fifteen Persian servants, fifteen English gentlemen and two Portuguese friars. Its purpose, according to the manifesto of the Shah, was to promote trade. "I do give this Pattent for all Christian Merchants to repaire and trafique

44

in and through our Dominions, without disturbances or molestations of any Duke, Prince, Governour or Captaine, or any of whatsoever office, or qualitie of ours: but that all Merchandise that they shall bring, shall be priviliged, that none of any Dignitie or Authoritie shall have Power to looke into it, neyther to make inquisition after, or stay for any use or person, the value of one Asper." An ulterior purpose of the mission undoubtedly was to create alliances against the ever-bellicose Turk.

In Moscow the mission was entertained by the Czar. Travelling overland to Archangel and by boat down the coast of Norway, it entered Germany, where three great potentates were propitiated; thence it journeyed to Prague in Bohemia, where Emperor Rudolf III magnificently regaled it during the winter of 1600. At Mantua, Italy, during a period of further joy provided by the Duke of Vincenzo, Gonzaga, it was learned that the Doge of Venice was entertaining a Turkish ambassador, and on that account declined to receive the Persians. At Siena, on the way to Rome, Ali Beg accused Sir Anthony of having stolen and sold for his personal profit the gifts of the mission, which now were sorely needed for the papal audience. The violent quarrel that ensued was annihilative.

After the Vatican reception, the loss of Sir Anthony Sherley by resignation and of three Persians, including the ambassador's cook, by conversion to the Catholic faith—a suicidal act if committed in Persia—a remnant of the mission proceeded to Spain, where at the court of Philip III, three of the four Persian secretaries apostatized; and Ali Beg in disgust went home to Persia by sea round the Cape of Good Hope, leaving the courts of England, Scotland, France, Poland and Venice to await a more propitious expedition.

Not to be frustrated, Shah Abbas immediately despatched a second mission, this one headed by Fethy Bey, who presented his credentials to Doge Marino Grimani in Venice in 1603. Among the gifts of the Persians were "a rug knotted in silk, gold and silver, a coat of gold brocade, a velvet with the representation of the Madonna and Child, and other silks." In Thuanus' *History of the Times* we are informed of further rug gifts: "In the year 1607 the Persian embassy brought to the court of Phillipp III of Spain two precious old carpets; the victories of Timurleng were represented on them." In 1609 Abbas sent a mission to Poland, Germany and Rome, headed by Robert Sherley, brother of Sir Anthony; and in 1622 a mission to Venice led by the Persian ambassador, Sassaur, who presented "among other gifts, four silk rugs, three of which are today preserved in the Treasury of St. Mark's."

Prompted by the Shah's advances, numerous missions of haughty Western monarchs were sent to Persia. Contemporary monarchs in England were Queen Elizabeth and James II, in Turkey Murad III and Ahmet I, and in India Akbar. The golden age was just beginning to wane.

SHAH SAFI (1629-1642) AND "POLONAISE" RUGS

The audience hall at Ispahan that Shah Abbas made famous, and the infamous Shah Safi who succeeded to the throne are effectively described by Olearius: "The hall was raised three steps from the ground, and was eight fathom broad and twelve in length. There was at the entrance a Partition with Curtains drawn before it of red cotton. On the left-hand, as you came in, there were some pieces of painting done in Europe, representing certain Histories. The floor was covered all over with Tapestry where-of the ground work was of Gold and Silver; and in the basin [pool] was abundance of Flowers, Citrons, Oranges, Apples and other Fruits, which swam upon the water. About the sides of the basin, there was a great number of Gold and Silver Flaggons and Bottles, which either had Garlands or Flowers about them, or posies in their mouths.

46

RUGS OF KINGS, CALIPHS AND SHAHS

"The King sat upon the ground, having a satin cushion under him, behind the Fountain, with his back to the wall. He was about seven and twenty years of Age, handsome Bodied, having a graceful Aspect, and of a clear and smooth Complexion, somewhat Hawk-Nos'd, as most of the Persians are, and he had a little black Hair upon the upper lip. There was nothing extraordinary in his Habit, save that his Cloths were of Brocade, and that at his Coiffure there was a Plume of Heron feathers, fastened with a bracelet of Diamonds. He wore also his Kurdi, that is a kind of Coat without Sleeves, which the Persians wear over their garments, two Sable Skins hanging at the neck. The Cymitar he had by his side glittered with Gold and Precious Stones, and behind him, upon the ground, lay a Bow and Arrows. On his right hand there stood twenty Pages. They were all very handsome as to their Persons, but it seems they had made choice of the handsomest among them to hold the Fan, wherewith he incessantly gave the king air."

An embassy from Shah Safi to Duke Frederick of Holstein Gottorp, in the year 1639, presented to the duke six silk rugs, including the superb coronation rug described and illustrated by Martin, which later were removed to Rosenborg Castle, Copenhagen.

Later Safavi Monarchs

Safi murdered right and left, and among his successors only Abbas II was a credit to the line. Sulayman was so vicious that a great noble always "felt if his head was on his shoulders," when he came from the royal presence; and Husayn was so tender-hearted that he exclaimed in terror, "I am polluted with blood," and ordered alms to the poor on wounding a duck with his pistol.

On the down grade, Persia still was high in the esteem of Europe. Alexis, Czar of Russia, sent two envoys and eight hundred followers;

and Peter the Great two missions. The French, Dutch and English all maintained commercial agents in the country. But the many functions of government had come more and more into the hands of mullas and eunuchs, and the army under the disintegrating influence of court factions. The pitiful state of affairs was due in part to the great Abbas himself, whose policy of mistrusting his sons, destroying nobles and tribal chiefs, and creating town factions to accomplish his ends, left Persia too weak to beat off so petty a foe as twenty thousand crude Afghans.

Afghan Dynasty, 1722-1730

The Afghans, under Mir Mahmud of Kandahar, had as their objective, at the beginning, only the termination of their dependency as a Persian province. Finding, however, no opposition to their raids around Kerman and Yezd, they pushed along toward Ispahan, and on a plain eleven miles east of the world-famous city found the Persian army. "Composed of whatever was most brilliant at court, it seemed as if it had been formed rather to make a show than to fight. The riches and rarity of arms and vestments, the beauty of horses, the gold and precious stones of harnesses, and the magnificence of tents made the Persian camp very pompous. On the other side was a much smaller body of soldiers, disfigured by fatigue and the scorching heat of the sun. Their clothes were so ragged and torn in so long a march that they were scarce sufficient to cover them, and their horses being adorned with only leather and brass, there was nothing glittering but their spears and sabres."

Once again the stout of heart and poor of purse won, and despoiled the rich and grand whose sun had set; and once again an understudy despatched a bandit leader, the Afghan victor, and Persia grovelled before a second Afghan potentate. Coincidentally, Peter the Great neatly appropriated Persia's Caspian provinces, and Turkey the cities and districts of Tabriz, Hamadan and Kermanshah—altogether a rather complete dismemberment.

NADIR SHAH, 1736-1747

More than a degenerate Safavi was needed to drive out the Afghans, and the need was supplied by an Afshar nomad, common soldier and robber, whose first-born, raised to affluence, gave his pedigree as "Son of Nadir, Son of the Sword, Grandson of the Sword, and Great Grandson of the Sword for Seventy Generations." Nadir, the Napoleon of Persia, dissolved the Afghans with an army of wild Turkmans, enthroned Tahmasp II the rightful ruler and as promptly dethroned him, defeated the Turks, retook the Caucasus, crowned himself, invaded India, devastated Delhi, where he repeated Timur's massacre of one hundred thousand citizens, and returned to Persia with the famous peacock throne and spoil valued at half a billion dollars. Incidentally, he terminated the period of the great rugs of India. Had he died at once he would have become a national hero. Unfortunately he lived to abuse his power and to deserve the assassin's dagger which removed him and his heirs, and again made Persia a cockpit of pretenders.

ZAND DYNASTY, 1750-1795

PERIOD OF IMPORTANT SHIRAZ RUGS

Eventually a triangular fight between three strong groups, the Zand of Shiraz, the Turkish Kajar of the Caucasus, and the Afghans, resulted in the victory of Karim Khan Zand, who made Shiraz a beautiful and prosperous national capital and incidentally a rug name. "So anxious was he that his subjects should be happy that if in any quarter of the town no music was heard, he invariably inquired what was wrong, and paid musicians to play there." During

49

his just and gracious reign Persia gained needed rest from infinite turmoil. His death precipitated the usual contest for succession, and produced an unanticipated result.

At the court was a boy of royal Kajar blood who was held as a hostage for the good behavior of the Kajar tribes. This lad, made a eunuch for the greater security of the Zand heirs, became famous in story for his practice of maliciously cutting with his knife the royal carpets that later were to become his personal possession. Escaping from the court by a clever ruse, during the fatal illness of Karim Khan, he instigated the revolt of the Kajar forces around Tabriz, and bribed or otherwise secured the powerful support of the mayor of Shiraz, Haji Ibrahim, who seized the capital. Out of the march of armies that ensued the Kajar issued the victor and executioner of the rightful ruler, Lutf Ali Khan, "the last chivalrous figure among Persian rulers."

KAJAR DYNASTY, 1796-1925

THE LESS SUCCESSFUL RUG PATRONS

Aga Muhammad Khan made Teheran the Persian capital. His energy and genius for government were magnificent, but avarice and revenge were his gods. "The Shah turned his attention to Khorassan, and Shah Rukh, unable to resist, yielded. But Aga Muhammad wanted more than the possession of Khorassan; he coveted with intense passion the jewels which he knew that Shah Rukh had concealed from every one, including his own sons. The wretched man denied the existence of any hidden treasure, but in vain. He was handed over to the torturers, and day by day some valuable jewel was produced from its hiding-place. Last of all, the famous ruby of Aurung-Zeb was extracted by pouring molten lead on a circle of paste which had been put on his head. The tale of the jewels was complete, and Shah Rukh, worn out by the tortures, died." The assassination

50

of this ogre monarch, the first Kajar, by two bodyguards whom he had condemned to death, occasioned Persian delight.

The second Kajar, Fath Ali Shah, constituted himself keeper of the toll-house on the highway of French ambition to India; and many fortunes in pounds and diamonds the English under George III paid the old miser for assurances and contracts to impede the plans of Napoleon. But not a shilling would he pay his own army to defend Tabriz against the Russians; and the army deserted. The result was the loss to Persia of all status as a nation, and an acknowledgment of a condition of dependency which only in recent years has been terminated.

In one particular Fath Ali Shah was a man without peer. He was the husband of one hundred and fifty-eight wives who bore him children, the father of fifty-seven sons and forty-six daughters who lived to maturity, and the grandfather of two hundred and ninety-six grandsons and two hundred and ninety-two granddaughters. To-day, it is said, ten thousand Persians revere him as a most puissant ancestor.

If ever a country was out of favor with the Fates, that country was Persia under the succeeding Kajars. Mohammed Shah was a vassal of Russia and a mortgager of the state. Nasir-u-Din Shah lost Herat to Afghanistan, and said that he preferred advisers "who did not know whether Brussels was a city or a cabbage." Muzaffar-u-Din Shah granted a constitution to his subjects, but made extravagant trips to Europe on money borrowed from Russia. Mohammed Ali Shah was deposed for opposition to the constitution and national parliament. Lastly, Sultan Ahmad Shah, sojourning in Paris, was deposed for neglect of the affairs of state, by the parliament which now pays allegiance to its recent efficient soldier and new ruler, Riza Shah Pahlavi. All rulers of the Kajar succession possessed fine rugs, inherited and woven to special order, but lesser rugs compared to earlier weavings.

51

ORIENTAL RUGS AND CARPETS

"Observe always," writes Marcus Aurelius, "that everything is the result of change. Get used to thinking that there is nothing Nature loves so well as to change existing forms, and to make new ones like them."

CHAPTER III

PERSIA'S GREAT RUGS

"In the vaunted works of Art,
The master-stroke is Nature's part."

GARDENS, physical source of the rug art of Persia, have a significance in the East wholly beyond the comprehension of the West. The Bible proclaims their divine origin, the Koran (634 A.D.) their heavenly recompense. To understand the theology of gardens the West must reread the sacred texts.

The Bible: "The Lord God planted a garden eastward in Eden. Out of the garden made the Lord God to grow every tree that is pleasant to the sight—the tree of life also in the midst of the garden, and the tree of knowledge of good and evil. And a river went out of Eden to water the garden. And the Lord God took man and put him into the Garden of Eden to dress and to keep it."

The Koran: "And when the heaven shall be rent in sunder, and shall become red as a rose, and shall melt like ointment, for him who dreadeth the tribunal of his Lord are prepared two gardens, planted with shade trees. In each of them shall be two fountains flowing. In each shall there be of every fruit two kinds. They [the elect] shall repose on couches, the linings whereof shall be of thick silk interwoven with gold; and the fruit of the two gardens shall be near at hand to-gether. Therein shall receive them beautiful damsels, having complexions like rubies and pearls. Besides these there shall be two other gardens of dark green. In each shall be two fountains pouring forth plenty of water. In each shall be fruits, and palm trees, and pome-granates. Therein shall be agreeable and beauteous damsels having fine black eyes, who shall be kept in pavilions from the public view. Therein shall they delight themselves, lying on green cushions and beautiful carpets. Blessed be the name of the Lord, possessed of glory and honor."

Plain, intriguing words these, that seem to justify Thomas Moore's shaft:

> "A Persian heaven is easily made;
> 'Tis but black eyes and lemonade."

But not so. Mohammed visualized for lean, unlettered Arabs, impossible to surfeit with animal pleasure, an unbridled garden party, whereas the heavenly garden of Persia is a radiancy in which each of us would wish to dwell, and its poet the immortal Nizami:

> "Now when once more the night's ambrosial dusk
> Upon the skirts of Day had poured its musk,
> In sleep an angel caused him to behold
> The heavenly garden's radiancy untold,
> Whose wide expanse, shadowed by lofty trees,
> Was cheerful as the heart fulfilled of ease.
> Each flow'ret in itself a garden seemed,
> Each rosy petal like a lantern gleamed.
> Each glade reflects, like some sky-scanning eye,
> A heavenly mansion from the azure sky.
> Like brightest emeralds its grasses grow,
> While its effulgence doth no limit know.
> Goblet in hand, each blossom of the dale
> Drinks to the music of the nightingale.
> Celestial harps melodious songs upraise,
> While cooing ring-doves utter hymns of praise."

That the Persian paradise should be a garden, rather than a palace or a fortified city, was ordained from the beginning. The high, vast sky-land of Persia is "limitless space and entire aridity," often possessed by merciless sands, dust, heat, winds, snows and floods. The endless, treeless, stony roads lead from sparse towns to sparser cities, from oasis to oasis, within which is the personal oasis, the one shelter, recompense, comfort and delight, the garden.

> "If there is a paradise on the face of the earth,
> It is this, it is this, it is this."

Out of this valuation arose the Persian name for habitation, "bagh," which means garden. The Persian refers to his house not as a house but as a garden. The little mud house always is "bagh," and sometimes the pretentious palace, such as the Bagh-i-Takht, or Garden of the Throne, in Shiraz. Probably in no other country in the world is the garden so much the heart of life and the object of thought. "As he thinketh in his heart, so is he," and his rugs. Persian gardens and rugs had a grand court wedding in the "Spring of Chosroes" carpet which the Arabs secured at the looting of the palace at Ctesiphon in the seventh century, and subsequent stresses and strains of national calamity served only to strengthen the bonds of union.

Historically, Persian rug design and color doubtless had in primitive nature-worship and religion far earlier sources. Fortunately for our mundane requirements, these springs ceased to function, or were diverted into the gardens that realistically and conventionally were transposed to rugs, with every least item of interest utilized, as a valuable by-product, to create some further artistic effect.

The small Persian garden, enclosed by high mud walls, appears from without a dense bouquet of trees, "set in a pitiless glare of unbroken leagues of sand." Within, the impression of density may be continued; sometimes in a small plot crowded trees and flowers create a wildwood. Commonly, however, the garden area, usually rectangular in shape, is divided by two raised intersecting paths into four equal beds whose flowers are watered by scarcely perceptible channels connected with some ancient water-system. Such are the little gardens that constitute the courtyard of many town and city houses.

A pretentious Persian garden is constructed on a large level site. Here the paths of the small garden become two intersecting axial avenues, one slightly more important, higher and broader than the other, to accommodate a canal. Both avenues are bordered by stately trees, "lofty pyramidal cypress, tapering plane-trees, tough elm, straight ash, knotty pine, fragrant masticks, kingly oaks, sweet myrtles, and useful maples." At the intersection of the avenues is either a shallow pool, lined with blue tile, or a pavilion, square or cruciform in shape, surrounded by four pools and surmounted by a dome.

Grander still, the stately Persian garden is located on an acclivity with a background of mountains. The pavilion, or casino, occupies the highest eminence; numerous planted terraces, watered by a cascading central rivulet, grace the hillside; and a pool of considerable area, the goal of the water, reposes at the foot of the hill. Beyond, a double avenue leads across a level space to a gate house, which is the exit to the city in direct and unimpeded view, a mile or more away.

In the royal garden at Ispahan, Sir Anthony Sherley, in the year 1599, attended a levee given by Shah Abbas, which subsequently he described in a passage that remains in one's memory.

"The King's entrance into Hispahaan was there of the same fashion that it was at Cassan, differing only in this, that for some two English miles, the ways were covered all with velvet, satin and cloth of gold where his horse should pass. For thirtie days continually the King made that feast in a great garden of more than two miles compasse under tents, pitched by certaine small courses of running water, like divers rivers, where every man that would come was placed

56

according to his degree, either under one or other tent, provided for abundantly with meate, fruit and wine, drinking as they would, some largely, some moderately without compulsion. A royaltie and splendor which I have not seene, nor shall see again but by the same King."

The words "certaine small courses of running water" are important. Water is never abundant in Persian gardens; all pools are shallow, channels miniature, land thirsty. Herein lies one of the chief differences between Persian and Italian gardens; the latter with water almost too abundant, the pools deep, dark and full of mysterious movement. In Persia the motionless pools are seldom deeper than eighteen inches, a defect cleverly remedied by linings of greenish-blue tile which give the effect of depth and tranquil sky.

To the surprise of most occidentals, the flowers of Persian gardens and rugs are the common flowers of Europe and America, many of which originally were secured in Persia, where they grow profusely in a wild state. The favorite is the narcissus, which prospers everywhere, and in huge bouquets gladdens every house. The roses are the china and moss varieties, from which rose-water is secured; yellow and orange single roses, noisette and nest-orange roses, the latter a delicately scented single rose whose tree grows to great size. Hafiz composed his famous garden ode about the rose, and one of his devoted followers wove the following stanza of it into the design of a rug now in the collection of the Victoria and Albert Museum:

"Call for wind and scatter roses; what dost thou seek from Time?
Thus spake the rose at dawn: O nightingale, what sayest thou?
Take the cushion to the garden, that thou mayest hold the lip and kiss the cheek
    of the beloved and the cup-bearer, and drink wine and smell the rose.
Proudly move thy graceful form and to the garden go, that the cypress may learn
    from thy stature how to win hearts.
To-day while thy market is full of the tumult of buyers, gain and put by a store
    out of the capital of goodness.
Every bird brings a melody to the garden of the King—the nightingale songs of
    love, and Hafiz, prayers for blessing."

Other common garden flowers are the zinnia, whose plant grows five feet high, aster, balsam, wallflower, chrysanthemum, marigold, convolvulus, marvel-of-Peru, portulaca, cockscomb, dahlia, Mary's flower, larkspur, sweet-william, pink, tulip, violet, lily, pansy, petunia, white and purple iris. Lilacs and grape-vines are everywhere. In shady corners are to be found small patches of mint, anise, fennel and parsley. Sometimes at intervals gourds and melons add their glories of form and color. Backgrounds and edgings are of broom-plant.

The fruit trees of the garden are apricot, date, fig, olive, orange, apple, pear, plum, peach, cherry, nectarine, mulberry, quince and pomegranate. The shade trees are cypress, willow, poplar, the semi-sacred plane-tree, alder, ash, beech, elm, juniper, maple, oak and walnut. The birds are nightingale, blackbird, bluejay, thrush, pastor, bee-eater, cuckoo and oriole. The Persian garden is a composite of flower-garden, orchard, park and bird refuge.

Garden Rugs

Little imagination, and yet sufficient to "body forth the forms of things unknown," is needed to visualize these gardens through their rug portraits. Designs with obvious axial avenues, paths and plots invariably astonish and captivate. Less commonly recognized as garden rugs are weavings whose designs reproduce only garden plots with unsymmetrical flowers and trees, and terraces whose banks of flowers, shrubs and trees seem to create only a pleasing perpendicular perspective. Many "tree" and "landscape" rugs are terrace-garden rugs. Of less importance, although effective when handled with skill, are the designs acquired from garden accessories—vases and arbors, swans and peacocks. Such is the panorama of garden-rug design that attained eminence primarily through magnificence of color, acquired from the source that most often rivals the incomparable sky.

Still the pattern itself has distinction. The central avenue has possibly three attractive circular pools embroidered with water plants, or three enticing pavilions surrounded by pools, or two central avenues separated by a brook containing fish, that converges with an equal brook in a central pool possessed by swan. The double avenues bordering the larger streams are superbly treed and planted. To right and left are numerous garden plots rich with flowers. Further beyond are other parallel lesser streams forever converging in pools with other streams, more paths and plots, the entire prodigy of truth and fiction encompassed by an avenue as stately as the heavenly-minded weaver can contrive.

That most of the many fine garden carpets of antiquity seem to have entered the service of the faithful in Paradise is an earthly tragedy in art. Seemingly the oldest and finest extant example is in the Figdor Collection, Vienna. It contains gold and silver thread, and is assigned to the end of the sixteenth century. The Naesby House, Sweden, and Vincent Robinson & Co., London, are said to possess complete important examples. The latter rug is believed to have been woven for one of the rooms of the Ispahan palace of Shah Abbas the Great, 1587-1628. Minor garden rugs of one hundred and fifty years ago, and yesterday's gardens executed in silk of Tabriz and Kashan, and in wool of Kerman and Bakhtiari, comprise the principal part of our inheritance. One of the largest and most magnificent Persian garden carpets known is in India in the Jaipur Museum. It was the work of Shah Abbas' weavers and, according to several entry labels, arrived in India August 29, 1632. The garden plots are bordered by a variety of trees and shrubs, with many of the birds and animals indigenous to Persia.

Seven Classes of Masterpieces

As a curtain of "darkness visible" drawn across a mountain landscape temporarily terminates a pleasing prospect, so present ignorance of the sources of our oldest rug possessions creates a barrier to unalloyed enjoyment of them. We know the paths of descent from antiquity, but not the precise camps and courts of indulgence.

Tamerlane at Samarkand, between the years 1369 and 1405, possessed superb rugs. Approximately the year 1400 is assigned by Doctor Martin as the date of the supreme old tree rug in the Joseph Lees Williams Memorial Collection, which, therefore, is a product of the Tamerlane era. Doctor Sarre terminates the jubilation of enthusiasts by reducing the probable age a hundred years. Agreement consists solely in the assignment of the weaving to northwestern Persia, which during the fifteenth century was ruled by the Black and White Sheep dynasties. Some day, by a miracle of grace, a Tamerlane rug may be discovered and authenticated.

Tamerlane's son, Shah Rukh, ruled the erudite court at Herat between the years 1404 and 1447, and his descendants maintained an ascendency there until 1494, when anarchy overwhelmed them. Shah Ismail captured the city in 1510. That Tamerlane and Shah Rukh created a standard of monarchical elegance in rugs, which was maintained and possibly surpassed in Persia during the two succeeding centuries, is the only fact about the rugs of these monarchs that can be positively asserted.

A likely source of a few old rarities is the court maintained at Tabriz by Jahan Shah (1437-1467), last important ruler of the Black Sheep dynasty and builder of the Blue Mosque. As yet, however, no rugs definitely have been attached to it. Only with the advent of the Tabriz court of the White Sheep dynasty and its grim ruler, Uzun Hasan (1466-1477), who killed Jahan Shah in battle and dispossessed his family, are we in contact with a seemingly certain source.

To Tabriz, in the year 1471, came, as already related, the Venetian envoy Josafa Barbaro, who testifies that the rugs of the court far surpassed the carpets woven at Cairo and Brusa. Whether the art so highly commended was displayed in the rugs of large medallions and delicate abstract pattern of flowers, commonly attributed to the district and asserted to be the oldest of existing groups, or in tree rugs resembling the Williams specimen, or in rugs of silk now assigned to a subsequent date, or in rugs comprehending all of these varieties, cannot be asserted. Suffice it that the court fits a scholastic requirement and provides almost as certain a source for some of the earliest of existing rug masterpieces as the dates on the Ardabil carpets provided a definite period.

From this point the succession of the important classes of rugs is seemingly established. The wool masterpieces among animal rugs, long in process of development, seem to have been woven at Tabriz and Herat during the reign of the courageous, red-headed Ismail (1502-1524). The great hunting rugs, woven at Tabriz, Kazvin or Kashan,—the latter the almost certain source of animal rugs of silk,— were undoubtedly the product of the era of the gloomy, introspective Tahmasp (1524-1577), which also produced the Ardabil carpets. Coincidently, the finest examples of a fourth group of superior rugs, distinguished by pattern of palmette and now called Ispahan, were woven at Herat. Concurrently a fifth group of rugs, known as Vase carpets, distinguished by vases, palmettes, diagonal vines and realistic flowers, was created probably at Joshaghan. Finally, during the latter part of the century, was begun the weaving of the Polonaise silk-and-metal rugs of the Ispahan court of Shah Abbas and his successors, woven probably at Kashan, Joshaghan and Ispahan. If to the foregoing groups are added a very few fine prayer rugs, no more than a corporal's guard, the tale of Persian rug masterpieces is complete.

Rugs decorated largely with inscriptions and called inscription carpets, and rugs displaying boating scenes with mariners dressed in the costumes of Portugal and Spain and called Portuguese carpets— both weavings of the seventeenth century—are too few in number to constitute important classes. Similar objection applies to the inclusion of the class of rugs known as arabesque-stem carpets, which are decorated with forms that the layman would describe as grape-vines. Parenthetically, *arabesques* are curving scrolls that cross and interlace, ornamented with the forms of leaves and flowers; and *stems* are the trunks or stocks of trees, shrubs and plants, and the stalks of flowers. The stems of arabesque carpets are thick black bands; the stems of floral-stem carpets are delicate scrolls in intricate convolutions. The important varieties of floral-stem carpets are the Ispahan and vase rugs.

As a river flows from source to delta gathering the substance of tributaries, so flows the stream of design, from Tabriz to Ispahan, in the important rug classes. The source group at Tabriz displays large medallions and floral scrolls. The first and second tributaries contribute human, animal and bird forms; the third adds a wealth of palmettes; the fourth, further along, brings vases and realistic flowers. At Ispahan a general assembly of these motives is exhibited in the rug Polonaise.

Cross-currents of pattern create admixture of ingredients. The medallions of the early rugs flow over into the majority of animal rugs and thence into hunting rugs. Doctor Bode reverses the statement in asserting that the animal forms were imposed upon the medallion art. The palmette, employed inconspicuously in medallion rugs and conspicuously in Herat brocade, becomes the chief ornament of Herat rugs. The certainty that this variety of palmette came direct to Herat from China does not annul the relationship. In the year 1419 Shah Rukh sent ambassadors to the Chinese Emperor with letters written by himself which are still extant. Finally, Chinese pattern, popularized in Western Asia by Chinese artists at the court of Hulagu Khan at Bagdad (1251-1265), as well as by direct contacts with the Celestial Empire, runs very like a gulf stream through all groups. So much for outline and generality.

PERSIA'S GREAT RUGS

The First Group: Medallion Rugs

Medallions, symbols of the earliest extant Persian rugs, are the pearls and diamonds of all Persian art. From the period of the sixth century, when the weavers of the fine fabrics of the Sasanian monarchs used them to frame the forms of huntsmen and lions, down to recent centuries when artists embossed them upon book-covers, silver and brass objects, tile and porcelain, never for a single day has the medallion been out of employment. Brilliance of expression is everywhere among artists a natural and stimulated ambition, and brilliant performance through the use of medallions the surest road to success in the decoration of large rug areas.

But not alone intricate medallions. As the kaleidoscope from revolving particles of colored glass magically creates constellations, so Persian rug artists created diamonds, disks and ovals that hang indefinitely in rug space, and again break into a thousand particles of light and color. The inordinate fondness of the modern Persian for displays of actual fireworks is only the natural concomitant of a related practice in art.

The zenith of medallion-rug art *per se* was attained in the earliest extant group of weavings, by this author associated tentatively with the court of Uzun Hasan (1466-1477). Depiction of medallion rugs in Persian miniature paintings by Bihzad, favorite painter of Shah Ismail, about the year 1520, presumably coincides with the end of the major production. Large central medallions, brilliant pendants, traceried spandrels and graceful floral scrolls "rise in glad surprise to higher levels." By general agreement, here is achieved the highest point of artistic abstraction.

Obviously the medallions are stars of eight and sixteen points. In the rug used for color illustration, both forms are employed, one within the other. In later examples sometimes as many as five diversi-

63

fied star shapes are imposed one upon another, the outer star terminating in ornate shield-shaped points. In such rugs four satellites, two above and two below, have the graceful forms of shields and elongated panels called *cartouche*. Stars and satellites are decorated with flowers and stems, which reappear in the surrounding field with floral scrolls, arabesques and palmettes. Chinese forms of palmettes and cloud motives are found in some examples. In the earliest specimens design is strong and angular, and color light and restrained. Curved and lobed design, with rich and variegated color, was attained only in rugs after the order of the masterpiece in the Altman Collection of the Metropolitan Museum of Art—rugs that consummated the first known period of the art and inspired the genius displayed in the decoration of two succeeding species.

Except for the Ardabil tomb carpets (1536-1539), later medallion rugs are less pretentious in size, more pretentious in design, with tendency to inclusion of animal, bird and Chinese forms, and fine in texture. In one group, now generally assigned to Tabriz, the medallions are round and the pattern a maze of arabesques. In the group of superlative silk rugs attributed to Kashan, and herein illustrated in color frontispiece by a rug from the Widener Collection, the medallions are quatrefoil in shape, deeply incised, and the art of arabesque brought to perfection. Color here rises to utmost regal splendor. The dominant hue is a brilliant crimson that would seem to have no counterpart. Only in the hunting rugs is equal color and texture attained, and regal splendor enhanced by living, exultant forms.

HUNTING

An account, obligingly supplied by Adam Olearius, of a hunting party given by the Shah Safi, out of Ispahan in the year 1637, greatly facilitates our understanding of hunting rugs:

"The hunting began the 17th. Betimes in the morning, there were

Horses brought for the Persons and camels for the Baggage. The Ambassadors got on Horse-back with about thirty persons of their Retinue. The Mehemandar conducted them into a spacious Plain, whither the King came soon after, attended by above three hundred Lords, all excellently well mounted, and sumptuously cloathed. The King himself was in a Vestment of Silver Brocade, with a Turbant adorned with most noble Heron's feathers, and having led after him four Horses, whereof the Saddles, Harness, and covering cloaths were beset with Gold and precious stones. The King at his coming up very civilly saluted the Ambassadors, and ordered them to march near him on his left side.

"The other Chans and great Lords marched after the King with so little observance of order that many times the Servants were shuffled in among their masters. There was, among the rest, in the King's Retinue, an Astrologer, who always kept very close to him, and ever and anon observed the position of the Heavens, that he might prognosticate what good or ill fortune should happen. These are believed as Oracles. We rode up and down that day above three Leagues, the King taking occasion often to change his Horse and upper Garments, which he did every day while the Hunting lasted.

"The morning was spent in hawking. The hawks were let out at Herons, Cranes, Drakes, nay sometimes at Crows, which they either met with by chance, or were set purposely upon. About noon, after the King had been brought by his Grandees into his Tent, they came for the Ambassadors, who with some of their Gentlemen and Officers dined with him. Fruits and conserves were brought in first, and afterwards the meat, upon a kind of Bier or Barrow, which was covered all over with plates of gold, and it was served in dishes of the same metal.

"The 18th betimes in the morning, the King sent the Ambassadors word that he would go with very few persons about him a Cranehunting, that the cranes might not be frightened by a great number of people; but the sport was no sooner begun ere they sent for all the retinue. They had made a great secret way underground, at the end whereof there was a field about which they had scattered some wheat. The Cranes came thither in great numbers and there were above fourscore taken. The King took some of their feathers to put into his Turbant, and gave two to each of the Ambassadors who put them into their hats.

"The next day was our greatest day for sport, the King having ordered to be brought to the field, a great number of Hawks, and three leopards taught to hunt; but very few dogs. Having spent some time in beating the bushes up and down, and found nothing, the King carried us into a great park, compassed with a very high wall, and divided into three partitions. In the first was kept Harts, Wild-Goats, Deer, Hares and Foxes. In the second were kept that kind of Deer, which they call Ahu's; and in the third wild Asses. The King first commanded the Leopards to be let in among the Ahu's and they took each of them one. Thence we went to the Wild Asses, and the King seeing one of them at a stand, spoke to the Ambassador to fire his pistol at it, and perceiving that he missed it, he took an arrow, and though he rid in full speed, shot it directly into the breast of the Beast. Another he took just in the Fore-head. He never failed, though he always shot Riding in full speed. He was as well skilled at his sword as at his Bow.

"Then we all went to another small partition, that was in the middle of the Park, to a little building after the fashion of a Theatre, into which the King brought us to a collection of Fruits and Conserves. That done, there was driven into the place thirty-two wild Asses, at which the King discharged some shots with the Fowling-pieces, and shot some arrows, and afterwards permitted the Ambassadors and other Lords to shoot at them. Having knocked down all, there was let in thirty wild Asses more, which they also killed and laid them all in a row before the King, to be sent to Ispahan, to the Court kitchen. The Persians so highly esteem the flesh of those wild Asses, that they have brought it into a Proverb.

"Some days afterwards it was published by the publick crier, all over the City, that all should keep within their houses, and that none should presume to come into the street; the King being to go that way abroad to give the court Ladies the Divertisement of Hunting. The King goes before, and the Ladies follow, about half an hour after, accompanied by their women, and a great number of Eunichs. When they are come into the field, they get on Horse-back, carry Hawks on their fists, and use their Bows and Arrows as well as the men. Only the King and the Eunichs stay among the Women; all the rest of the men are about half a League from them and when the sport is begun, no man is to come within two Leagues, unless the King send for him by a Eunich. The Lords of the Court in the meantime hunt some other way."

Persian monarchs of the Achæmenian dynasty hunted lions about Persepolis, where they are said still to persist; but only the lion on the Persian coat-of-arms is of much account throughout the country. Tigers, infesting the Persian coast along the Caspian, were somewhat aloof from Persian courts and kingly hunting parties, but not too far removed from Rome's arena to be caught and transported there. Leopards in Persia both hold with the hare and run with the hound. "One, excellently well taught, started with as much swiftness as a greyhound, and gave us all the satisfaction hunting could afford." Wolves hunt in couples and packs in the Meshed district, and supply the eyes and knuckle-bones which inspire courage when worn as talismans. Jackals also hunt in packs and with silver-gray foxes deplete vineyards during the fruit season. Hyena are common mammals that share uncleanness with the wild boar, which is considered so foul an animal that a Mohammedan killed by one is purified only by the

67

fires of hell. Herds of gazelle and fleet wild ass roam the plains, and small gray bear, ibex and wild sheep the hills and mountains.

To these objects of hunting ambition must be added many varieties of small game and wild fowl, that equally with the brutes sought cover from shotgun, rifle, bow and arrow, sword, hawks, leopards, horses, dogs and the noisy reckless ardor of the hunting party. Because of scarcity of food and water, the Persian plateau was never the paradise of hunters that the natural propensity of the people for the pursuit of wild life would have warranted.

HUNTING RUGS

The most famous of hunting carpets and most marvellous of all existing rugs is the silk and silver masterpiece in the rug collection of the present Austrian State, now exhibited by the Museum of Art and Industry, Vienna, that according to tradition was acquired by the Austrian Imperial family about the year 1698 through gift of Peter the Great of Russia, who secured it by inheritance from Czar Feodor Ioannovitch. One of our authorities as to original Russian ownership is Arsenius, Bishop of Elasson, city of old Thessaly, who wrote that the audience-hall of the Imperial Palace at Moscow, in the year 1589, was covered with "Persian carpets from silk and gold, artistically decorated with hunting scenes and animals."

The design represents a large court party, mounted on spirited steeds, hotly pursuing lions, foxes, jackals, antelopes, ibexes, wild boars and hares. The field of salmon-pink color, lavishly flowered, has for central ornament an unrivalled, scalloped, green medallion containing four pairs of fighting dragon and "phœnix" appropriated from Chinese art; and, for corner ornaments, segments of the medallion; and, for border, an unsurpassed frieze of Persian genii participating in a fruit ceremony performed against a crimson background.

68

The design is believed to be the work of the great Sultan Muhammad, court artist and head of the painting school of Shah Tahmasp at Tabriz (1524-1549). Here at least is perfection of design, color, material and weaving. Only ages of utmost kingly luxury and belief in the divinity of kings could produce so sumptuous a carpet.

The world's supply of important hunting rugs is meagre, a scant half dozen, the result both of original rarity, due to high cost, and of wanton destruction by fanatical orthodox Mohammedans, to whom the Mischat-ul-Masabih, "Niche of the Lamps," or "Collection of the Most Authentic Traditions Regarding the Actions and Sayings of Mohammed," was equal law with the Koran. The law against the employment of human, animal and bird forms in works of art, observed until recent years by all of the faithful except Persians and other dissenters and the rich and profligate everywhere, is most interesting.

Abu-Talhah: "The angels do not enter the house in which is a dog, nor into that in which are pictures."

Ibu-Abbas: "One morning his highness [Mohammed] got up silent and sad and said to me: 'Gabriel promised to visit me last night, but did not come; by God, he never acted contrary to his promise before.' Then when his highness considered about Gabriel's not coming, he was struck by the reason of a puppy being near the curtain, and he ordered it to be taken away. Then his majesty took water in his hand and washed the place where the puppy had lain. And in the evening Gabriel came to his highness, who said to him: 'Verily, you promised to meet me last night.' Gabriel said, 'Yes, I did, but we angels do not go into a house in which are pictures or dogs.' Then in the morning of the following day, his highness ordered the dogs to be killed, even to those kept for the protection of small gardens; but ordered those kept for orchards not to be touched."

Aayeshah said: "His highness would not allow a single thing to be in his house with a picture on it, but would break it. I bought a bed [rug] on which were drawings, and when his highness saw them, he stood at the door but would not come in. Then I perceived displeasure in his countenance, and said: 'O Messenger of God, what fault have I committed that you will not come in?' His highness said: 'What bed is this?' I said: 'I bought it for you to sit and recline upon.' His Majesty said: 'Verily, the makers of these pictures will be punished at the day of resurrection, and it will be said to them "bring to life these pictures which you have made." ' After that his Majesty said: 'Verily, the angels do not enter into that house in which are pictures.' "

Aayeshah said: "I had a house with a curtain [rug] at the door of it, with paintings upon it; and his highness blotted them out. Then I made two beds of it, and his highness used to sit upon them. His highness went to fight with infidels and I purchased an elegant fine bed, and used it as a curtain for my door; and when his highness returned and came into my house, he saw the bed which I had put up to cover the door, and pulled it down, and tore it to pieces, and said: 'God has not ordered me to cover stones and clay. Those will be punished the most severely, at the day of resurrection, who draw likenesses of God's creation.' "

Abu-hurairah said: "I heard his highness say that God said: 'Who is more unjust than that person who makes resemblances to my creation?' Let them create a small ant or a grain of corn."

Ibu-Abbas said: "I heard his majesty say: 'Every painter is in hell fire; and God will appoint a person, at the day of resurrection, for every picture he shall have drawn to punish him; and they will punish him in hell. If you must make pictures, make them of trees and things without souls.' "

One must infer from this dialogue, transcribed about 1336 A.D. from earlier manuscript, that during Mohammed's lifetime the rugs

70

of Mecca and Medina commonly were decorated with "likenesses of God's creation," which fell under Mohammed's malediction, because with idols they violated the law of creation. According to Doctor Bode, "Omission of all figural representation was a self-understood requirement in all rugs intended for sanctuary use," even in Persia, a thousand years after Mohammed's time.

ANIMAL RUGS

Animal rugs, progenitors of hunting rugs, are the descendants of the Sasanian floor-coverings which the Chinese traders (750 A.D.) reported to contain designs of "birds, beasts, human figures and dead objects," and in still more remote times of Persian-Alexandrian "beast carpets." Beyond shadow of doubt the designs of the finest and most pretentious of existing examples were made by great artists, ordinarily engaged in miniature painting and other arts, employed at the courts of Shah Ismail and Shah Tahmasp. Except for figures of horsemen and other hunters, animal rugs duplicate in general character the decoration and substance of hunting rugs, and consequently suggest the appearance of the more monumental weavings. Their number is none too great, but sufficient to provide a reasonable survey.

The animal rug held in highest esteem is the wool masterpiece in the collection of the Victoria and Albert Museum (see illustration), whose ten medallions are organized as two identical constellations, one balancing the other on either side of a small, round, central pool containing fish. Each constellation consists of a large central eight-pointed star filled with lace-like vines, flowers and leaves, surrounded by four oval medallions decorated with pairs of ducks flying among clouds. Chinese flower vases, decorated with geese and supported by dragons; and fine palmetto leaves that later were to become famous in "Ispa-han" rugs, alternately fill the areas between the encircling medallions. Dragons, lions, bullocks and antelopes move among almond and pomegranate trees filled with birds, and in consequence are subordinate features of decoration, as in all animal rugs of the medallion type. As if to stamp the design as kingly, an undulating pattern of Chinese cloud-ribbons in the border creates the forms of numerous crowns. The color of the field is reddish-brown, of the ten medallions black, and of the border half of each. The color note of black and the double measure of design are unique and magnificent features. The period of weaving is approximately 1502, the date of the coronation of Shah Ismail, founder of the Safavi dynasty.

To the eight varieties of animals already enumerated as the indicted content of hunting and animal rugs, must be added tigers, panthers, monkeys, fallow deer, dogs and the masks of lions, panthers and demons, employed in other examples of the art. To hunters must be added musicians and feasters; and to birds, peacocks, parrots, pheasants and falcons. Trees are cypress, plane, medlar, pomegranate, almond, magnolia and many varieties of fruit. Flowers are difficult to identify because the forms are floral essences. The most important are the lotus and peony, generally called palmettes, which at an earlier time simulated vine-leaves and flower petals. Curving scrolls, called arabesques, crossed and interlaced, decorated with palmettes, leaf and flower motives, are extensively, magnificently employed. Inscription of the verses of poets adds further ornament to a scheme of decoration lacking nothing, because the motives include the entire property of Persian art.

In ancient times animal designs had meaning. In early Persian art, the lion was the symbol of victory, virtue, sun and day; the antelope the symbol of defeat, vice, moon and night; but not in these rugs of utmost maturity. Here the motives that once had meaning and diverted the mind from the whole to the part had long since gained mature significance as decorative pattern. Even the date-tree, which was the original "*hom*," or tree of life, symbol of the eternal renewal of persons and things, was soon displaced by trees too beautiful to bother with religion or philosophy.

The quantity of Chinese ornament in animal and hunting rugs is formidable. Most important are the dragon and "phœnix," forever engaged, against all the practice of Chinese art, in mortal combat. Explanation of the antagonism is supplied by Persian and Arabian mythology. "The nagas or uragas are large serpents, and the garudas or supernas immense birds called rokhs by Arabian fabulists, or mere creatures of the imagination like the Simorg of the Persians, whom Sadi describes as receiving its daily allowance [of serpents] on the mount of Kaf."* The roc that carried Sindbad above the clouds and deposited him in a field of diamonds, picked up and carried away a serpent.

Other Chinese ornaments are the Kylin, mythological composite of stag and dragon; bats, cranes and ducks flying through clouds; the cloud-band, one of the forms of the Tschi, holy Chinese fungus, emblem of immortality, which often is represented in its original spongy and gnarled form; the globe pattern called Tschintamani, holy symbol of the teaching of Buddha, which in the form of three globes is the seal of Tamerlane; and finally a representation of the Chinaman himself, dressed in long ceremonial coat and elevated shoes.

The extensive employment of Chinese art in the rugs of the Safavi dynasty (1502-1736) was a sequel to its use in Persian book-paintings, book-bindings of stamped leather, lacquer painting and textile decoration, beginning in the last decade of the thirteenth century. The famous Manafi al Hayawan in the Morgan Library, dated 1291; the decoration of the mosque of Veramin, built about 1322; the potteries generally attributed to Sultanabad; and a miniature in the manuscript of Khwaju Kirmani, written about 1396, are a few of the cited evidences of the growth of admiration.

* *Remarks on the Arabian Nights' Entertainments.* R. Hole. London, 1797.

73

The decoration of animal rugs has three forms. In the vast majority of the weavings the medallion is the conspicuous ornament. Fields surrounding the medallions are either wholly floral or partly treed. The flowers are charming; the forest, magnificent. In a small minority of the weavings the animals are the chief feature, appearing only with vines and flowers. Finally, in a few precious creations of amazing beauty and force, the central field is broken into numerous panels in which the animals are enclosed or framed as pictures. These are the famous compartment or cartouche rugs that rank high among rug masterpieces. Materials of animal rugs are both silk and wool, the latter used generally in the earlier period.

OTHER SCENIC RUGS

Garden, hunting and animal design has long been compounded in scenic rugs that trail a lessening art down to the present hour. An old example is the rug in the Musée des Arts Décoratifs, whose scenes fuse illustrations of hunting with illustrations of story-telling. Here is depicted the romantic meeting of Shirin and Prince Khusru, the former bathing in a pool, the latter guided by an intelligent horse; and Majnun dying in Laila's arms. In another rug, the national hero Rustam and his horse Rakhsh are shown in the act of destroying a serpent.

In modern examples, if digression is permissible, the subjects are taken less from Persian romantic literature and more from romanticized general history. One widely advertised and exhibited rug displayed the effigies of an assortment of persons, assembled on the steps of a Greek temple—or was it an American "movie" theatre? The group included Christ, Moses, Mohammed, Napoleon, Washington and other leaders, sacred and profane. As an offset to this test of tolerance, an occasional modern Kerman weaving exhibits a praise-worthy attempt to depict delicately an oriental garden scene containing merry-makers indulging the old delights.

Comparison of old scenic rugs with new clearly exhibits the artistic superiority of the former. Always, in the old rugs, fact is subordinated to fiction and make-believe, as in the paintings of John Constable human and animal forms are subordinated to landscape. Never is fact allowed to monopolize the stage. By simplicity of treatment, as when figures are well spaced on a few simple planes, and again by an ordered complexity of treatment,—by a veritable deluge of small decorative forms,—fact is made artistic.

HERAT RUGS CALLED ISPAHAN

Ispahan design differs from garden, hunting and animal pattern in having no similar obvious and intriguing source, and consequently in being what Milton calls "a fairy vision." The forms employed are purely imaginative, and the composition is as abstract and intricate as a Persian religious discussion. So superior was the genius of the original designers, so talented were the dyers, so competent the weavers, that the product sometimes became a fantasy endowed with life, a garden of the poetic mind with constantly waving foliage within a labyrinthine tangle of vines. Analysis of such a work of art invites the soul no more than the parsing of poetry.

Palmetto leaves (palmettes), cloud-bands, lancet leaves, spiral tendrils and arabesques are the essential substantives of the pattern. Three of the five are imported motives. The palmette and cloud-band were derived from Chinese art, where the former appears as lotus and peony, and the latter as ribbons of lightest grace, once having the meaning of immortality. The arabesque is Arabian and its appear-

75

ances comport with the common use of the word as indicating interlaced curving scrolls. Greece as the source of these arabesques and palmettes is too remote in time and out of position. Persian art, at this period, was facing east.

To visualize these spirit forms, conceive the palmettes as flower-decorated leaves that somehow have the faculty of resembling shells of mother-of-pearl, the cloud-bands as floating ribbons of silk, the tendrils as webbing of frost, the lancet leaves as plumed fronds, and the arabesques as carved vines. Conceive each item as in itself a work of art, exquisitely shaded and outlined, but reticent of self-assertion: the palmettes in pairs, distributed symmetrically about a common axis; the cloud-bands floating free or serving as aerial anchorage to tendrils curved with weight of buds and leaves. Impose this decoration, rendered in gold, green, orange, blue and black, on a field of claret or deep crimson; surround it with a border of further palmettes held in place by proud arabesques on a ground of moss-green or deep blue, and the charm is complete.

Such is the superlative Ispahan of the sixteenth century, without medallion or decorated corner areas, the upper half identical with the lower half, doubling from a suggested centre, the color rich and harmonious, the pile of choicest wool, the foundation of silk or linen, the fabric hard and firm, sometimes stiffened by double warp. The best examples of the art were produced in the years preceding the installation of Abbas as Shah of Persia, and consequently before the selection of Ispahan as his capital city. Rubens, Van Dyck and many other painters utilized the original beauty and contributed to its European fame, which, overtaken by the fame of Ispahan, probably secured for the rug the city's name. That the art should fall from its apex of perfection was but to follow Babylon. Popularity did not completely ruin it, but with increase of demand and reduction of cost, which originally was enormous, colors lost their finesse, designs forgot their details, motives became large and crowded or small and insignificant, materials and workmanship inferior, until finally resemblance vanished and a new style was established.

In all probability several places participated in the weaving, exactly as many villages to-day produce the modern Saruk. The variations are too great to warrant the supposition of a common source—so great that the class constitutes a style rather than a weave. The fine early work came from Herat, Persian metropolis between India and Ispahan, recently the great court of the Timurids. The reasons for the assignment are convincing. Here were still executed many of the finest examples of Persia's many fine arts, including the brocade that in pattern and color is almost identical with the finest Ispahan rug art. Here was the reputation for the best rug-weaving of Persia. Close at hand in the Afghan mountains were sheep that yielded the finest qualities of wool, lacking which no rugs can be great. Not far away was India, that imported many of the rugs; and in India were the Dutch and Portuguese traders who carried them to Europe.

Concerning the possibility that the weaving was taken up and continued at Ispahan, Olearius, who visited Ispahan in 1637, says: "There are near and about Ispahan one thousand four hundred and sixty villages, the inhabitants whereof are all in a manner employed in the making of tapestry [carpet] of wool, cotton, silk and brocade." The weaving soon languished, however. Raphael Du Mans, a French priest who lived in Ispahan about 1650, asserts that only a very few poor rugs were being woven, and that the weavers could barely make a living.

VASE RUGS

During the regency (1500-1600) of the Ispahan rug in eastern Persia a second variety of rug, decorated with all-over design of palmettes and scrolls, was maintaining a courtly standard of floor-covering in a still unidentified but important city of Persia, possibly in Joshaghan. Attribution of this art to south Persia and Kerman, favored by the earlier authorities, is no longer in vogue. Among other reasons it seems reasonable to assume that so elegant a weaving must have emanated somewhere in the district of courtly taste.

The rug derives its name from a representation of a flower-filled Chinese vase that appears at widely separated intervals within the profusion of leaves and flowers, and consequently is often difficult to locate. Shah Abbas I and his father, Shah Tahmasp, incidentally, were both ardent collectors of Ming porcelain—the former so devoted a collector that a special treasury for his acquisitions was built adjoining the tomb-mosque of his ancestor, Sheikh Safi, at Ardabil. Other, secondary design of the rug consists of flowers that are readily recognizable as bluebells and asters. Vases and identifiable flowers are, however, rather unimportant items of realism in a pattern dominated by the most romantic of all palmettes and scrolls. The palmettes resemble supernaturally ornamented and variegated palm-leaf fans, each obliquely tilted to the customary angle of usefulness. The fan-like appearance is abetted by the stem-like scrolls, which are the diagonal lines on which the palmettes seem to grow. Perpendicular rows of resplendent eight-petalled rosettes keep the pattern upright and flowing between narrow single-stripe borders, which to the uninitiated seem meagre and inadequate until their charm of simplicity is emphasized.

Field color is either rich red or deep blue, and rarely dull ivory. Usually the weaving is executed upon double warp, which being hard and resistful accounts for the badly worn condition of most surviving examples. The scarcity of complete rugs and the treasuring of meagre fragments is doubtless the result of small original production. It is not impossible that the pattern was a court or family property, upon which there was little encroachment. Certainly the art was not commercialized.

Rare as vase rugs are, the species nevertheless indulged the usual penchant for variation. The design of one of the variants consists of numerous large lozenge-shaped compartments, like the prisms of honeycomb magnified. Each lozenge or prism is decorated with one of several varieties of ornament—either a flowering tree, a palmette, a rosette, a bulb-shaped lily that resembles a vase or, finally, in one or two specially favored prisms, the long-searched-for flower-filled vase itself. The prisms are further distinguished by individual colors, each beautiful and magically blended to its environment. The net result is the most gorgeous display of prismatic design and color that the art exhibits. Allied rugs of the seventeenth century display rows of elaborately designed flower-filled vases, rows of flowering plants to which roots append and, finally, charming arabesque and mille fleur patterns.

Polonaise Rugs

Loss of identity as Persian fabrics, through foreign residence, was the astonishing fate that befell the rugs of silk, gold and silver that at this time shared court favor. How these rugs of fairyland acquired their European color-scheme, became the property of European monarchs, and eventually secured their European name is a romance worthy of their beauty.

Gifts ever were exchanged between friendly oriental monarchs, and during the sixteenth and seventeenth centuries between Persian and European monarchs. "There were withal thirty-two camels carrying the presents," according to Don Juan, member of the embassy sent to Europe by Shah Abbas in 1599; who further recounts that the Grand Duke of Muscovy signalized his appreciation by presenting the Persian ambassador with "three most rich robes of cloth of gold, a cup of gold big enough to hold half a gallon of wine, and further

79

three thousand ducats for journey expenses. And to each of us secretaries, the Grand Duke sent three robes, with eight yards of cloth to each person to make us travelling clothes. Further a silver cup to each and two hundred ducats to each a free gift."

Persian rulers also purchased European elegance. Arthur Edwards in his letter of June, 1567, lists an astonishing order given him by Shah Tahmasp for "good velvets, to wit cramosins, purples, reds, greens and blacks—these colors because they are most worn; also good damasks and satins."

From these fabrics and from European tapestry which the court weavers copied, a new color-scheme for rugs seems to have been obtained and applied to rugs of silk and metal—richest gold against cool silver, pale green consorting with rare orange, light and deep blue hand in hand with rose and crimson, salmon cheering mauve, violet and brown—all delicate, pastel hues, sometimes balanced by passages of deep, pure color. Frequently variety of color is so great as to obscure the structure of the design.

The forms to which these picturesque colors were applied are the palmette, lanceolate leaf, arabesque, cloud-band, floral scroll, rosette, shrub, bird, animal and human form—plus the coats-of-arms of the royal families of Europe when the rugs were intended as gifts to specific monarchs in Poland and Moscow, where many of them went.

Designs are of four varieties: medallions, oval and lobed in shape, and some formed by arabesque palmettes; compartments, arranged symmetrically about a central panel and again distributed as parts of an all-over pattern; scrolls that emerge from centres decorated with coats-of-arms or rosettes; and finally all-over pattern of palmettes arranged in rows and connected with short stems. The border design most commonly employed is the palmette, leaf and scroll decoration of Ispahan rug borders. Other border motives are compartments and trefoils. In design, therefore, the rugs are echoes of previous court rugs and carpets.

The sumptuous materials, silk, silver and gold, accorded with the vast wealth and the belief in the divinity of the Safavi monarchs. Gods exact the last atom of attainable art and disdain all but the finest atoms of substance. Shah Abbas, Safi and Abbas II, jointly covering the period from 1588 to 1667, expressed their self-esteem in the Polonaise style. Shah Tahmasp (1524-1576) possessed silk and gold rugs executed presumably in native color-schemes. To Sultan Selim II of Turkey he gave, as already recounted, "twenty large silk carpets and numerous small ones, decorated with birds, beasts, flowers and embroidered with gold." Tamerlane (1369-1405) possessed "a crimson carpet beautifully ornamented with gold threads." The use of silk and metal thread in the construction of Polonaise rugs was therefore old custom.

The innovation of the intervening years was the use of silk and metal in wool rugs. During the fifteenth century far the greater number of fine rugs were all-wool products. In the early part of the sixteenth century silk and sometimes linen were substituted for wool as foundation materials. Subsequently gold and silver thread were employed sparingly to emphasize special patterns in wool surfaces.

The production of this thread was an art practised by a special group of workmen. Sir John Chardin, who made trips to Persia in 1666 and 1672, says: "The Gold Wire-Drawers and Thread-Twisters are very dextrous Workmen. Their tools of several sizes are like our wire-drawing irons; they wind on Bobins and Drums, and buy at the Mint small wire the bigness of a pin. Their thread is the best and the smoothest that can be imagined. All the art they use to give it that lively and lasting colour is to guild the wire very fine and very thick." "The Persians call Brocade Gold Tissue. The Gold and Silver does not wear off whilst the Work lasts, and keeps still its color and brightness. The finest Looms of those Stuffs are at Yezd, at Kashan, and likewise at Ispahan."

Technically, Polonaise rugs compose three groups—knotted, tapestry-woven and embroidered rugs. Far the larger number of examples contain two techniques,—knotting of the Sehna variety conjoined with brocading of metal threads, five of the latter to each row of knots. Texture, averaging two hundred and fifty knots to the square inch, is coarse, compared to the weaving displayed by most important silk rugs, because of the employment of cotton, commonly, for warp and weft. By contrast, tapestry or khilim weavings of the Polonaise class are fine in structure, their materials wholly silk and metal and their designs varied by the use of human, animal and bird forms, which weavers of the knotted variety avoided. Nevertheless, decoratively, the knotted rugs are the superior fabrics, despite the fact that tapestry-woven carpets and rugs of magnificent character constituted part of the dowry of the Polish princess, Anna Katharina Kostanza, on her marriage in the year 1642.

The place of Polonaise rug-weaving is not finally determined. Tavernier, the French merchant who had an audience with the Shah in Ispahan in the year 1664, informs us that "The *Karkrone* is the House for the Royal Manufactures, where the Gold and Silver carpets are made, as also those of Silk and Worsted, together with Tissues, Velvets and Taffetas." Another important source of silk rugs was Kashan. In the seventeenth century Polish kings sent Armenian merchants to Kashan to order rugs of silk and gold threads. Several tapestry-woven rugs, part of the dowry of the Polish Princess Anna Katherina Kostanza, are in the Residenz Museum at Munich.

John Fryer, travelling in Persia in 1676, found Polonaise rugs for sale in the bazaars of Ispahan: "Besides these common Buzzars, there are others set apart for choice commodities, as Silks and Velvets, Gold Brocade, that is Gold and Silver cloth, Embroidery, Persian carpets, both woollen and silk, intermixed with Gold and Silver very costly, which are the peculiar manufacture of the country." *

Approximately three hundred specimens are preserved in European court-collections, in the richer museums and in private possession. They are treasured no less than in former years. When Shah Abbas II (1642-1667) entered a room spread with gold and silver carpets he was attended by "two old men whose office it was to pull off his shoes, and to put them on again when he went forth." That to-day some faded colors and worn surfaces indicate the use of poorer dyes and cheaper materials than were employed in the silk rugs of earlier date, which are the super-masterpieces, is no great detraction.

Why the name Polonaise? In the year 1878 several fine examples of the art were exhibited in the Paris Exposition, held in the Trocadéro, by Prince Czartoryski of Warsaw. All knowledge of their source had with time departed, and the only clew to their identity were Polish coats-of-arms embroidered upon them. Due to this decoration, the fame of a Polish family of silk-weavers, and the knowledge that silk rugs had long been made in Poland and were not known to have been woven in Persia, the work was mistakenly attributed. By comparison, true Polish silk rugs are ordinary weavings.

With Polonaise rugs the important classes of masterpieces of Persian rug art come to an end, but not the possibility of instruction in them. The obvious fact that Polonaise rugs are allied to European textiles, hunting and animal rugs to Persian miniature painting, and Ispahan rugs to Herat brocade, opens an interminable avenue of thought and investigation. If three important classes of rugs have a source or relationship in allied art, others may have similar origin or alliance; and so they have. Knowledge of Persian rugs is meagre that fails to include some knowledge of all Persian art, that in variety and brilliance of accomplishment is most impressive.

* Hakluyt Society Pub. Series II, vol. XX, pt. II.

ORIENTAL RUGS AND CARPETS

PERSIAN ART

In architecture the Persians produced the superb buildings at Persepolis, the palace at Ctesiphon, numerous huge historic bas-reliefs, elegant mosques and tombs. Among their accessories of architecture are the enamelled tiles of Susa and Kashan, glazed brick, stained glass, mural decoration, stucco façades, carved and fretted woodwork. For interior decoration they created the supreme lustre-ware of the world, porcelain of beauty and elegance learned from the Chinese, repoussé and incised silver work of unbelievable perfection, inlay articles of ivory, mother-of-pearl, metal on wood and letter-seals used for signature to accompany papier-maché pen-boxes and mirrors. To this array of amazing accomplishment must be added imperial attainment in lacquer ornamentation, miniature-painting and calligraphy, book-covers and illumination, damasks, brocades, velvets and embroideries, shawls used for coats of honor and incredible varieties of carpet. These arts are the brilliant subjects of a scholarly work issued by the Metropolitan Museum of Art, entitled *A Handbook of Muhammadan Decorative Arts*, by M. S. Dimand (third revised and enlarged edition, published 1958).

All of the foregoing arts are venerable, some antedating others by a few centuries, but all essentially coming down the years together, always seemingly on good terms, mutually helpful. Whether the artists in rugs were commonly the patrons of other artists through greater facility in invention, or whether they were the chief beneficiaries of an unusually talented and enthusiastic brotherhood is of little consequence. Appropriation of motives is obvious.

PRAYER RUGS

From mosque architecture and mihrabs, the sacred shrines of mosques, Persian weavers created the most elaborate and spirited prayer patterns anywhere devised. One rug displays a vast and noble dome with spandrels of sky-blue, supported by solid masonry of border pattern, arching a crimson field containing cloud-forms in sunset gold; another, a dome supported by columns with elaborately wrought bases and capitals, sheltering a chalice decorated with temple lamps. For good measure of appropriation, borders commonly are filled with inscriptions from the Koran or books of poetry, the latter preferred because the devout Mohammedan has no desire to trample the text of the sacred word. But Persian prayers ordinarily are said on embroidered and printed cotton cloth, which makes Persian prayer rugs a rarity compared to Turkish prayer rugs, the account of which will suffice for both.

Sometimes, of course, Persian prayers, like European and American prayers, were neglected. "We have cast aside the prayer mat and the rosary," writes Maghribi; "we are wholly delivered, and are now worshippers of wine." Hafiz became the historian of this defection, in his famous verse to Mahmud Shah Bahmani, King of India, who had sent money for his journey to the court:

> "Down in the quarter where they sell red wine,
>   My holy carpet scarce would fetch a cup.
> How brave a pledge of piety is mine,
>   Which is not worth a goblet foaming up."

Under these circumstances the wishes of mosque benefactors sometimes are disregarded. Important among the rugs of mosques are the long, narrow weavings that cover the steps of the mimber, or pulpit. Three magnificent rugs formerly so used have found their way into the market. One bears the inscription: "I, Fatima, daughter of Kabalei Glumriza, bequeath this rug to the mosque forever. Whosoever sells, buys or covets it is cursed by God, condemned by the guardian angels, and pursued by the maledictions of the weaver and testator."

The appropriation of mural decoration by rug-weavers is well

85

exemplified in the Ardabil carpet of the Victoria and Albert Museum. The central design consists of an elaborate medallion surrounded by sixteen ogee panels and two pendant lamps. Obviously a ceiling decoration somewhere inspired the composition. One hundred and sixty years later the pattern was employed again, except for the lamps, upon the ceiling of the vestibule of the "College of the Mother of Shah Sultan Hussein" at Ispahan. The ornament of panels and octofoils in the border of the rug is antedated on the walls that remain of the Blue Mosque of Tabriz, which probably contained also the original ceiling decoration. This magnificent carpet and its companion piece in the Paul Getty collection, were made in the time of Shah Tahmasp, to order of Maksud of Kashan as an offering to the holy shrine of Shaikh Safi at Ardabil, and finished in 1539. The intricate floral pattern with arabesques and palmettes, placed on a dark blue background, is one of the most elaborate Safavid designs known. It is rendered more naturalistically than in other early Safavid rugs.

"The pavement before the Gate of the Tomb," writes Olearius, "was covered with tapestry [meaning rugs] to express the holiness of the place, and we were told that for the said reason, it was expected we should put off our shoes. We passed thence into a very fair spacious gallery hung and covered with tapestry." To know this carpet, now like a mummy encased in museum glass, one should endeavor to visualize its rich blue-and-gold beauty in the old surroundings of solemn light, before the iron grate that bars the resting-place of saints, "over whose high tombs are carpets of yellow damask; at head and feet, wax candles and lanthorns upon great brass candlesticks; above, from the roof of the vault, certain lamps." Only in this manner is the genius of any rug comprehended.

The famous inscription on this tomb carpet, "I have no refuge in the world other than thy threshold. My head has no protection other than thy porchway," is an appropriate contribution of the art of poetry to the art of rug-weaving. The little panel on which it is inscribed has no decorative significance; the sentiment is incorporated wholly for itself. Comparable rug inscriptions are many and beautiful. Here is one:

> "Raise thy head and see the trees, which at daybreak
> Make their prayers for the ruler of the world."

The appearance of poetry in Persian rugs seldom, however, conveys the impression of plain living and high thinking. Its form, ordinarily, is very much full-dress. This is the contribution of the art of calligraphy, the profession of the scribe, patronized by royalty and revered by the commonalty, to the art of weaving, as to the arts of pottery, brass and book-illumination. Persian poetry without a physical appearance equal to its spiritual attainment is considered of very little account. To comprehend this well-bred exaction is difficult, if not impossible, for nations of illegible writers and typewriters. Only a great poet and artist like William Blake, in happy mingling of text and ornament, approximated it among the English. Nevertheless, the fine writing in the border of the supernaturally beautiful rug from the old Marquand Collection demonstrates the reasonableness of the requirement, and the comprehensive nature of the art of rug-weaving as a symposium of art. This writing, covering twelve panels, is ornament as full of charm as the text:

> "O Saki, the Zephyr of the spring is blowing now;
> The rose has become fresh and luxuriant;
> The drops of the dew are like pearls in the cup of the tulip,
> And the tulip unfolds its glorious flag.
> Narcissus keeps its eye on the stars,
> Like the night-watch throughout the night.
> To sit alone in the desert is not
> Isolation, with company of wine.
> When Saki passes the beautiful cup around,
> The rosy cheeks of the beauties become violet for love of the rose,
> And look like the purple robe of a horseman."

87

ORIENTAL RUGS AND CARPETS

By reason of its draft of motives and suggestions from innumerable arts, the art of oriental rugs is comprehensive to a degree wholly unrealized. Many arts feed principally upon their own forebears. It is recorded that when the mediæval Vilard d'Honnicort was commissioned to build the church of St. Stephen at Prague, he spent two years travelling about Europe studying and sketching other churches. His notebooks contain comments like this: "Here's a good tower. If it were changed thus, I could use it for my church." After this manner, continues the historian, all architectural design was created. Each style was logically evolved from the study and revision of the work immediately preceding it. A diet as limited as this would have restricted the art of rugs almost to the requirements of tents.

In Summary

From the foregoing narrative it would appear that a marvellous richness of floral motives, medallion forms and pictorial figures, all expressed in graceful, flowing, rhythmic lines of utmost decorative quality, distinguishes the rug masterpieces of Persia. It would appear also that artists, such as only centuries of culture could produce, applied to this creation not only all of the appropriative forms of nature, which they combined in every conceivable way, but also a vast multiplicity of invented forms—flower imposed upon flower, sometimes to the number of three within a single unit; medallion imposed upon medallion, scene added to scene, until genius in ornamentation could accomplish nothing further.

Kings, claiming divine origin, officiated at this carnival of artists that lasted almost three hundred years. By dependable and indispensable patronage they promoted the special grandeur of an art which, obviously at its zenith, is one expression of the perfect blending of artistic brilliance with worldy magnificence. But not all the wealth of all the kings could produce a silk rug from an ahu's ear. Persian rugs, as well as Persian kings, have a higher source.

The Persian mind first created a great religion, still impressive, and two earth-convulsing empires. Dominated by the warrior propagandists of Mohammed, it proceeded instantly, through a host of heterodox sects, to create a second great state religion, wholly its own, and a third great empire. Frustrated eventually of its ambition for world domination, it struggled to solve the only remaining problem, like the Titans who piled mountains upon mountains to scale heaven. Against the wall of eternity it speculated, regardless of consequences, and ruthlessly destroyed whatever solution of the hereafter it had with infinite pains created:

> "O God, although through fear I hardly dare
>   To hint it, all our trouble springs from Thee.
> Had'st Thou no sand or gravel in Thy shoes,
>   What prompted Thee to bid the Devil be?
> 'Twere well if Thou had'st made the lips and teeth
>   Of Tartar beauties not so fair to see.
> With cries of 'On!' Thou bid'st the hound pursue;
>   With cries of 'On!' Thou bid'st the quarry flee." *

Hafiz, in blazing words, summarized the splendid defeat of the Persian of his time: "They are calling to thee from the pinnacle of the Throne of God. I know not what hath befallen thee in this dust-heap—the world." To-day this inquiry is answered. The Persian in his dust-heap, balked of his ambition, created great art. It is the old story of talent, aspiration and accomplishment travelling the world together. The intricate, graceful design of the Persian rug is the visible labyrinth of the versatile, subtle, contemplative, speculative mind which "essayed to unravel a knot from the skein of the universe, and made the tangle worse."

* Browne, E. G., *A Year Amongst the Persians*. The Macmillan Co.

89

Such is the mental and spiritual source of the great rug art of Persia, which is clothed in color warm, rich and sensuous, befitting an environment hard, bare and austere.

"Snow mountains in the distance, on the rim of the plain, blue and white; foothills nearer at hand, tawny in the curious, intense light, tawny through every shade of brown, from yellow through ochre to burnt umber. This color of the hills cannot be exaggerated. The rockier portions look painted, artificial; patches of blue-green rock appear, looking as though they had been sprayed with copper sulphate—copper overgrown with verdigris, rocks of pale malachite; then a ridge of blood-red rock; rocks of porphyry.

"It is not a waste of time to absorb in idleness the austerity of this place. Crudely speaking, the plain is brown, the mountains blue or white, the foothills tawny or purple; but what are those words? Plain and hills are capable of a hundred shades that with the changing light slip over the face of the land and melt into a subtlety no words can reproduce. The light here is a living thing, as varied as the human temperament and as hard to capture, now lowering, now gay, now sensuous, now tender; but, whatever the mood may be, it is super-imposed on a basis always grand, always austere, never sentimental. The bones and architecture of the country are there, whatever light and color may sweep across them; a soft thing passing over a hard thing, which is as it should be."*

Passenger to Teheran, by V. Sackville-West. Doubleday, Doran & Company.

CHAPTER IV

PERSIA'S SEMI-ANTIQUE AND MODERN RUGS

FROM one of many mountainous piles of rugs that fill an importer's loft, a rug having a border of inscriptions is disinterred and opened. As if it were the only existing copy of some sacred manual from a mosque library, four modest scholars intently peruse the script of five hexagonal panels, and dictate the translation:

"Woven during the reign of Nasir-u-Din-Shah, King having the power of the world. Titles."
"Woven in Kerman by Mirza Mehdi Khan. Titles."
"Woven in the recess beyond the arch where the bazaar street ends."
"Whosoever sells or buys this rug is reminded to respect it."
"Whosoever heeds this admonition, may his business continue forever."
"Whosoever wishes to know the date of this weaving—the master finished it the eleventh month of the year 1250." (1835 A.D.)

RUGS OF KERMAN (KIRMAN)

Kerman rugs, city and province product of high, aloof, southeastern Persia, are a long succession of weavings distinguished by style of ornamentation. As the cave-men of Europe, during one period, shaped their stone weapons and tools in one way, and during another period in another way, so the weavers of Kerman, Persia, and all Asia, were slaves of fashion. Style is the yardstick of time and place.

91

Marco Polo tells us that the Kerman rugs of the thirteenth century were decorated with birds, beasts and other ornamental devices:

RUG MAP
OF
PERSIA

"The women and young persons work with the needle, in embroideries of silk and gold, in a variety of colors and patterns, representing birds and beasts, with other ornamental devices. These are designed for the curtains, coverlets and cushions [rugs] of the sleeping places of the rich; and the work is executed with so much taste and skill as to be an object of admiration."

Between the thirteenth and the seventeenth centuries the record is wanting. In the latter century we are advised by Sir John Chardin, the French jeweller who made two trips to Persia (1666-1672), and himself an authority on Persian matters, that the "finest looms for carpets are in the Province of Kerman, and especially in Sistan." We are told that Nadir Shah, after his ascension to the throne of Persia in 1736, employed Kerman weavers in Ispahan—a diversion of Kerman rug talent that was repeated in the institution of the Turkish Imperial looms at Hereke.

In the seventeenth century came into use formal patterns of flower-filled vases that prompted the inference that classic vase rugs were Kerman products; interlocking panels filled with birds and flowers, and finally tree and garden motives, all elaborately floral and wholly devoid of the Chinese ornament that found favor among the rug-weavers of the great courts. Lack of a great court and aloofness, that court vogue seemingly could not penetrate, lessen the probability that these patterns were incorporated in rugs of first importance.

Subsequently came a flood of fine inventions, mostly small repeated motives applied to medium rug sizes: numerous vases containing realistic roses; cypresses, three and four to a row, disposed upon natural setting; battalions of large palmette medallions with centres pyramided with flowers; numerous rose bouquets obtained from European sources; and finally pictorial designs revived—landscapes containing human figures, animals, birds, trees and flowers naturalistically rendered.

Additionally, some fifty years ago, large flower-strewn medallion patterns with graceful pendants and floriated corners were devised and applied to large carpets by weavers working for Tabriz rug-merchants who saw in the fine Kerman workmanship opportunity for commercial enterprise. These rugs and carpets were called Kermanshah, to permanent confusion with the rug-weavings of the city of that name located miles to the west in the province of Ardelan.

The Tabriz venture in Kermanshah rugs spread quickly and widely over the Kerman province. To-day, with design greatly altered to meet the present Western requirement for repeated pattern, and with color changed from delicate pink and gold to richest reds and blues, these rugs, at last generally called Kerman, are woven in the city of Kerman, in the towns of Mahun and Zarand, which can be located on any good map of Persia, and in Joopar, Shahrokhabad, Mayabad and numerous other villages which no map will indicate. Incidentally, villages and towns have the human faculty of using common names. Ten Alibads and five Sultanabads, with more of each awaiting recognition, correspond to our numerous Watertowns and Centervilles.

Of all the villages weaving Kerman rugs, Rawar only has general rug fame. Commonly spelled Laver or Lavher, Rawar is the name applied to rugs of specially fine weaving, or rugs having a predominance of rich blue color. Therefore, in the market, Rawar bears the same relation to Kerman as Mir bears to Saraband.

Notwithstanding an obvious multiformity, the art of the rugs of Kerman is a consistent as well as a superior performance. It is an expression of a distinct variety of thought and feeling; like language, superficially altered by time, but unchanged in essential character. Coherence over several generations is attributed to the dominating influence of strong families, such as those of Hasan Khan and his father Mousin Khan, men of keen artistic sensibilities who owned entire villages of weavers and took infinite pride in maintaining a tradition of superior rugs.

Naturalistic treatment of forms, found in the rugs of India but

94

consistently in no other rugs of Persia, is the basic characteristic. Seemingly, roses are woven to be plucked, as in a garden, and leaves need only a wind to blow them away. This illusion and its development in perspective, an art of which Kerman weavers are masters, is created by infinite outlining and shading upon grounds carefully chosen to abet the deception. Even abstract forms, like medallions, are molded and incised to a point just short of vibration. It has been asserted that this realism is attributable to the influence of India weaving. Rather, the influence would appear to have flowed the other way. In any event, the two together came to support an ancient Persian conception of rug ornament.

General brilliancy of color is the product of fine highland wool, pure water and superior dye technique; and the appearance of smartness that the rugs seldom lack is the result of fine Sehna knotted texture and short-cropped pile.

Afshar and Shiraz

Afshar rugs, marketed in Kerman, and Kashgai rugs, traded in Shiraz, together constitute the textile bridge across southern Persia. Rugs of greater merit, called Laristan, from the city of Lar, seem to be extinct. Both Afshar and Kashgai rugs are Caucasian nomad transplants that maintain with considerable firmness the conceptions of art to which their infancy was inclined. The Caucasian home of the Afshar tribe was near the nomad port-of-call once designated as Gengha, after Jenghis Khan, now Elizabethpol, located south of Tiflis. On the journey to Kerman, part of the tribe settled on the western shore of Lake Urumiah in northwestern Persia. This halfway lot weave no rugs whatsoever, but only felt mattings for tents. Only the Kerman Afshars, the virile persistent group sometimes called Phutchaghtchi, meaning knife-bearers, weave and market the quanti-

95

ties of small rugs of crude rectilinear pattern, executed in madder red, yellow and blue, interspersed with much white, that resemble Shiraz rugs in their checkerboarded ends and sides selvaged in many colors. In the curriculum of the rug business, Afshar rugs are poor-grade Shiraz.

Shiraz rugs, weavings of the powerful Kashgai tribes of Turkish origin, exhibit an art more Caucasian than Persian. Designs consist of medallions, single and multiple, often in tandem arrangement, usually barbed with latch-hooks and encompassed by small flora and fauna ornaments to fill otherwise unused spaces; rectilinear pear patterns, larger in scale than the native Persian device; and many shawl patterns of perpendicular and diagonal stripes that decoratively are as unsuitable to Western floors as the soft texture, commonly Ghiordes-knotted, in which they are executed, is incapable of maintaining an assigned position upon them. Colors are a wealth of glowing reds and blues often set off by white. Restored to a Caucasian setting, a few of these rugs would scintillate; compared to rugs of comparatively pure Persian art, they are no more than artistic trinkets.

Broad web ends, decorated with colored horizontal bands or with flat-stitch ornament, and sides overcast with yarns of various colors, sometimes supplemented by tassels, are the reputed features of Shiraz weaving. This superfluous artistry, never indulged by court weavers, is, on the contrary, a nomadic characteristic. Not only Shiraz and Afshar weavers in southern Persia, but Lor, Bakhtiari and Kurd weavers in western Persia, all more or less employ it. The distinction of Shiraz rugs is only greater elaboration of finish, conjoined with utmost softness of fabric.

Shiraz rugs are country, not city, products. The city of Shiraz to-day contains only a few looms, some recently set up for experiment in the weaving of Kerman rugs. When Shiraz was the capital of Persia, during the reign of Karim Khan, 1760-1779, a real Shiraz rug art existed, examples of which are to be seen in collections. The name Mecca, as applied to this weaving, came of a long-established pilgrim custom of selling or trading the rug-bed in the sacred city. Not weaving, but hundreds of transactions, therefore, produced the Mecca rug.

WESTERN NOMADS

Northwest of the Shiraz or Fars district are the districts of Khuzistan and Loristan in whose deep valleys live the tribes of Bakhtiari and Lors, semi-nomadic peoples whose vast herds of sheep and goats occasion the amazing yearly migration from lowlands to highlands so marvellously portrayed in the moving-picture "Grass." For years, until the advent of the present Shah, these tribes maintained an essentially independent government and an aloofness from commercial intercourse so complete as to make their rug-weavings a matter of conjecture. Only with their surrender to the authority of Shah Riza did the rugs emerge to add a fillip to a market already thought complete. Of the two groups, the Bakhtiari are the more important, because they include a surprisingly large number of carpets, woven at home during the winter, whereas the rugs of the Lors seldom exceed eight feet in length and include numerous bags and miscellaneous trappings.

BAKHTIARI

The designs of Bakhtiari rugs are the largest, boldest and most forceful in the entire Persian art armory; they are the heavy artillery of the company. Here are big diamond- and hexagonal-shaped panels set in rows of five to fifteen, each ornamented with rough floral or geometrical motives; and designs of Persian gardens coming rather too full-bloom from the loom. Only in the smaller rugs, designed in plant and tree-forms set in rows, is there suggestion of compromise with dainty delicacy. Strong shades of orange, yellow, light blue and rose further animate the weaving, and plead for the discipline that American use will apply in unstinted measure. Once subjugated, like their makers, these weavings will attain no mean social position. The materials, consisting of fine, long strong wool, sometimes half from goats, imposed upon wool, cotton or "half-and-half" foundations, finished with either wool or goat-hair selvage and webbings laced with gaily colored yarns, seem indestructible. The best weaving is called Bibibaff, compliment to Bibi, admired wife of a Bakhtiari chief.

LORISTAN

The designs of the rugs of Loristan are floral geometrics rendered in deep colors that suggest the rugs of "Beluchistan." The field motives consist of palm-leaves composed of small flowers, numerous small box-forms containing flowers, trellis-work similarly decorated, or small plants resembling fleur-de-lis, imposed upon areas contracted by numerous narrow borders of small leaves and vines. In dark recesses are to be found unusual quantities of green against blue, creating a peacock tone. The fabric is heavy wool throughout, finished with particolored blue-and-green overcasting, and ends containing ornament in Soumak stitch, features of the rugs of Shiraz likely to confuse the novice who insufficiently stresses the words heavy and dark. The chief market for Lor rugs is Burujird, which has no weaving of its own.

KURDISTAN

North of Loristan is the Kurd country, where until recent years could be witnessed, on occasion, one of the most picturesque and interesting assemblies of the Orient—"the court of a great Kurdish chief, who like another Saladin ruled in patriarchal state, surrounded by his clansmen with reverence and affection, and attended by a bodyguard of young Kurdish warriors, clad in chain armor, with flaunting silken scarfs, and bearing javelin, lance and sword, as in the time of the Crusades.''

Kurd rugs continue the ring of rugged weaving that fortifies Persia's western textile frontier. Of little account in the lowlands toward Mosul, they improve with every mile of ascent up the mountains, until, coming into contact with Persian art in the outpost cities of Kermanshah, Bijar and Sehna, they attain to fame as Persian Kurdistans. Not as an imperial family of rugs, but as a high-class democracy, the rugs of the province of Ardelan, which include Persian Kurdistans, true Kermanshahs, Bijars, Sehnas and Suj Bulaks (the latter within the group although outside the province), may be said to have established through dependable service a large following of buyers in the Western world.

Persian Kurdistans

Persian Kurdistans may be defined only negatively, as the rugs of the group that do not obviously fall into one of the other classes. As they are undistinguished by design or color, they must be identified by fine wool that the expert recognizes; full pile of medium length executed in the Ghiordes knot; web ends through which are run one or more strands of colored yarn, sometimes developed into flat-woven pattern; warp ends webbed and knotted; sides finished with heavy double overcasting, dark in color, usually brown wool; and finally shaded and sometimes emphatically broken colors throughout the field. Noticeable "Abrash," by which is meant arbitrary and accidental change in the shade of any color that results in contrasting bands of color, is almost inseparable from the weaving. Whether the designs consist of Caucasian medallion forms, salted with Persian elements, or of the Persian repeated motives of Herati, Pear and Mina Khani, the latter a particular favorite in blue, yellow and red, depends upon environment, the needle of pattern here pointing north and there east. Undoubtedly the fine Persian rugs that were woven not many years ago in the governor's palace at Kermanshah became the fulcrum that lifted the weaving of the Persian Kurds above the rough products of the Kurd family.

True Kermanshah

Kermanshah, city of Kurdistan, is said to have acquired its name from a circumstance associated with one of its early governors. Coming from Kerman in southeastern Persia, he was the Kerman Shah, and persons going to see him went to Kermanshah. That confusion of place should extend to product was only the natural course of events. Kermanshah rugs, even when completely disassociated from the rugs of Kerman, are, in the beginning, an illness to identify and always a plague to bound. They include both the surviving scattered rugs woven in the governor's palace and under its influence, and the rugs woven in the surrounding hills, which are very different types. The former are dominantly Persian in design—numerous eight-pointed star medallions set upon a secondary all-over design of leaves and flowers; or of utmost popularity, a design of large leaf forms waving after the manner of cloud-bands, and seemingly a residue of Chinese art. Color is Persian, texture firm, and the use of cotton for warp and weft a Kerman practice that came into vogue probably with the Kerman Shah. With this group the rugs of the suburbs have nothing in common. Color of the latter resembles Turkish red and yellow; design is a mixture of Turkish-Caucasian medallions and latch items; material is wholly wool and texture, Ghiordes-knotted, loose and coarse. Nevertheless, these country rugs are uncommon and of much interest. Both groups belong to the antique or semi-antique class. To-day Kermanshah is a great wool market, not a rug market or a rug-weaving city.

PERSIA'S SEMI-ANTIQUE AND MODERN RUGS

BIJAR

Bijar rugs, woven both in the town of that name and in the surrounding country, are the dreadnaught battleships of all rug weaving, so heavy, thick and compact are they of fine wool lavishly expended. Exceptional thickness is due not to extra length of pile, as in most heavy rugs, but to exceptional depth of foundation, from which emerge a short, sharp, erect pile and clarity of pattern that high and overlapping pile never produces. Bulk is the result of the insertion of extra weft, called filling, between the rows of knots, and compactness the result of hard hammering with extra-heavy mallets.

But not all Bijar rugs completely answer this description; there are grades. Some, although heavy, are soft and even flimsy, due to lack of filling and packing, and some have foundations of cotton, which violate the rule of all-wool. The hard-woven masterpieces are the product of Halvaye, meaning sweetmeats, in the language of Turkey, but, in Persia, the name of a little town that attained to great rug fame. Second in rank are the rugs produced in Bijar and in Tiran Tepe, or thorn hill, a town to the north which sometimes lowers its standard to the level of the Gehrous district about Bijar, that weaves only the soft variety.

Bijar design extends the full gamut of Persian rug ornament from large medallions to small repeats, but always scale and detail are commensurate with the strength and vigor of the Kurd in the fabric, never dainty and lacy as in the rugs of Kerman, which are a complete antithesis. In consequence, one walking on a Bijar carpet feels no urge to mince steps or wear patent-leather. In brief, Bijar rugs in texture and design are living-room upholstering as distinguished from parlor ornament, and the color, inclining strongly to-day to deep, rich effects, supports the distinction. Nevertheless, Bijar color, like the American tariff, is a local issue, one district favoring red and rose, another blue, gold and green. In theory, any Bijar rug should be traceable to its lair through its color. Shaded and broken colors and much irregularity of pattern, to avert the evil eye, both sudden Kurdish changes of mind that shock and distress systematical persons, contribute indispensable personality to the weaving.

Thirty years ago the outstanding design of Bijar weaving was a large central blue medallion gracefully defined and heavily ornamented, imposed upon a field of solid red shading in streaks to rose, bounded by corners and borders continuing the theme of the medallion. This was sophisticated city style, whose country counterpart consisted of impromptu patterns containing human, animal and bird forms rendered in cartoon manner. These types are obsolete, replaced by effective shield devices on fields of blue, by fine Herati designs with and without small medallions, by lattice-work patterns that all Kurds love and by frames containing French rose clusters and bouquets.

Among the most interesting and delightful of small rugs is the Bijar Vagireh, or Orinak, which displays sections of numerous patterns artistically combined. The purpose of the weaving was to produce models of draftsmanship and color combination for use in the creation of carpets. Some Vagirehs contain as many as five incipient carpet designs. An ulterior purpose, undoubtedly, was the preservation of pattern and color, generation after generation. These records should not be neglected; genuine art treasure is found among them.

SEHNA

Sehna (Senneh or Senna) rugs, delicate sisters of stalwart Bijars, are distinguished by masterful accomplishment in small pattern. The knot, ordinarily but not always employed, often slight as any curl of hair rhapsodized by poets, was in former times so completely identified with the city as to give its name to all similar knotting, no mat-

Meshed Carpet. Minute floral pattern of Herat with multiple band border. Small flowers in outer stripe used to determine texture

Khorassan Prayer Rug. Characteristic minute floral pattern, Herati, with border of narrow bands

PLATE XXIV

Modern Kashan Silk Rug. Extreme elaboration of the palmette design of the Herat (Ispahan) rug

Modern Kashan Prayer Rug. Floral design of realistic character and detailed execution that made the weaving famous

PLATE XXV

Feraghan Rug. Characteristic small Herati motive surrounded by border of extreme elaboration

Bakshis Rug. Small Herati design with decorated corners. Herez leaf-rosette border

Herat (Ispahan) Carpet, Seventeenth Century. Large Herati design, two leaves about a rosette. Source of patterns to right

PLATE XXVI

Feraghan Rug.   Herati pattern of lattice effect
about a central medallion

Feraghan Rug.   Guli Hinnai Pattern

Feraghan Rug.   Mina Khani Pattern

Saraband Rug.   Palm Leaf Pattern

PLATE XXVII

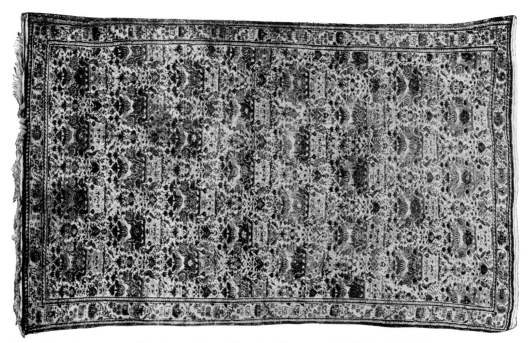

Zellé-Sultan Rug (Shadow of the Sultan). Vase and nightingale design on cream
ground with characteristic narrow border

Fine Old-Style Medallion-Patterned Saruk

PLATE XXVIII

Joshaghan Rug, Late Eighteenth Century.   Intermediate variety of Herati pattern

Joshaghan Rug, Eighteenth Century.   Shah Abbas Design

Plate XXIX

Baber, 1526-1530

Akbar, 1556-1605

Jahangir, 1605-1628

Shah Jahan, 1628-1658

PLATE XXX

Fountain Bath, Jasmine Tower. Dado decoration of flowering plants employed in rugs of the seventeenth century

India Rug, Early Seventeenth Century. Design of flowering plants: rose, lily, sunflower, narcissus, each in separate compartment

Victoria and Albert Museum

India Rug, Seventeenth Century. Design of flower-covered trellis. Variety found at Jaipur

Benjamin Altman Collection, Metropolitan Museum of Art

India Carpets of Seventeenth Century from the Palace of the Maharaja at Jaipur. "Rows of flowering plants each delineated separately and entire to the roots, as if planted in a garden."

Collection of Mr. Lionel Harris

PLATE XXXI

India Silk Rug from Ardabil, Seventeenth Century. Design of flowering trees and cypress along water-courses edged with stones and plants

Formerly in the Yerkes Collection
Now in the Frick Collection, New York

India Prayer Rug of Shah Jahan Period

Joseph V. McMullan Collection,
Metropolitan Museum of Art

India Rug of Persian star, palmette, rosette, and leaf design with border of realistic flowering plants.

Benjamin Altman Collection, Metropolitan Museum of Art

Mogul Rug, Lahore, about 1620. Persian pattern of rhythmic grace combined with Mogul floral design

J. Pierpont Morgan Collection, Metropolitan Museum of Art

Indian Pictorial Rug with scenes derived from Mogul miniatures

Museum of Fine Arts, Boston

India Bird and Tree Rug. Date about 1620. Commonly known and famous as the "Peacock Rug"

Austrian State Collection, Museum of Art and Industry, Vienna

PLATE XXXII

Masulipatam Copy of Indo-Ispahan Rug

Agra Copy of Jaipur Plant Rug

Modern India Copy of Rare Variety of
Persian Vase Rug

Part of Working Drawing of Vase Rug

PLATE XXXIII

PLATE XXXIV. India Rug, about 1640
Benjamin Altman Collection, Metropolitan Museum of Art

PLATE XXXV. India Animal Rug, Seventeenth Century
Joseph E. Widener Collection, National Gallery, Washington, D.C.

Egyptian-Turkish Rug, Sixteenth Century. Design of Egyptian Mosque Pavement

James Franklin Ballard Collection, City Art Museum, St. Louis, Mo.

PLATE XXXVI

Mohammed II, 1451-1481, Turkish Conqueror
of Constantinople

Siege of Constantinople, 1453 A.D.

Portrait of Georg Gyze with Turkish Rug of Octagon Design and Kufic Border. By Hans Holbein the Younger, 1497-1543

"Holbein" Rug, Late Fifteenth Century. Probably woven at Ushak during the period of Mohammed II

PLATE XXXVII

Painting by Lorenzo Lotto, Executed between 1520 and 1540.
Displays Turkish Rug of Arabesque Design and Kufic Border

Similar Turkish Rug. Late Fifteenth or **Early**
Sixteenth Century
Metropolitan Museum of Art

Bordone's Painting of Fisherman and Doge at Venice,
about 1550, showing Turkish Rug of Star Motive

Similar Turkish Rug, Called Star Ushak.
Sixteenth Century
Metropolitan Museum of Art

PLATE XXXVIII

Persian Medallion Rug, Early Sixteenth Century. Rugs decorated with round medallions are assigned to a later period than rugs showing star medallions. (See color plate.) Obviously the art displayed in the rug illustrated to the right was inspired by Persian art

Turkish Medallion Carpet, Called Ushak. Displays adaptation of the design of Persian medallion carpets. Woven during the sixteenth and early seventeenth centuries, and exported to Europe

PLATE XXXIX

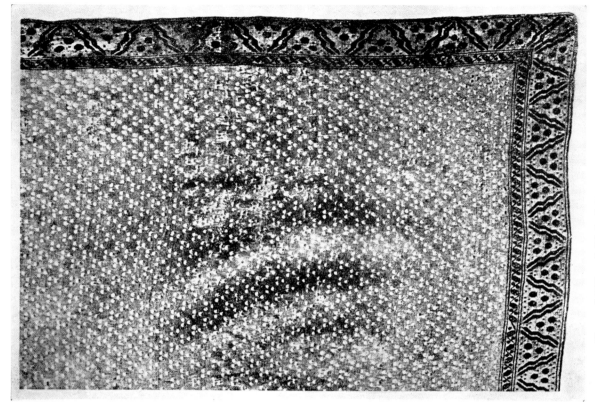

Rug of "Cloud-Globe" Pattern, Same Period

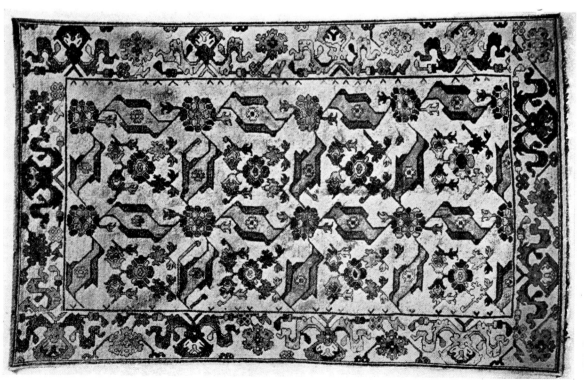

"Bird" Rug, Late Sixteenth and Early Seventeenth Centuries

PLATE XL

Portrait of Abraham Grapheus by Cornelis de Vos, 1585-1651. Shows two borders of a Bergama Rug

Bergama Rug, Seventeenth Century. Similar to example in de Vos painting

Turkish Version of Persian Flowering Shrub Pattern, Late Sixteenth Century

Davis Collection, Metropolitan Museum of Art

Turkish Adaptation of Persian Vase Design, Early Seventeenth Century

Ballard Collection, Metropolitan Museum of Art

PLATE XLI

ter where employed. Thus far in this survey, only the weavers of Kerman and some of the weavers of Shiraz employ it. The rug, in its finest expression, is distinguished by knots so tiny that four hundred often are crowded into a square inch of surface, by pile so short and erect as to feel like an assembly of needle points, by back as rough as coarse sandpaper and by texture as thin as heavy canvas.

The finest materials—silk, linen or very light cotton—compose the foundation, and only a whiffet of weft is inserted between the knot rows. Naturally, such a technique is the medium of the finest rug engraving. Sometimes numerous concentric diamonds are woven, but never for themselves. Always they are forms used to confine and organize the most minute floral patterns. Similarly, numerous serrated medallions, full, half and quarter size, are the jewel boxes of delicate floral ornament.

Sehna design, therefore, is a compilation of minute pattern nowhere surpassed. It includes the Herati, large and small palm-leaf, rose-bush and cypress-tree motives, shawl patterns, lattice with flower inserts, and finally floral diagonals, complex and ornate, with cone-tipped branches loaded with dancing green leaves. Borders ordinarily are narrow frames. Color ranges from the delicate gaiety of rose and ivory to the dark rich and restful harmony of deep reds, blues and greens, all applied pin-point with variations that are a trial to count. Many saddle rugs and khilims, for which the city is famous, are precious color charts. The status of the weaving in Persia is indicated in "Sanctuary," a rug story by A. Cecil Edwards, in a volume entitled *A Persian Caravan*.

Sehna-Kurd

Sehna-Kurd is the name applied to rugs woven by the Kurds in emulation of the Sehnas. By reason of heavier substance they have a desirable quality of durability on Western floors, which pure Sehna weavings sometimes lack. Always excessive refinement pays the penalty of impermanence. Partly on this account, beautiful old Sehna rugs are a rarity, and Sehna-Kurd rugs the only Sehnas that the market commonly offers.

Suj Bulak

Suj Bulak rugs are Kurd weavings to which the man who knows gives respectful attention; often there is valuable art among them. In design special fondness is displayed for small flowering shrubs, variations of the conventional rose-bush pattern, utilized either to create a compact field of flowers, or to decorate a central diamond-shaped medallion, placed sometimes on a solid rose-red ground having the usual Kurdish shading of color. French pattern too has considerable vogue. Dominant colors are the same as in Persian Kurdistans, dark red and blue; texture commonly is stiffer and heavier, due to the use of slightly coarser yarn.

Rugs of Tabriz

Modern Tabriz rugs constitute a forty-year-old revival of weaving that began at least as early as the Caliphate. Tabriz is one of four places mentioned as the source of the carpets of the super-beings of Bagdad. That Tabriz was also the source of some of the fine silk and medallion rugs of northwestern Persia of the fifteenth and sixteenth centuries, is now reasonably established fact. The report of the rugs contained in the palace of Uzun Hasan at Tabriz will be supplemented shortly by the chronicle of the requisition of Tabriz weavers by Sultans Selin I and Suleyman the Magnificent of Turkey. Seemingly, Tabriz has been cheated of a fame in rugs that would have anchored her recent career in the art, and given it an assurance and individuality for want of which it has greatly suffered.

About the year 1885 the English firm of Ziegler organized looms in Tabriz for the creation of rugs suitable to the Western market. Exactly what this firm accomplished, and what rugs were woven in Tabriz for local consumption during the years prior to the advent of this firm, are facts not to be ascertained, so fleeting are things inconsequential. The Ziegler work was extended to Bakshis and subsequently to Sultanabad, where it made its only impression.

But Tabriz, with its large population at the teller's window nearest Europe, presented rug-weaving advantages which three Persians, Kurban Dai, Hajji Jalil and Sheik Safi, soon seized and made memorable. They requisitioned designs, color schemes, dyers and loommasters from the city of Kerman, where only a few years previously Tabriz rug merchants had organized the most successful of all modern commercial rug enterprises. Working from Kerman models, they created brilliant, elaborate floral medallion carpets, often with borders containing the verses of poets. For texture, they employed a fine Turkish knot, often to the number of three hundred and more to the square inch; they selvaged the sides of their weavings, used a pink weft, and a distinctive ruby note in the color scheme, and in these particulars created a distinctive fabric.

Additionally, they copied Sehna and Feraghan carpets, and reproduced the rugs of Herat, even going to the trouble of securing wool for this purpose from the Meshed market. Sheik Safi made many copies of the Ardabil carpet, and executed orders for important weavings given him by Russian nobles. Hajji Jalil made himself famous by creating superb silk carpets that dealers to-day prize more than currency. Then Hajji Jalil was shot and the work came to an end, at once praised and derided as "beautiful, perfect in ornamental quality, but having no spontaneity or atmosphere." If endeavor is made to secure one of these fine carpets to-day, derided "spontaneity" and "atmosphere" will be discovered to exceed the requirements of all but the most palatial rooms.

Following these famous Persians, came the German firm of Petag, whose looms and warehouses were wrecked and sequestered by the Russian soldiers who entered Tabriz at the beginning of the World War. Subsequently, weavers were employed to make copies of Ghiordes prayer rugs and other standard types, the general weaving populace pirating the unguarded achievement, embodying it in Dabakhana, or slaughter-house wool, which, failing to wear well and to hold color, brought all Tabriz rugs into disrepute.

To-day Persian interests own more than three thousand looms, operated, as in Kerman, by boys serving for wages. No specific design, color scheme, material or texture distinguishes the product, but only diversity, even in name, on the theory that any name, even one un-known, is better than a name that stands for nothing in particular, or contains a tarnished letter. If reproduction is made of a Yezd rug, the weaving itself, no matter how commendable, is attributed to Yezd. Other fine and commercially important weavings are called Sahand, Leishah and Teheran. The wool employed excellently illus-trates the rug's cosmopolitanism. From the region adjacent to the Caspian Sea is secured the lamb's wool, "Talish Gusam," which is converted into the best carpets. From Ardabil comes wool derived from the sheep of the nomads who drive their flocks south in summer and north in winter, the reverse of custom. From Urumiah is ob-tained wool grown by the Afshar tribes, kin to the rug weavers living west of Kerman; and from Suj Bulak the fine wool of Kurdistan. Tabriz, therefore, is the present world of rugs in miniature.

SEYSSAN

Seyssan rugs are the wage products of four or five villages of Ba-bists, located out of Tabriz on the road to Teheran. Designs are vase, cypress, palmette, as the owners of the looms direct. Colors are too dark to be popular, and texture too coarse for fine Tabriz and too fine for good Gorevan. Rug weaving has been practised in these villages for at least thirty years, and on some five hundred looms, without attracting sufficient attention to give currency to the name, or even to secure it a place in the literature of the subject. Throughout Persia innumerable villages produce rugs insufficiently individualized or commercialized to secure foreign recognition.

HEREZ

Gorevan and Serapi rugs are the Castor and Pollux of modern rug mythology. Certainly they are twins, long of doubtful parentage, and the petty villages of Herez, Bakshis, Gorevan and Sirab that sponsored them, in the rôle of *mater Leda*, forever afterward had their constancy questioned.

Before the advent of Gorevan and Serapi rugs the name Herez was applied to local native rugs, a mediocre lot, of Hamadan appearance, and also to the old weavings of Bakshis, on the principle that all rug names can conveniently mother a brood. When in the course of events the women of Bakshis produced an inexpensive commercial carpet styled by concentric hexagonal medallions and strong rectilinear corner devices, deploying copper red, buff and white on a ground of blue—altogether a virile, archaic-looking performance with trowelled color—this weaving too, forsooth, was called Herez; but not for long, because almost instant commercial success resulted in hasty production and deterioration of quality, which brought the name into disrepute.

Near at hand was the insignificant village of Gorevan, with hardly enough fingers to work fifty looms, if it had them, but with a good enough name for an average christening, if the rug stork flew that way, as it did. So the new "Herez" or Bakshis rug became a Gorevan; and Gorevan's brother, who arrived a little after, described as a "light and bright carpet with clear grounds for display of elaborate vine and flower design," became, for similar reasons, Serapi, although the poor little town of Sirab contained not a single loom of carpet dimension.

To-day the cheapest grades of Gorevan are woven in the villages of Djangur and Malkit, the next to worst in Bakshis, Gorevan and Heravan, the second best in Berverdi and the finest grades in Herez, all Turkish knotted on cotton. Sirab is consoled for exclusion from the enterprise by being honored with the privilege of weaving "Mosul" rugs for the firm of Oriental Carpets Merchants, Ltd.; and old Herez and Bakshis, observing the success of things "limited," are back in business on their own account.

Recently, Gorevan weaving was started at Ahar, which would mean nothing to the reader if rug knowledge were an equipment of standard parts rather than an aggregation of miscellaneous facts. Therefore it is worth knowing that at Ahar the rugs all came deformed, one shoulder higher than the other, or of a disturbing rotundity, where prevailing style required a straight, trim line. Undoubtedly Allah had willed the calamity. But expert examination disclosed the use of new, wet wood in the construction of the looms, which had sprung and buckled under the tension of tight-strung warp.

BAKSHIS (BAKHSHESH OR BAKSHAISH)

Old Bakshis rugs, often sold as antique Herez, and on that account little known under their true name, probably have contributed more sheer charm to modern Western interior decoration than any one variety of nineteenth-century Persian weaving other than Feraghan. Never produced so extensively, or in such large sizes, or in the Sehna-knotted workmanship of the Feraghans, they have nevertheless supplied to a small group of discerning buyers adaptable color harmonies of great beauty. Fine variegated color is to this older Bakshis what fine workmanship is to the rugs of Sehna; and what color it is! It includes much cobalt blue, some Chinese lacquer red and green, reds of ruby, rose and plum, and tans of richest camel color. Some color schemes are tenderly warm, the reds old and magnificent; others are austerely cold in blues and grays that glisten.

The source of this extensive and fascinating color repertoire has been the subject of considerable inquiry. What magic was conjured in these rugs that other weavers could not invoke? The answer, probably, is that the introduction of the first Western dyes, called aniline, into Persian rug production, coincided with the weaving of these particular Bakshis, and that these rugs display the first amalgamation of Western and Eastern dyes.

It is well known, because widely proclaimed, how vicious the use of Western dyes was considered in Persia. The continuance of the entire rug industry was believed threatened by them. In consequence, a law was promulgated decreeing the loss of ears and hands to dyers who employed the iniquitous substitutes. Thereafter, dyers both earless and handless, or partially maimed, were not infrequently encountered, and it is not unlikely that some of them once pursued their vocations in Bakshis and Suj Bulak, where the governor was most severe.

That men should have paid so dearly for a part in creating so obvious a beauty, that matured naturally without artificial drugging, loss of textile strength or least particle of flooded color from repeated washing, is a sad thing to contemplate. To-day many thousands of dollars are spent yearly to bleach tons of new dye in new Persian rugs; yesterday it was a crime to employ for shades of color otherwise unobtainable the precursors of these same pigments. And by far the larger quantity of the dye used in these Bakshis was of vegetable origin, as examination will prove. Most of the dyes are as sturdy as the colors are ripe. What a vastness of ignorance has always pervaded the dye subject!

Rumor says that the firm of Ziegler had Feraghan rugs copied in Bakshis, as well as in Sultanabad. If such was the case, the Bakshis weavers employed their own border designs, as well as their own color schemes. Furthermore, old Bakshis rugs contain a design of intricate, diagonalled vines, bearing palm-leaves resembling fruit, that is highly distinctive and allied only to a somewhat similar pattern in the rugs of Sehna. Other choice patterns, too, have an individual twist and a firmness of expression that no amount of innuendo can reduce to a parasitical basis. Always the weavers of Bakshis had among the Persians a high reputation for knowing what they were about.

MIANAH

Mianah rugs, woven southeast of Tabriz in the environs of the town of that name, which incidentally contains no looms, present designs and color schemes, except for red, that bear so striking a resemblance to the rugs of Hamadan as to explain their mistaken classification as such. Intermarriage and trade are the simple explanations of the phenomena.

KARAJE OR KARADAGH

Karadagh or "Black Mountain" rugs are the all-wool weavings of shepherd tribes located on the Caucasian fringe of Persia, immediately north of Tabriz. Naturally, designs are a Persian-Caucasian blend, the former ingredient always the stronger. The Herati motive, for example, is given a saw-tooth leaf or geometrical vine-pattern border, and the Mina Khani design appears with rosettes geometrically wrought, and an eight-pointed star border. Border designs, therefore, are far more geometrical than the designs commonly employed in Persian borders; and geometrical or archaic treatment of old Persian field patterns is common practice. Usually small repeated patterns completely fill all available space, and medallions when admitted seem to have crowded their way in. Abhorrence of open spaces and cultivation of all available ground are therefore a second design characteristic. Exceptional softness of wool attributed to special properties of water in which it is cleansed, glowing dark blue color, occasional plum tones and predominance of runner shapes are other distinguishing features.

Teheran

Teheran, capital of Persia, although possessed of five or six hundred looms operated by men and women employed by Persian firms and by children learning to weave in orphanages, is not a city of much account in rug commerce. The reason is lack of rug tradition, and high wages. When Teheran weaves, it experiments, and when Teheran patterns and textures can be produced in Kashan at a saving of twenty per cent, capital invested in rug manufacture finds labor conditions unpropitious. Nevertheless, of the five grades of Teheran rugs, the best are superior products. The wool is excellent, texture compact, pile short, full and Sehna-knotted; backs resemble the admired foundations of the first Saruk rugs; colors need no bleaching to be beautiful, and designs are intricate and old-fashioned, some copied from the inventions of Joshaghan. All grades bear the city name, except an orphanage product called Shemran, after a summer resort in the neighboring mountains. In this and other schools two hours each day are devoted to instruction in rug and tapestry weaving. When, as sometimes happens in rug kindergartens, these two arts are confused, rugs depict yoked oxen negotiating hard roads and flamingoes inspecting quiet streams. But honesty and high ambition are obvious attendants, and neither beasts nor birds will endure in vain their unaccustomed hardships.

Rugs of Khorassan

Khorassan as applied to rugs has two meanings. In its broadest sense it represents the entire grand division of the art, old and new, free and controlled, city and country-bred, that is created in a district which comprehends one-quarter of the area of Persia. Obviously, the name thus applied is too inclusive for usefulness in rug exposition. Narrowly and specifically, it is the dealer's name for the antique and native rugs of Dorosch, Birjand, Gahyn and numerous undetermined villages. Allied but distinct are the native rugs of Herat, always Persian, regardless of geographical line. Dominating both, as a Goliath, are the new commercial rugs of Meshed, capital of the province and most holy city of Persia.

Meshed

Meshed to-day is the source of the great "baff" family of carpets: Turkbaff, which means Turk-woven (Ghiordes knot); Tiebaff, which means single-woven (Sehna knot); and Farsbaff, which means Persian-woven. All of these weavings, mostly of large size, are the latest and most successful models of an ancient production of rugs. Here the new is deep-rooted in tradition and prestige.

Turkbaff rugs secured their name from the conspicuous and exclusive practice of the Turkish knotting system on the part of Persian weavers of Turkish speech who came to Meshed from Tabriz. Common local practice favored the Persian knot, and only condoned the use of the Ghiordes. In color, too, the weaving took an individual course, showing preference for light, delicate effects—cream, sky-blue, and rose—in opposition to the Meshed preference for richer and more sombre colors. Naturally, also, Tabriz rigidity of expression was graved on Turkbaff rugs—that look of precise molding that is far from nonchalance and near to formality. In a market now inundated with sinuous richness, Turkbaff effects would provide needed variety.

Tiebaff rugs are single or Sehna-knotted fabrics, sold commonly as Ispahan-Mesheds, which meant originally Meshed rugs of Ispahan design. To-day the design is any graceful arrangement of delicate floral items executed in colors increasingly dark and rich. Farsbaff or Persian-woven rugs are Sehna-knotted, like the Tiebaffs, but each knot is tied on four warp threads instead of two, a practice which is said to have originated in Birjand, where to-day a part of the Farsbaff product is created. To undersell these improved modern carpets, Gahyn, famous with Birjand for antique Khorassans, to-day produces a soft-backed, shoddy carpet woven in the Sehna knot, and the district of Tersheez an equivalent substitute, so that no one wishing a cheap Meshed carpet may be deprived of his desire.

Turkbaff, Tiebaff and Farsbaff carpets are being produced by men and boys—no women—on a thousand looms, mostly the property of five American firms, which unquestionably secure the best product. Rugs made under Persian auspices find their market in Teheran, Constantinople and London. Rugs undergoing production for Riza Shah's palace at Teheran, a gift of Persian officials located in Khorassan, have been the objects of unstinted praise. Three years have been devoted to their making and the work is still far from complete.

Semi-antique Meshed carpets, a term which now signifies pre-war and late-nineteenth-century weavings, are the magenta and blue fabrics, large and inclined to squareness, with multiple border stripes, sometimes nine to fifteen in number, that enclose pretentious medallions surrounded by plain fields, unless the gracious Herati pattern asserts its rights. The weaving is characterized by the extensive omission of weft, which crosses only above each five or six rows of knots; and the material by the use of short autumn-clipped wool, which, although fine, is of insufficient length and strength to withstand hard wear. Both practices, thanks be to Allah, have been discontinued in the new weaving.

Identifying Meshed rugs is one of the easiest and least known of practices. Always the outside border stripe—the merest ribbon, an inch wide—contains numerous minute flower forms connected by curved leaves. These flowers are woven nine, ten or eleven knot rows apart. The weavers are paid by the mokata, which is twelve thousand knots. To compute the total number of knots the paymaster has only to walk his first and second fingers on the flowers, up one side and across one end, and multiply the two counts to determine the number of squares, each known to contain eighty-one, one hundred or one hundred and twenty-one knots. Emphasis has been given an undulating vine-and-leaf pattern that commonly decorates the main border stripe, as if it were the identifying feature. Compared to its little inconspicuous neighbor, it is of minor consequence.

Sixty years ago, Meshed contained a number of talented loom-masters who made a practice of signing their weavings. One was Hajji Rajah, whose name came to have much the same significance in Khorassan as the name Gainsborough in England. A hundred and more years ago, the rugs of Meshed were inextricably allied to the rugs of Herat, and were not without correspondence, through the rugs of Gahyn and Birjand, with the rugs of Kerman. Always art in rugs is a current that comes to rest somewhere, for a few years or a century, only to be amplified, if virtue and vitality are in it, to be sent farther for more distant utility. To-day it has vitalized, one might say raised from the dead, the machine-made rugs of America.

PERSIA'S SEMI-ANTIQUE AND MODERN RUGS

Never is the position of Meshed as the religious centre of Persia, the second Mecca of all Shiite Mohammedans, as Kum is the third, to be overlooked in the rug equation. For three hundred years all persons of rank and wealth in Persia, to the number of hundreds of thousands, have made the Meshed pilgrimage, to venerate the shrine of Ali Riza, the eighth Imam, to present to the mosque the finest of rugs, and incidentally, on the part of the rank and file, to get home again by selling and bartering the magic carpets on which they had come. The result was a permanent exposition of rug masterpieces that influenced beneficently all contiguous weaving, giving it exceptional versatility, breadth and depth. That the able minds engaged in the trade of rugs should long have been confused by the miscellaneous assortment of weaving that was exported from Meshed was but a temporary embarrassment demanding and largely accomplishing the solution of the problem of original sources.

"Persian Beluchistans and Bokharas"

Numerous little villages east of Meshed produce the ubiquitous Beluchistan rugs that spring from the soil along Persia's entire eastern frontier. These are collected by brokers and conveyed to the city for sale. Meshed is one of the largest "Beluch" and "Persian Bokhara" markets, the latter weaving hailing from the neighborhood of Sarakhs.

Semi-Antique Khorassans

Khorassan rugs, products of Gahyn, Birjand and Dorosch during the last century, and formerly of Toon, Nishapar and other towns still to be honored with recognition, are the wholly splendid, native, antique floor coverings that among all rugs still reasonably obtainable are closest to one of the highest thrones of rug art, the sixteenth-century atelier at Herat. Certainly, the available rug art of Khorassan and Kerman, on Persia's sunrise side, far surpasses the general accomplishment of Persia's western frontier. From the high peak attained at Kerman, the art, as thus far reviewed, fell into a deep abyss with the Afshars, climbed a knoll with the Shiraz, held the gain with the Lors, rose slightly with the Bakhtiari and abruptly with the Persian Kurds, reached the highest elevation of the west in Sehna and Bijar, levelled off for Western business in Tabriz, Teheran and Meshed, and rose again to mountain heights in Khorassan. Always it is to be remembered, however, that individual performance, not family reputation, is the acid test of art.

The color scheme of Khorassan rugs is founded on the rich reds that the old Herat weavers disseminated. To complain that the coursing wine tones of the "Ispahan" are not maintained in their integrity is to overlook as remarkable a series of experiments in color as the later art exhibits. Purple and plum have a field-day; gaiety ascends to rose, and regretting the indulgence, expresses its despondency in magenta; excitement vibrates in sharp brick tones, to be mercifully quieted by consoling greens, level-headed blues and wise old golds, that are impeccable. Therefore, in spirit, color is both brilliant and restrained, voluble and quiet.

Design, too, has its root in Herat. First lessons in weaving seemingly were given in the Herati pattern, and in all variations of accent and scale. Rosettes, leaves and diamond-forming vines advance and recede, expand and contract, in accord with the rhythm of individual temperament. Small medallion and corner-ornament inserts are outward evidences of pretension. When, as sometimes happens, ambition overleaps itself, design becomes wholly medallion, sometimes with the forms of men, birds and animals in "everlasting poses" upon a field of solid blue. When, similarly, talent in the creation of fine and numerous border-bands becomes an obsession, an entire field of vertical stripes, each involved with curving vines, results, which at best is fine art misplaced. The most individual pattern is the famous "mother-and-child" overlay of cones in sprawling postures, forerunner of the mood that finds expression in our comic supplements. But nowhere in rugs is the simple small palm-leaf in battalion formation so masterfully handled. Beyond a doubt the famous Feraghan and Saraband patterns here find most attractive rendering, and possibly their intermediate source. Years ago, Feraghans often were sold as Khorassans.

Wool in these rugs is a silky substance, knot fine Sehna, and pile short or medium in length, sometimes irregularly clipped. Foundation is fine cotton. Warp often is "underslung" as a result of crowding, and weft reduced to a spider's thread or completely omitted between many lines of weaving, in order to make room for additional knots. But why generalize, when only precision will register the three principal varieties?

Gahyn

Gahyn (Ghayn, Cayn, Kain) rugs are the most colorful and cheerful. Joyous reds, blues and golds possess an integrity and transparency that is refreshing, and a modest assurance in rising from their silky divans that few masters of dye etiquette can surpass. Design always is some minute floral pattern, commonly the steadfast friend from Herat, executed in the Sehna knot, which as common property is of no assistance in segregation. Only two features, in addition to color, stamp the variety: light, pliable backs and fleecelike surface due to uneven shearing. Both features are accounted for by the purpose of the weaving, which was the covering of divans. Therefore our best use of it is over plain carpeting, which to-day is an increasingly fashionable use for antique rugs of superior character. It is equally useful, however, on hard-wood floors, if equipped with lining. The principal occupa-

117

tion of the inhabitants of Gahyn is the raising of silk, which is sent to Yezd.

BIRJAND

Birjand has a reputation for rugs that is always expressed in superlatives, such as "incomparably good, superior workmanship, exquisite designs, marvellously blended colors." Generally the variety is composed of quiet, restrained fabrics, having something of the quality of etching through the use of small pattern in delicate colors over an ivory or light-toned ground. Compared to the rugs of Gahyn the color is low, the pile short and evenly clipped, and the backs heavy and hard, often due, it is asserted, to the practice of doubling the warp, as in the modern Farsbaff. Together, Birjand and Gahyn rugs are the eastern Feraghans, rare and costly because never spoiled by exploitation.

DOROSCH

Dorosch (Duroshkt, Durukh) rugs, however, are reputed the supreme Khorassans. This reputation is founded on an outstanding achievement in weaving that combines the fineness of Sehna rugs with the fulness of Bijar rugs, and on an achievement in art that unites Khorassan with Kerman. Always the weaving is superior and frequently the art. Important designs are engaged with the decorative rendering of cypress and plane-trees rising from flower-strewn and landscaped grounds, or similar imaginative ornament, executed in the engaging make-believe of Kerman. Attendant color is light and buoyant. The conventional patterns of cone, leaf and vine forms are rendered commonly in dark tones. The weaving is said to have been terminated by an earthquake that all but destroyed the town some thirty years ago. At any rate the weaving is ended, and the strongest textile link between Khorassan and Kerman severed.

PERSIA'S SEMI-ANTIQUE AND MODERN RUGS

HERAT

Herat, applied both to the "Ispahan" weaving of the sixteenth century and to the blue Herati-patterned rug of the nineteenth century, is, rightly or wrongly, the outstanding name in rugs. "Big and small make a great wall," according to an old Greek saying. Nevertheless, the present generation of rug appraisers considers the nineteenth-century Herat one of the most important of Persian rugs, equal to the best Khorassans, excepting only the Dorosch, and superior to all but the finest Feraghans. Additionally, it considers the Herat rug the prototype of Khorassans, Feraghans, Bakshis, Kurdistans and all other varieties extensively employing the Herati pattern, including, for good measure, the Sarabands, whose palm-leaves alternate the direction of their stems only to reduce their obligation to Herat, whose palm-leaves all incline in one direction. The worth of these beliefs is difficult to determine. Suffice it that the later Herat is a sterling fabric of decoratively useful art, employing the Herati and palm-leaf patterns on blue or red grounds, usually with dominant blue effect, and with white, green, yellow and sometimes purple as subordinate colors. Accented borders with conspicuous centre stripe are a characteristic not to be overlooked. The design of this border is employed probably in half the important rug-weaving centres of Persia. Usually the knot is hard-hammered Ghiordes, which creates a stiff fabric in comparison with most Khorassans; and occasionally the entire foundation is wool.

THE COMMERCIAL CENTRE OF RUGS

The district of Irak-Ajemi, called Aragh, constitutes the corolla of modern Persian rug weaving, whose stamens are Hamadan, Sultanabad and Kashan, cities of great concentration of rug investment. Its rug flowers of yesteryear are the famous Feraghans, Saruks, Sarabands and Joshaghans.

ORIENTAL RUGS AND CARPETS

HAMADAN

Hamadan was the first capital of Persia. "Cyrus the Great," says Herodotus, "having appointed Pactyas, a Lydian, to bring away the gold, took Crœsus with him and departed for Ecbatana," which means "treasure-house" and was Hamadan's ancient name. Here, in the palace, according to Ezra, a roll was found during the reign of Darius concerning the house of God at Jerusalem: "In the first year of Cyrus the King, Cyrus the King made a decree. Let the house be builded, the place where they offer sacrifices, and let the foundations thereof be strongly built, and let the expenses be given out of the King's house." In Ecbatana the first Persian kings had their summer residences, Alexander the Great his recreation of several months in the year 324 A.D., and there later the Parthian kings held their courts. To-day Hamadan is a city shorn of every vestige of greatness except the greatness of modern oriental-rug industry.

Thirty years ago one of the best known of Persian rugs was the rug of camel hair. It had a broad brown outer-border stripe, a field of similar color, and a medallion or compact diaper pattern filled with crude floral forms. The fabric was heavy and durable, although it was held together by only a single weft above each row of Ghiordes knots. This was the one known Hamadan rug. To-day this rug is obsolete, but as a result of its technique almost every central Persian weaving featured by a single weft thread, which makes conspicuous on the back every alternate warp string, is called Hamadan, regardless of the fact that Sehnas, Lilihans, Kamaraes and numerous other rugs are woven in this manner.

Hamadan is not a unit but a congeries of weaving. Possibly thirty varieties or grades of rugs of every conceivable size, design and color, native and foreign, are produced by the weavers of innumerable villages and tribes that surround the city and make it a great market not only for modern rugs but for semi-antiques. Large carpet sizes are woven mostly in Hamadan, Borchalu and Kabutrahang; fine "Mosol" rugs, canopies and mats in Mehreban, Dargazin, Gumbat and Rahaty; and cheap grades in Koumat and Faminin. Rugs of Feraghan pattern are produced in Kara Geuz, Mesrobian and Amsagird, and orders for fine weaving are executed in Kara Geuz, which is famous for its Kurd qualities. The subject is vast and controversial. Forty authorities, native and foreign-resident, will express as many conflicting opinions: "There is no village named Vin; Feraghan-styled rugs are not called Angelees; Nobaran I never heard of; Daulatabad produces this but not that." England and the United States secure three-fourths of the product, which somehow the trade-winds quickly seize and scatter.

SULTANABAD

Sultanabad, officially known as Arak, chief competitor of Hamadan in the creation of modern Persian rugs, is a new city laid out with a rectangular street system, like a Western metropolis, and is still growing, thanks to numerous strong occidental firms of rug manufacturers and, formerly, to two influential families, Mahajarani and Mahomed Saduch. Like Hamadan, Sultanabad is the centre of three or four thousand looms producing rugs of such varying sizes, qualities, designs and colors as to contradict any description.

All towns within the environment are "Mahals," meaning places or localities. With us Mahal means the lowest grade of Sultanabad weaving, Muskabad a slightly better grade, Arak a lesser grade of Saruk, and Saruk the utmost attainment. The best Saruks are now all woven in Sultanabad, because strict supervision is there most easily exercised, and only rugs of second grade are made in the town of Saruk, which has lost prestige. The popular Lilihan rugs are woven by Armenians of the district and in the village of Kamarae, in a quality corresponding to Arak weaving, from which it can be distinguished by numerous white knots on the back. All the weaving of the district, including the Saruks that once contained art of enviable distinction, is of pattern that the investing firms conceive or stylize for a specific clientele, whose penchant for rich reds and blues seems to be insatiable.

KASHAN

Among the cities of first importance in modern rug weaving, Kashan probably presents the most surprising anomalies. The thought that beauty of art, which the rugs frequently display, is the reflection of beauty of soul and environment, is here nullified by mental suffering, excruciating heat and death by scorpions. In Kashan, beauty of rugs is release from torture. In desert heat, among deadly vermin and within dilapidated buildings set upon the ruins of ancient habitations, live and labor for trifling compensation hundreds of weavers, desperately poor, ignorant, improvident and seemingly incapable of improving their condition. Still, out of an area that commonly is compared to the region beyond the Styx comes a weaving, both in silk and wool, that in quality of art, material and workmanship is generally to-day unsurpassed.

Another surprising fact. Kashan rugs, always important, were so far unrecognized as a separate weaving thirty years ago that no mention of them was made in the first modern rug books. Seemingly, the weaving was then temporarily submerged in the maelstrom of rugs called "Iran" or Persian, and this in spite of the fact that possibly half of the quantity of Persian silk rugs created during the nineteenth century were woven in Kashan. Historically no city, not even Herat, takes precedence over Kashan as the source of the great rug art of the sixteenth century; and of all rug artists Maksud of Kashan is by far the most famous.

PERSIA'S SEMI-ANTIQUE AND MODERN RUGS

Modern Kashan weaving displays ancestral traits of superior talent, in inclination toward realistic rendering of floral motives, in careful execution of details of pattern, in delight in multiplicity of borders, and in the exclusive use of fine Sehna knots held in place by blue cotton weft.

During the past two years six hundred looms for the production of Kashan rugs have been established at Kazvin, located three hundred miles to the northwest. Kazvin will be recalled as the capital of Persia in the period of great art between 1549 and 1576, and as the probable source of some of the rug masterpieces of the resident monarch, Shah Tahmasp. The higher quality of the new product is very superior, almost too good to last. It duplicates Kashan weaving at its best. Equally, the lower qualities resemble the present rugs of Tabriz, which means that their art is more formal and less realistic. Possibly in emulation of this enterprise, the city of Resht, not very far distant, famous for raw silk and cheap but effective embroideries, is experimenting with sixty looms.

SEMI-ANTIQUE RUGS

Feraghan, old Saruk, Saraband and Joshaghan rugs constitute the important rugs that in Aragh flourished amazingly until forty years ago, when intriguing commerce settled in the poor little villages and diverted the art of the talented but innocent weavers.

FERAGHAN

Feraghans were woven in some seventy villages located upon the high plain, seven thousand feet in elevation, between Hamadan and Sultanabad. Already the names of these villages are difficult to collect, but the principal places were Saruk, Temerez, Daulatabad, Kezas, Gorban and Tafrish, most of which famine greatly reduced in

1918. Here were woven four superior types that have obvious relationship: Feraghans, old Saruks, Zellé (Zil-as) Sultans, and old Muskabads. Except for a small number woven in medallion pattern upon a plain field, the Feraghans were produced in all-over design—Herati, Guli Hinnai, vase and nightingale, and miscellaneous small flower devices arranged in rows. Of these the Herati with blue field, rose-colored pattern and green border is the favorite; and when executed in fine wool and Sehna-knotted workmanship, no rug better accords with fine tapestry. Comparatively few examples answer this description. Many have rose, and some, ivory, grounds, which reverse the salient colors. Often details are lacking, and borders are too conspicuous from over-use of white and pale tints. With commercialization, inferior wool and coarse Ghiordes knots grounded the weaving and created a less artistic result.

More brilliant than the Herati pattern on blue is the Guli Hinnai pattern on red, with green, gold and blue garnishment. Comparatively, this is a rare weaving, particularly in carpet size, the result of special order, presumably, like many of the fine Feraghan weavings known as Zellé-Sultan, distinguished by vase design conjoined with narrow single-stripe border.

SARUK

That the old-type Saruk rugs were developed on the Feraghan plain and out of Feraghan weaving there is no least doubt; the earliest examples bear the family birthmark. When and how the prodigal expansion of the art took place no one appears to know; but that an amazingly fine blossoming of talent occurred is now generally recognized. Sumptuous medallion carpets, rugs with designs of cypress and willow realistically rendered, and mats of exquisite tracery, all executed in fine shades of deep blue and red, delicate green and ivory, are now a memory except for the fortunate few who possess them.

124

PERSIA'S SEMI-ANTIQUE AND MODERN RUGS

These rugs had no common design; seemingly, the weavers mastered a hundred patterns and went to their reward. To-day, in substitution, there are the Saruks of Sultanabad, Khonsar, Melair and a score more of little struggling villages: popular and serviceable rugs, but all much alike and restricted in art—whose weavers next year will go to their reward and give place to new weavers with bright fresh hopes.

SARABAND

That the makers of the fine rugs known as Saraband, once created in villages adjacent to the Feraghan plain and located about the Seribend Mountains, fifty miles southwest of Mount Elwund, should have left no rug-weaving progeny is but another oriental enigma. Explanation may lie in the assertion that all the fine Sarabands, known as Mir from the town of that name which an earthquake destroyed, were "Farmayashti," or special-order weavings; or in the supposition that the old weavers gave up in disgust when neighbors, for purposes of common commerce, pilfered both pattern and color scheme, which seem to have been an ancient inheritance. In any event, an unmistakable mastery of rug weaving came to an abrupt end in the villages of these hills. The rugs were Sehna-knotted, the finest double-warped; the material was unexcelled, the colors quiet and rich, the border stripes multiple to the point of prodigality, and the little pear pattern, facing alternately right and left, as delicate an ornament as the art of rug weaving displays. To-day a thousand imitations flood the market, and the genuine old superb Saraband is rarer than the Ovis Poli.

JOSHAGHAN

The rugs of Joshaghan merit a new study. Rugs of real importance were created in the city that found a market for its weaving, in Ispahan and India, during the sixteenth century. The probability of the weaving of vase and Polonaise silk rugs in Joshaghan has already been asserted.

The popular design during the eighteenth and early nineteenth centuries was the so-called "Shah Abbas" version of the vase-rug pattern—rows of large palmettes and rows of diagonalled floral "turtle" forms, separated by rosettes and small flowers. Then came a version of the later Ispahan pattern—long, prominent saw-toothed leaves, curved about shrunken palmettes. This was the early form of the small Herati design, which attained such extensive use that experts formerly attributed the first Feraghan rugs to Joshaghan. To the foregoing floral patterns the weavers added a design of linear draftsmanship that displays numerous crosses and eight-pointed stars. Whatever the pattern, the treatment has a pronounced expert quality and equitable co-ordination of parts, which is the deftness of art so much admired in the best Ispahans.

Colors either are rich rose or blue, combined with secondary greens, yellows and ivory. Always the weaving is hard and substantial, due to the employment of fine, well-hammered Ghiordes knots. Always the pile, composed of finest wool, is the least bit longer than was common in Feraghan and Saraband practice. To-day in this famous rug city, on approximately one hundred looms operated by women, are being woven carpets that might be called "Near Kashans," the field color some shade of rose, the design rhomboid.

Modern Ispahan

Below Joshaghan is the city of Ispahan. "If the world had no Ispahan," said an ancient poet, "the world-creator would have no world. *World* is the word and *Ispahan* is the meaning." Fallen on evil days, Ispahan is now the humble market for the rugs of the tribes of Bakhtiari and Lor, and of the Armenibaff rugs of the contiguous Armenian villages.

PERSIA'S SEMI-ANTIQUE AND MODERN RUGS

YEZD

Beyond, on the road to Kerman, is Yezd. "We presently entered the sandy plain wherein lies the ancient city of Yezd," writes Browne, "towards which we wound our way through gardens and corn-fields. As we approached I was much puzzled as to the nature and function of numerous tall chimney-like structures. I was disposed to regard them as a new variety of minaret; but I soon learned that they were really wind-chimneys, designed to collect and convey into the interiors of the better class of houses such breaths of fresh breeze as might be stirring in the upper regions of the air which lay so hot and heavy over the sun-parched plain." *

Marco Polo found Yezd "a considerable city of much traffic, where a species of cloth of silk and gold is manufactured and carried thence by merchants to all parts of the world." Silk manufacture always has been the great industry, but carpet weaving has not been wholly unindulged. Rugs, not over seventy-five years of age, display mostly a large form of the Herati design, the leaves the longest anywhere employed, but well proportioned to carpet sizes. Always colors are low and well co-ordinated, the reds inclining to old browns and tans, the blues and ivory-white cool and refreshing.

To-day in Yezd, rugs of excellent quality are being woven in the patterns of Herat, Rawar and Kerman, on approximately one hundred looms. The work lags, however, and the town sinks from its position of affluence attained during the World War, when Persia had no other outlet and contact. Zoroastrians, Babis and Musselmans, who compose the population, have renewed their interminable disputes, and settled into the state of mind where "Haste is of the Devil, and tardiness from the All-Merciful."

*E. J. Browne, *A Year Amongst the Persians*. The Macmillan Co.

CHAPTER V

INDIA'S GREAT RUGS

MEN who did superlatively great things and wrote superlatively fine things are rare in history. Europe produced two men possessed of this double genius, Cæsar and Napoleon. The Orient produced at least one, Baber, author of *Memoirs* that rank with Cæsar's *Commentaries*, and founder of the Mogul dynasty of India, which, next to the Safavi dynasty of Persia, contributed most to the fine art of rugs.

The vast talent of Baber for high thought and pure expression is displayed in an exhortation, to cite only a single instance, addressed to a victorious but tired, intimidated and vacillating Afghan army facing crucial encounter with a powerful Hindu confederacy of enraged, maniacal Rajputs. "Gentlemen and soldiers: Every man that comes into the world must pass away. God alone is immortal, unchangeable. Whoso sits down to the feast of life must end by drinking the cup of death. All visitors to the inn of mortality must one day leave this house of sorrow. Rather let us die with honor than live disgraced.

> With fame, though I die, I am content;
> Let fame be mine, though life be spent.

128

God Most High has been gracious in giving us this destiny, that if we fall we die martyrs, if we conquer we triumph in His holy cause. Let us swear with one accord by the great name of God that we will never turn back from such a death, or shrink from the stress of battle, till our souls are parted from our bodies."*

Baber was more than a great prose-writer in his native Turki language; he was a poet in the Persian language and a facile interpolator of poetry in speech and writing. He was devoted to learning and nature, held great artists in high esteem, especially penmen and singers, and had a sense of honor bright as a Damascus blade. He had the "urbanity and culture of the Persian, and the most captivating personality in oriental history." Physically he was so powerful that "he could take a man under each arm and run with them round the battlements of a fortress, leaping the embrasures."

At the age of eleven he inherited from his father a petty kingdom east of Samarkand, and the right to fight with numerous other heirs of Tamerlane over the remnants of the ancestral empire. Twice as a young man he established himself on the great throne at Samarkand, only to be unseated and driven out. For ten years he lived vagrantly in huts and camps, and then set up his fourth throne in Kabul, among the Afghan mountains. Eventually from Kabul, first with bands of wild citizens and then with armies, he made four unsuccessful attempts to conquer India, and finally a fifth and successful venture. On April 21, 1526, he faced in war, on the plain of Panipat, the mighty Sultan of Delhi, and, employing the famous encircling manœuvre of the Mongolians, defeated the Hindu army of one hundred thousand men and one hundred elephants. To his officers and men he gave the entire vast wealth of the Delhi kings, and earned for himself a nickname, "the begging friar." He was content with fame, which fortune increased to the status of founder of an empire. He is the connecting

* Stanley Lane-Poole, *Mediæval India*. G. P. Putnam's Sons.

129

link between the predatory hordes of Central Asia and the imperial government of India.

Humayun (1530-1556), "whose presence," his father wrote, "opened our hearts like rosebuds and made our eyes shine like torches," was a gallant and lovable fellow, a gentleman, but as a king a failure. His position called for boundless energy and soldierly genius, neither of which he possessed. Treachery of brothers and the opposition of a gifted Afghan general dethroned him, and made him an unwelcome guest at the Persian court of Shah Tahmasp, who nevertheless assisted him to retrieve Kabul. Years later, from this dais, he recovered the Delhi throne, only to die within six months from the effects of a fall down the marble steps of his palace. "His end was a piece with his character. If there was a possibility of falling, Humayun was not the man to miss it."

The recorded story of the rugs of splendor produced in India under the Moguls begins with Akbar (1556-1605), son of the precipitous Humayun. Our informant is Abu'l-Fazl, author of the *Institutes of Akbar*. "His majesty has caused carpets to be made of wonderful varieties and charming textures; he has appointed experienced workmen, who have produced many masterpieces. The carpets of Iran [Persia] and Turan [Turkestan] are no more thought of, although merchants still import carpets from Goskhan [Joshaghan], Khuzistan [southwest Persia], Kerman [southeast Persia] and Sabzwar [northeast Persia]. All kinds of carpet weavers have settled here, and drive a flourishing trade. These are found in every town, but especially in Agra, Fathpur and Lahor."

That the rugs in the palaces of Baber and Humayun were imported from Persia and Turkestan is a reasonable inference. That the palace of the Sultan of Delhi, whom Baber deposed, contained the carpet depicting a nightmare of grotesque animals engaged in consuming or disgorging rodents, rabbits and serpents—whose famous fragments are

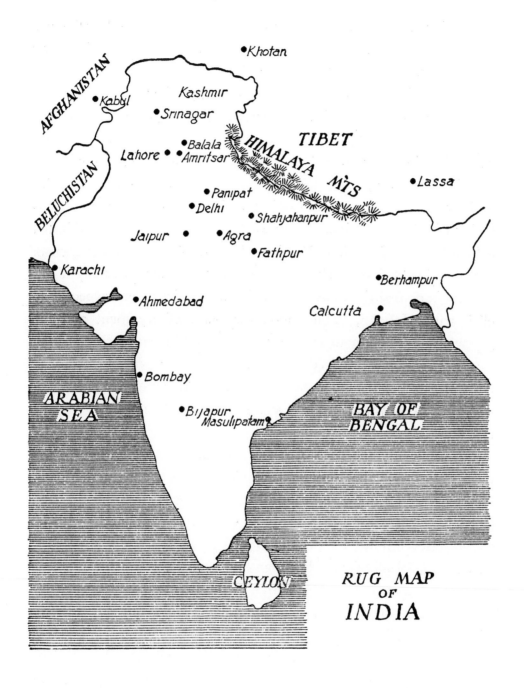

Khotan

AFGHANISTAN
•Kabul

Kashmir
•Srinagar

TIBET

BELUCHISTAN

Lahore • •Balala
•Amritsar

HIMALAYA MTS

•Lassa

•Panipat
•Delhi

Jaipur • •Agra
•Shahjahanpur

•Fathpur

•Karachi

•Berhampur

•Ahmedabad

Calcutta •

•Bombay

ARABIAN
SEA

•Bijapur
Masulipatam•

BAY OF
BENGAL

CEYLON

RUG MAP
OF
INDIA

now assigned to India of the year 1500—is also a reasonable inference. Certainly, if ever a rug was also a prophecy, this carpet of feasting monsters was a portent of wholesale disaster.

The royal factory established by Akbar supplied two peremptory requirements—rugs for a huge harem and for the new vast palaces of Fathpur. "There were more than five thousand women, in various capacities, in the harem," Abu'l-Fazl remarks, "which created a vexatious question, even for a great statesman, and furnished his majesty with an opportunity to display his wisdom." The harem, consisting of Hindu, Persian, Mogul and Armenian women, constituted a "parliament of religions," which Akbar duplicated for the men of the court in the famous Hall of Worship. Here, each Thursday night, debates upon doctrinal and philosophical questions were expected to elicit truth. Instead, "abuse took the place of argument and the plainest rules of etiquette were forgotten, even in the presence of the Emperor, who was inspired only with compassion for the futility of reasoning and contempt for narrowness. To Akbar's open eyes there was truth in all faiths, but no creed could hold the master-key of the infinite."

Pre-eminently the rugs of Akbar are the rugs of Fathpur, "the town of victory," the Versailles and Pompeii of the greatest Mogul. "Nothing sadder or more beautiful exists in India than this deserted city—the silent witness of a vanished dream. It still stands, with its circuit of seven miles, its seven bastioned gates, its wonderful palaces, peerless in all India for noble design and delicate ornament, its splendid mosque and pure marble shrine of the hermit saint, its carvings and paintings—stands as it stood in Akbar's time, but now a body without a soul. Reared with infinite thought and curious care, it was deserted fourteen years later. In the empty palaces, the glorious mosque, the pure white tomb, the baths, the lake—at every turn, we recognize some memory of the greatest of Indian emperors. We may

132

even enter his bedroom and see the very screens of beautiful stone tracery, the same Persian couplets, the identical ornament in gold and ultramarine on which Akbar feasted his eyes in the long sultry afternoons of the Indian plains."*

Akbar's flower rugs are the Fathpur dream executed in silk and finest fibred wool. The animal and bird rugs, produced probably in the succeeding reigns, tell another story. "The chase was his keenest delight, and he would break the tedium of the long marches of his many campaigns by hunting elephants or tigers on the way. We read of three hundred and fifty elephants taken in a single day; at another time he stalked wild asses for thirty-five miles, and shot sixteen. He had names for his guns, and kept records of their performances. There were vast battues when thousands of deer, nilgao, jackals and foxes were driven by the beaters in a circle of forty miles, and the lines drawn closer and closer, till Akbar could enjoy at his ease several days' shooting and hawking, and still leave a few thousand head for his followers to practise on."* Like his grandfather he was a man of titanic strength and wholly without sense of fear. Time and again, during his reign of forty-nine years, with hardly a year free from war, he personally led attacks upon forces that outnumbered his own ten to one. He expanded the boundaries of the rich but little state which he inherited at the age of thirteen years, until it extended from Kandahar to the Bay of Bengal and included the whole of Hindustan down to the southern plains.

Akbar was also a scholar. "From his youth he had delighted in the conversation of professors and philosophers and shown the greatest deference to real learning. He had books read aloud to him daily from his rich library, and would go through them again and again. The age was one of great literary abounding and superb art."* Nobility, however, is the true synonym for Akbar, as for Confucius. The

* Stanley Lane-Poole, *Mediæval India*. G. P. Putnam's Sons.

133

lines introduced into the bidding prayer of the service in the great mosque of Fathpur one Friday in 1580, when the King assumed the rôle of priest and caliph, epitomized his life:

"The Lord to me the Kingdom gave,
He made me prudent, strong and brave,
He guided me with right and ruth,
Filling my heart with love of truth;
No tongue of man can sum His State—
Allahu Akbar!   God is great."

Jahangir (1605-1628), whose birth Akbar celebrated by building magnificent Fathpur, the "town of victory," proved a great collector and connoisseur of art. In his memoirs Jahangir writes as follows: "My love of painting and my practice in judging them reached such a degree of accuracy, that any time a work is presented to me, whether by deceased or contemporary artist, I immediately guess the name of each painter who executed it." Jahangir was a great lover of beauty in nature and ordered such artists as Mansur and Murad to paint the most beautiful specimens of birds, animals and flowers, chiefly of Kashmir, which he called "the garden of eternal spring." According to Jahangir Mansur painted more than one hundred flowers found in Kashmir.

Among the court festivals was one set apart for the weighing of the monarch. Sir Thomas Roe, who succeeded William Hawkins as the representative of England, witnessed and described one of these curious performances: "The first of September was the King's Birthday, and the solemnitie of his weighing, to which I went, carried me into a very large and beautiful Garden, the square within all water, on the sides flowres and trees, in the midst a Pinacle, where was prepared the scales, being hung in large tressels, and a crosse beame plated with Gold thinne: the scales of massie Gold, the borders set with small stones, Rubies and Turkeys, the Chaines of Gold large and

massie, but strengthened with silke Cords. Here attended the No-
bilitie, all sitting about it on Carpets until the King came; who at
last appeared clothed or rather loden with Diamonds, Rubies, Pearles,
and other precious vanities, so great, so glorious; his Sword, Target,
Throne to rest on, correspondent; his head, necke, breast, armes, above
the elbows, at the wrists, his fingers every one, with at least two or
three Rings; fettered with chaines or dyalled Diamonds; Rubies as
great as Wal-nuts, some greater; and Pearles such as mine cycs were
amazed at. Suddenly he entered into the scales, sate like a woman
on his legges, and there was put in against him many bagges to fit
his weight, which were changed six times, and they say was silver,
and that I understood his weight to be nine thousand rupias, which
are almost one thousand pounds sterling: after with Gold and Jewels,
and precious stones, but I saw none, it being in bagges might be
Pibles; then against Cloth of Gold, Silk, Stuffes, Linen, Spices and
all sorts of goods, but I must believe for they were in sardles. Lastly
against Meale, Butter, Corne, which is said to be given to the
Banian."*

The era marks the beginning of English trade, which culminated
in the investment of considerable sums for carpet manufacture; and
the continuation of that investment even to the present day. The
first traders were Arabs and Egyptians, whose purchases went to
Venice by way of the Persian Gulf and the Red Sea, through Syrian
and Egyptian ports. Between 1498 and 1580 the Portuguese monopolized the traffic, through command of the Indian Ocean and numerous forts built along the Indian coast. In 1600 the English organized
the first East India Company, and with the aid of the Dutch drove out
the Portuguese, and began the movement toward the final conquest.
But this is anticipating a long train of events and the "era of splendid
ease" which Shah Jahan, "the pinnacle of splendor," instituted.

* Stanley Lane-Poole, *Mediæval India*. G. P. Putnam's Sons.

Shah Jahan (1628-1658) produced in the Taj "the supreme masterpiece dedicated to supreme love"; in the New Delhi, or Shahjahanabad, "the most magnificent royal residence in the world," and "the most magnificent palace in the East—perhaps in the world." To discharge the cost of these indulgences the Shah had at his disposal not only the "Revenue coming in from the great kingdoms, but also the Escheats falling to him at the death of great Lords and Favorites, who make the Mogul Heir to what they have gotten by his favour; insomuch that the children have no hope to enjoy ought of their Father's Estates, either Reall or Personall. For the Mogul's Authority is such, and his Power so absolute, that the Estates of all his Subjects are at his disposal." When he was weighed, "bowls of costly gems were poured over him, and all these riches, to the value of a million and a half [pounds], were ordered to be distributed among the people." He was the most popular of the great Moguls, his rule resembling that of a father over his children. His manner was stately and magnificent.

Agra, the first capital of Shah Jahan, was so large that it was as much as a horseman could do to ride round the city in a day. "Its Streets are fair and spacious, and there are some of them Vaulted, which are above a quarter of a League in length, where the Merchants and Tradesmen have their shops; every Trade and every Merchant having a particular Street and Quarter." There were eighty caravanseries for foreign merchants, "most three stories high, with very noble Lodgings, Store-houses, Vaults and Stables belonging to them." In the New Delhi, "streets opened in every direction from the palace, and here and there were seen the merchants' caravanserais and the great workshops where the artisans employed by the emperor and the nobles plied their hereditary crafts of weaving, embroidery, silver and gold-smithery, gun-making, lacquer work, painting, turning and so forth. It was only under royal or aristocratic patronage that the artist flourished; elsewhere the artisan was at the mercy of his temporary employer, who paid him as he chose."*

Aurangzib (1659-1707), sixth and last of the great Moguls, employed François Bernier, a Frenchman, as court physician. Bernier immortalized as well as medicated his royal patron. The scene was the Hall of Audience on any great occasion. The Emperor's approach was heralded by the shrill piping of the hautboys and clashing of cymbals from the band-gallery over the great gate:

"The king appeared seated upon his throne at the end of the great hall in the most magnificent attire. His vest was of white and delicately flowered satin, with a silk and gold embroidery of the finest texture. The turban of gold cloth had an aigrette whose base was composed of diamonds of an extraordinary size and value, besides an oriental topaz which may be pronounced unparalleled, exhibiting a lustre like the sun. A necklace of immense pearls suspended from his neck reached to the stomach. The throne was supported by six massy feet, said to be of solid gold, sprinkled over with rubies, emaralds, and diamonds. It was constructed by Shah-Jahan for the purpose of displaying the immense quantity of precious stones accumulated successively in the treasury from the spoils of ancient rajas and Patans, and the annual presents to the monarch which every Omrah is bound to make on certain festivals. At the foot of the throne were assembled all the Omrahs, in splendid apparel, upon a platform surrounded by a silver railing and covered by a spacious canopy of brocade with deep fringes of gold. The floor was covered entirely with carpets of the richest silk, of immense length and breadth.

"A tent, called the aspek, was pitched outside [in the court], larger than the hall, to which it joined by the top. It spread over half the court, and was completely enclosed by a great balustrade, covered with plates of silver. Its supports were pillars over-laid with

* Stanley Lane-Poole, *Mediæval India*. G. P. Putnam's Sons.

silver, three of which were as thick and as high as the mast of a barque, the others smaller. The outside of this magnificent tent was red, and the inside lined with elegant Masulipatam chintzes, figured expressly for that very purpose with flowers so natural and colours so vivid that the tent seemed to be encompassed with real parterres. As to the arcade galleries round the court, every Omrah had received orders to decorate one of them at his own expense, and there appeared a spirit of emulation who should best acquit himself to the monarch's satisfaction. Consequently all the arcades and galleries were covered from top to bottom with brocade, and the pavement with rich carpets."*

Contrary to public belief, a state is a delicate organism, as the complete ruin of the magnificent Mogul Empire by Aurangzib demonstrates. The Puritan in the man, a common disease among legislators, must overgovern. The Koran, which he knew by heart and copied twice with fine calligraphy, must be the accepted law. So he persecuted the Hindus, destroyed their temples, and involved himself and his vast army in a fruitless effort of twenty years to quell a southern rebellion. In camp Doctor Gemelli Careri of Naples found him "an old man with white beard, trimmed round, contrasting vividly with his olive skin, sitting upon rich carpets and leaning against gold-embroidered cushions." Defeated, he returned to Delhi only to find the north antagonistic. Even to the end he failed to realize that the Mogul domination of India was really an army of occupation. As his physician wrote: "The Great Mogul is a foreigner in Hindustan; he finds himself in a hostile country or nearly so; a country containing hundreds of Gentiles to one Mogul, or even to one Mohammedan."

The dregs of the line of incomparable Baber, philosophic Akbar and magnificent Shah Jahan had now only to be swept away, and the vast wealth of the dynasty transported to another country. The ser-

---

* Stanley Lane-Poole, *Mediæval India*. G. P. Putnam's Sons.

vice was rendered by Nadir Shah, the famous soldier who drove the Afghans out of Persia. In November, 1738, Nadir crossed the Indus, entered Delhi with the last Mogul as his captive guest, and, in revenge for the murderous onslaught of the populace, gave the capital over to despoilment. After two months of colossal pillage, he returned to Persia, taking with him "the famous jewelled Peacock Throne, valued by Tavernier at thirty million dollars, spoil to the value of forty million dollars in money alone, besides an immense treasure of gold and silver plate, jewels, rich stuffs, and a crowd of skilled artisans, with herds of elephants, horses and camels." "The dynasty of Baber ended in nothingness, like all its many predecessors. The conquerors of India have come in hordes again and again, but they have scarcely touched the soul of the people."

The superior rugs of the Moguls were woven during the reigns of Akbar, Jahangir and Shah Jahan (1556-1658). The attempt to assign them specifically to a single ruler awaits future data. The work was executed either upon imperial looms located at Agra, Fathpur, Lahore and doubtless at Delhi, or upon looms of princes, nobles and plutocrats, who made a practice of installing specially gifted weavers in palaces and houses, paying them fixed salaries in addition to food and lodging, and sometimes allowing them to contract for outside work. Extra honor and emolument were the reward of superior accomplishment; and continuity of employment, son succeeding father, the recompense of fidelity. This system was continued until the overthrow of the monarchy by Nadir the Persian.

The finest single collection of unquestionably authentic carpets is said to be the possession of the Maharaja of Jaipur. The mosques at Berhampur, Bijapur and Ahmedabad contain examples. The most famous specimens in Europe are the peacock rug in the Vienna Collection, and in London the Girdlers' Company rug (date 1634), containing the arms of Robert Bell, director of the company. In America the specimens in the Altman Collection at the Metropolitan Museum of Art, the Ardabil tree rug formerly in the Yerkes Collection, the "Current Events" rug in the Boston Museum of Fine Arts, and the elephant rug of Mr. Joseph E. Widener are best known and esteemed. Many other pieces are still in the hands of dealers in New York and London.

The designs of the rugs in the palace at Jaipur represent "rows of flowering plants, each delineated separately and entire to the roots as if planted in a garden, or else set in the interstices of a trellis as though climbing." These are two of the three classic flower patterns, the third consisting of single flowering plants enclosed within frames or compartments. In all three patterns, every flower, bud, leaf and vine is represented as a living organism, exactly as in nature. This literal depiction contrasts sharply with the freehand, imaginative drawing of the Persian rug weaver. It secures greater clarity and symmetry of composition; it loses scope and rhythm. Almost certainly it was appropriated from the velvets of southern Persia and northern India during the seventeenth century. Sometimes the Mogul weaver merged the two styles, as in the fine Altman example which contains a romantic centre framed by a realistic border. Whether or not the three realistic Indian flower patterns hailed from Persia, always Persia was the teacher, as the many "Indo-Ispahan" rugs, copied after the palmette style of Herat, demonstrate.

The Mogul animal rugs of India, equally with the flower rugs, are photographic. Animals are full of life and energy, scenes landscaped, and motives balanced but unsymmetrical. In the Widener rug an elephant and rider are in the midst of running leopards and gazelles, two fighting giraffes, a crocodile threatening a winged lion, a dragon seizing a goat, a rhinoceros and a tiger. The Boston Museum rug depicts a household scene, a temple, a chained leopard on a cart drawn by a bullock, a mythologic creature mastering seven elephants, and

140

a lion chasing gazelles. Here also is definite location of the event. By contrast, the Persian weaver rendered every animal form abstractly, usually as a subordinate part of an artistic composition.

The motives of the prayer rugs of the Moguls were taken from Indian design. One splendid example, now in the collection of Joseph V. McMullan, in New York, shows a profusely growing shrub with large semi-naturalistic blossoms and leaves on a red background. Another rug displays a thistle plant that teaches the beauty of thistles.

Color generally is lighter than Persian color, and the use of pink distinctive, particularly for contrast and outline. Technique is the finest anywhere employed, the weaving of the best examples ranging from seven hundred and two to one thousand two hundred and fifty-eight knots to the square inch. A silk fragment in the Altman Collection is said to contain two thousand five hundred and fifty-two knots to the square inch. Materials are both wool and silk, the latter sometimes imposed upon cotton warp. All-silk rugs are generally attributed to the reign of Shah Jahan and the period of the Taj Mahal.

The decline of the art was due to four drastic consecutive events. With the overthrow of the dynasty, the patronage of royalty, upon which the work depended, almost completely ceased. The East India Company exported to England the obtainable masterpieces, and so far as possible turned the country toward the production of merchantable carpets. The weaving of rugs by the convict labor of the prisons greatly reduced former wages and drove weavers into other occupations. Finally, European firms supplied the patterns and dyes and inaugurated a new era.

In ancient times the Hindu wove simple flat cotton mats, and between the Mohammedan invasion (712 A.D.) and the Mogul conquest (1526 A.D.) inferior rugs of wool. Following the Mogul debacle came a flood of carpets woven to sell in Europe. The varieties still to be encountered, of the manufacture of fifty and one hundred years ago, are Agra jail weavings of exceptional charm and distinction, and rusty Marsulipatam reproductions of Ispahan pattern executed in melancholy magenta color relieved by light blue and ivory.

To-day the great rug centres are the cities of Amritsar, Srinagar, Agra and Balala, all located in northern India. The Amritsar weaving is said to have been begun by shawl weavers who, by change of clothing fashion, were thrown out of employment about the year 1870. Men and boys to the number of fifteen to twenty thousand, varying with financial conditions, now create rugs of Persian pattern executed in compact Sehna knotting. Except for supervision so exacting that the product often appears too rigid and perfect to have been created by hand, the work could pass as Persian, and thereby acquire a merited increase in prestige. Approximately ten thousand weavers find employment in Srinagar, three thousand in Agra, and fifteen hundred in Balala. The largest employers of this labor are the Oriental Carpet Manufacturers, Ltd., C. M. Hadow & Company, Amar Dass, and Sheik Sahib, who know the art by long experience and control its destiny.

CHAPTER VI

RUGS OF TURKEY

IN the year 629 A.D. Yuan Chwang, a Chinese priest of the faith of
Buddha, made a journey lasting sixteen years through western
China, Turkestan and India. In his journal he described the
Turk as he found him, thirteen hundred years ago, on his native
heath in central Asia.

"The Khan of the Turks was a magnificent person in green satin,
with his long hair tied with silk. The gold embroidery of his grand
tent shone with dazzling splendor. The ministers in attendance sat
on mats in rooms on either side, all dressed in magnificent brocade
robes. The rest of the retinue stood behind. It was a case of a frontier
ruler who yet had an air of distinction and elegance. The Khan came
out of his tent about thirty paces to meet Yuan Chwang, who entered
after a courteous greeting. After an interval, envoys from China were
admitted and presented their despatches and credentials, which the
Khan perused. He was much elated, and caused the envoys to be
seated.

"Then he ordered wine and music for himself and them, and
grape-syrup for the pilgrim. Hereupon all pledged each other, and
the filling and draining of the wine-cups made a din and bustle, while

the mingled music of various instruments rose loud. Although the airs were the popular strains of foreigners, yet they pleased the senses and exhilarated the mental faculties. After a little, piles of roast beef and mutton were served for the others, and lawful food, such as cakes, milk, candy, honey and grapes for the pilgrim. After the entertainment, grape-syrup was again served, and the Khan invited Yuan Chwang to improve the occasion, whereupon the pilgrim expounded the doctrine of the 'ten virtues,' compassion for animal life and the emancipation. The Khan, raising his hands, bowed, gladly believed and accepted the teaching."

But not for long. Almost immediately Arab envoys attuned the wild Turk, still on his native heath, to a frenzied Mohammedanism that a ruling family named Seljuk utilized to overrun Persia, capture Bagdad (1055), then governed by a degenerate, unorthodox Abbassid caliph, and finally to take possession of the major lands of Asia Minor. This conquest was a continuation of the purest Arabic tradition of the faith, fanatical and insolent enough to foment the Crusades (1096-1270 A.D.), and so far to expend its energy as to stand in dire need of help, one fateful day at the end of the thirteenth century, when the forces of Kay-Kubād, the Seljuk Sultan, near Angora, now capital of the Turkish Republic, faced almost certain defeat by an enormous horde of roaming Mongolians.

"The enemy was rapidly gaining the mastery, when suddenly the fortune of the day was reversed. A small body of unknown horsemen charged upon the foe, and victory was declared for the Seljuks. The cavaliers who had thus opportunely come to the rescue knew not whom they had assisted, nor did the Seljuks recognize their allies. The meeting was one of those remarkable accidents which sometimes shape the future of nations. Ertoghrul, son of Suleyman, a member of the Oghuz family of Turks, which the Mongol avalanche had dislodged from its old camping grounds in Khorassan, Persia, was journeying to the more peaceful seclusion of Anatolia. Unexpectedly he had come upon the battlefield of Angora. With the nomad's love of scrimmage, and the warrior's sympathy for the weaker side, he led his four hundred riders pell-mell into the fray and won the day. He little thought that by his impulsive and chivalrous act he had taken the first step towards founding an empire—the Turkish Empire that was destined to endure in undiminished glory for centuries."*

The Seljuk Sultan rewarded his accidental allies and "cousins" by locating them in the territory of Asia Minor immediately south of Constantinople, where in a comparatively short time they grew in numbers and power beyond the wildest dreams of their fearless rulers. "Like the circling ripple that springs up in a pool when a stone is dropped into its midst, the sway of the new Turks spread in ever enlarging rings."

At Sugut, the capital, in the year 1258, a new son of Ertoghrul was given the name of Othman, and the fate, by the will of Allah, to become the first Sultan of the Othmanlis or Ottoman Turks. Before his death, his cavalry had captured all the ancient and important cities of the surrounding territory, and his vessels the entire coast. Succeeding Othman, came "Orkhan, the taker of Nicæa and founder of the Janissaries; Murad I, the conqueror at Kosova; Bayezid I, the victor of Nicopolis; Mohammed I, the restorer of the shattered empire; Murad II, the antagonist of Hunyady and of Skanderbeg; Mohammed II, the conqueror of Constantinople; Selim I, who annexed Kurdistan, Syria and Egypt; and Suleyman the Magnificent, the victor on the field of Mohacs and the besieger of Vienna. Never did eight such sovereigns succeed one another, save for the feeble Bayezid II, in unbroken succession in any other country; never was an empire founded and extended during two such splendid centuries by such a series of great rulers."*

* Stanley Lane-Poole, *The Story of Turkey*. G. P. Putnam's Sons.

ORIENTAL RUGS AND CARPETS

The oldest remains of Turkish rugs are accredited to the Seljuks, assigned to the thirteenth and fourteenth centuries and exhibited by the Evkaf (Ewqaf) Museum, Constantinople. They comprise three carpets in dilapidated condition discovered by Doctor Martin in the Ala ed-Din Mosque in Konia, the ancient Iconium, capital of the Seljuk Sultans of Rûm. The patterns consist of interlaced geometric forms and primitive diapers, surrounded in two rugs by borders of archaic Kufic lettering. Colors are strong shades of blue, red and yellow.

Of contiguous source, but of the first half of the fifteenth century, a fragment of a rug containing two panels of Chinese dragon and phœnix design is preserved by the Kaiser Friedrich Museum in Berlin. Its counterpart in literature is Coleridge's *Kubla Khan*. Probably the pattern resulted from Mongolian conquest of the region, temporary but sufficient to produce a textile result. About the year 1440 Domenico di Bartolo reproduced in a fresco in the hospital at Siena, Italy, a rug of similar character. In the Historical Museum, Stockholm, is a rug, approximately of the same age and source, that displays a crude design of two birds in a tree. This is the total discovery to date of very ancient Asia Minor weavings. Obviously only a good beginning has been made in recovering the remains of rugs of the first Turkish practitioners, who were liberal patrons of the fine arts after serving a Persian apprenticeship in them.

The oldest group of rugs remaining to us of the weavings of the Ottoman Turks, and certainly the most indigenous, are the fifteenth-century products now handsomely called Holbein rugs in compliment to Hans Holbein the Younger (1497-1543), who accurately reproduced their patterns and colors in his paintings. Jan van Eyck, Memling, Gerard David, and Italian painters of the same period similarly employed them. The patterns consist of octagons that resemble the present common motive of the rugs of Turkestan; and combinations of octagons, squares and diamonds of different sizes, outlined by knotted chains of arabesques. Borders often display interlaced pattern that obviously is an imitation of Kufic writing. Similar borders constitute a connecting link with the rugs of arabesque design seen in pictures, painted between 1520 and 1540, by Lorenzo Lotto, Girolamo dai Libri, Bronzino and Luca Longhi, and copied by Spanish weavers although Spain and Turkey were at war. Field color of the Holbein rugs is sage and olive green and deep rose; pattern blue, red, purple and black; general effect dark and rich. Field color of the Lotto rugs is scarlet, the dominant pattern yellow, and the general effect brilliant.

A third group of early rugs, known as star Ushaks, is represented in a painting by Paris Bordone (1495-1570), in the Academy at Venice, showing the fisherman in the act of restoring the lost ring to the Doge; and again in a portrait of Henry VIII (1491-1547) at Belvoir Castle. Executed in a new spirit of art, a blue or yellow star, sometimes with four and again with eight points, is repeated on a blue or red field, sometimes in tandem arrangement and again intricately as an all-over design, each star a maze of arabesque work. This variety of rug, forerunner of the "Turkey carpets" that overran Italy and England during the sixteenth and early seventeenth century, is believed to have constituted the shipment of sixty pieces received from Venice, October, 1520, by Cardinal Wolsey, the first Englishman known to import pile carpets. Incidentally, a portrait of Henry VIII in Earl Spencer's collection at Althorp represents the king sitting at a table with the Princess Elizabeth. On the table is a small oriental rug. Numerous paintings of Flemish, Dutch and Italian artists show similar use. Obviously, imported rugs were first used as table-cloths.

The location of the looms on which Holbein, Lotto and Bordone rugs were woven was probably Ushak in Asia Minor. The date commonly assigned to the earliest examples is the latter half of the fifteenth century, because all varieties are known to have been in foreign possession approximately by the year 1535. Inference is not proof, but often inference has excellent texture. The latter half of the fifteenth century is in Turkish history the period of Mohammed II (1451-1481), conqueror of Constantinople, and of Josafa Barbaro, envoy (1471) of the Signoria of Venice to Uzun Hasan, King of Persia. Barbaro compares the court rugs of Persia with the rugs of Brusa, presumably the rugs of the Turkish court. It is not unreasonable to assume, therefore, that the oldest examples of all the foregoing varieties are the rugs of Brusa during the period of the Conqueror. In the interval of thirty years during which Mohammed II reigned, style of rug decoration would be assumed to change, particularly with the acquisition of Constantinople, when the native "home-spuns," or Holbein rugs, would give way somewhat to a new model, in this case to a rug of star forms suggested by the star motives contained in Persian carpets. Furthermore, uniformity and continuity of art would be an anomaly in a period dominated by a man created after the fashion of the Conqueror.

Mohammed II, like all newly risen barbarians, was a person compounded of extreme virtues and vices. His spare time was devoted to writing poetry, to the society of men of learning, and to philanthropy, which included the endowment of colleges and "pious foundations." He made a practice of pensioning poets, one of whom compared his mustachios to "leaves over two rosebuds, and every hair of his beard was a thread of gold." Nevertheless and notwithstanding, he was a savage. His first act as monarch was to destroy his baby brother, and almost his second to saw a governor in two. He flayed princes alive, and garrisons that surrendered to his forces, upon his most solemn pledges of amnesty, were ruthlessly slaughtered. Secrecy and lightning rapidity of action were the key and cornerstones of his military arch. Asked concerning his plans for a campaign, he replied: "If a hair of my beard knew them, I would pluck it out." His military genius is most quickly comprehended from a passage of Gibbon's narrative of the fall of Constantinople.

After weeks of arduous assault with artillery, "the reduction of the city appeared to be hopeless unless an attack could be made from the harbor as well as from the land. But the harbor was inaccessible. In this perplexity, the genius of Mahommet conceived and executed the bold and marvellous plan of transporting his vessels and military stores from the Bosphorus into the higher part of the harbor by land. The distance was about ten miles; the ground uneven and overspread with thickets. A level way was covered with a broad platform of strong and solid planks; and to render them more slippery and smooth, they were anointed with the fat of sheep and oxen. Eighty-eight galleys and brigantines of fifty and thirty oars were disembarked on the Bosphorus shore, arranged successively on rollers and drawn forward by the power of men and pulleys. Two guides or pilots were stationed at the helm and prow of each vessel; the sails were unfurled to the winds; and the labor was cheered by song and acclamation. In the course of a single night, this Turkish fleet of large boats painfully climbed the hill, steered over the plain, and was launched from the declivity into the shallow waters of the harbor, far above the molestation of the deeper vessels of the Greeks." The feat was accounted a miracle. The value of cannon was for the first time conclusively demonstrated. Appreciation of the rugs of the period is enhanced tenfold by historical perspective.

The ambition of the Ottoman rulers of Turkey having been attained at Constantinople in less than two hundred years after the establishment of the family in Asia Minor, the fever of conquest subsided under Bayezid II (1481-1512), a ruler melancholy, dreamy, mild and inefficient. The art of rugs, during his dispensation, probably only perpetuated the styles already discussed, therein reflecting the general lethargy and incapacity of the state. If so, the inertia was the stillness and condition of expectancy commonly observed before a storm. For with Selim the Grim (1512-1520) mighty conquest was unleashed again, and through it the art of Turkish rugs radically changed.

Selim was another poet and dangerous man. He wrote flowery verses in the Persian language and executed with mathematical calculation deeds of cruelty, which included the execution of numerous male relatives and the decapitation of seven Grand Viziers. Preeminently he was a fanatical fundamentalist in religion. His vis-à-vis in Persia, Shah Ismail, was a dissenter. Spies sent by Selim into Asia Minor disclosed the pernicious doctrine of the dissenter everywhere, and seventy thousand heretics in the orthodox domain. The results were an efficiently planned massacre of the apostates, the battle of Chaldiran, in which Shah Ismail was injured and narrowly escaped capture, and the Turkish occupation of Ismail's capital, 1514.

"The Sultan entered Tabriz in triumph, massacred all his prisoners, except the women and children, and sent back to Constantinople a trophy in the shape of a thousand of the skilful workmen for which Tabriz had long been famous, and who had supplied architects, carvers, workers in metal and on the loom, to Cairo, Damascus, Venice and all places where fine workmanship was prized. The artisans were established at Constantinople, where they continued to ply their trades with success in embellishing the Turkish capital."*

The result in rugs can be only surmised. Probably it was the beginning of a century and a half of production of the Turkish counterpart of the Persian medallion carpets. There are two types of Ushaks: one type has a decoration of several large stars, floral scrolls, and arabesques; the other has a large central medallion or several small ones with arabesques as the chief feature of the decoration. Ornamented with a frost-work of arabesques, which is executed in dull gold, dark green and blue on a red field, it possesses at once

---

* Stanley Lane-Poole, *The Story of Turkey*. G. P. Putnam's Sons.

strength and opulence equal to the utmost requirements of throne-rooms, fine halls, and the canvases of European painters. "The famous Lansdowne portrait of George Washington, in the Academy at Philadelphia, shows the father of his country standing on a rug that seems to be allied to the Ushak type."

Hung side by side, original and early derivative display striking resemblance, the copy a bit more stiff and staid as a result of multiple medallion structure. Later copies were quieted in color to meet the requirements of the taste of the Western market, which the emissaries of Turkey had opened in Venice. Its instant success upon the floors of Italian and English churches and palaces, and its merited appreciation to-day, illustrate the vagary of art that bewitches in many guises.

The extremely practical nature of Selim the Grim is demonstrated by his very next move. Having avenged the insult to his religion, and taken as compensation for its injury all of the apprehendable art and talent of the Persian capital, he, without provocation, led his forces against the Mamluks, whose capital, Cairo, contained further enticement. The fact that the Mamluks, although descendants of the white slaves of the grand-nephew of Saladin, were gentlemen and scholars, and probably the best rulers that Egypt ever had, made no particle of difference to the Sultan, now a collector of capitals. His artillery annihilated the fine cavalry of the defenders, Cairo was occupied, Egypt became a Turkish province, and the "Grim" himself the great Caliph, head of the Mohammedan religion, by receipt of the symbols of the office from an inactive caliph, who maintained a "shadowy court" in the metropolis.

Because of the obliteration of the Egyptian art of rugs as an independent entity, through the conquest of Selim, and the subsequent complete absorption of the art by the Turks, whose importations and reproductions always were accredited to the purloiner, the high character of the appropriation can hardly be overemphasized. Quoting

ORIENTAL RUGS AND CARPETS

Stanley Lane-Poole: "The Mamluks made Cairo and Damascus, their two capitals, homes of civilization, art and literature. Merciless to their enemies, tyrannous to their subjects, they yet delighted in the delicate refinements which art could afford them in their home life, were lavish in the endowment of pious foundations, magnificent in their mosques and palaces, and fastidious in the smallest details of dress and furniture. Altogether they were the noblest promoters of art and literature and of public works that Egypt has known since the time of Alexander the Great."*

Thanks to Doctor Sarre, two styles of Egyptian rug decoration have now been segregated from the native and Persian patterns of Turkish weavings. The more important resembles somewhat the fifteenth and sixteenth century floor mosaic in the principal court of the Mosque Sultan Hasan in Cairo. Obviously the pattern is intended to simulate the plan of a mosaic pavement that displayed stars, octagons, squares and triangles, interspersed with palm and cypress trees. An unusual scheme of cherry red, yellow-green and pale blue adds color distinction to masterly draftsmanship. Material is both silk and wool. When the wool is of Angora variety, the rug has sheen that resembles the lustre of faience. The knots, eighty to one hundred and twenty to the square inch, are the Persian or Sehna variety. "Tabriz had supplied architects, carvers, workers in metal and on the loom to Cairo."

The second pattern consists of numerous squares, each containing a hexagon, which in turn encloses stars and cypress trees. A rug of this design is to be seen in Venice in a painting by Lorenzo Lotto, date about 1530. In Venetian inventories the attribution "tapedi damaschini" led to the assignment of rugs containing both patterns to the northern rather than to the southern Mamluk capital, which at most was only half in error. Specimens of both types have been

* Stanley Lane-Poole, *The Story of Turkey*. G. P. Putnam's Sons.

found in Italian and South German churches, to which they were transported from Cairo, probably by way of Constantinople. Thevenot, in the year 1660, found a large carpet industry in Cairo, whose product he said was exported to Constantinople and subsequently to Europe, under the name "Turkey carpets." In Europe, even Persian carpets were generally called Turkish until the seventeenth century.

The culmination of appropriation of Persian art in Turkish rugs came during the reign of Suleyman the Magnificent (1520-1566), the super-Sultan, "tall and thin, with a smoked complexion, fine black eyes, long nose, a thin mouth with long mustaches, and a forked beard," who raised a slave, the famous Roxalana, to the position of Queen-regnant. According to the historian, "the age which boasted of Charles V, the equal of Charlemagne in empire; of Francis I of France; of Henry VIII and Elizabeth; of Pope Leo X; of Vasili Ivanovich, founder of the Russian power; of Sigismund of Poland; of Shah Ismail of Persia; and of the Mogul Emperor Akbar, could yet point to no greater sovereign than Suleyman of Turkey."*

His military renown was won in countries as distant as Hungary and Persia, in Rhodes, and by his admirals in the seas about Spain. His empire included the area of Europe south of Vienna, between the Adriatic and the Black Seas, the whole of Asia Minor and the country eastward to the Persian Gulf, and, additionally, Syria and Egypt. His Persian campaign, made in part to find occupation for his janissaries, who were always prone to turbulence while inactive at the capital, resulted in a second Turkish occupation of Tabriz within twenty years, and a second draft of highly talented Persian weavers to create superior Turkey carpets. This appropriation (1534) took place during the reign of Tahmasp, the monarch of the period of pre-eminent Persian rugs, and two years before the date woven into the first of the renowned Ardabil tomb carpets.

* Stanley Lane-Poole, *The Story of Turkey*. G. P. Putnam's Sons.

Suleyman chose not only the right decade but the right moment to pluck the ripe fruit of Persian weaving. The late medallion rugs and the finest Ispahan carpets, fresh from the looms, were the world's standard of elegance in floor covering, a position they retain to this day. That the Sultan acquired examples and with his new weavers established a new line of royal carpets in Turkey is the verdict of the circumstantial evidence. The sumptuous court sorely needed a great art of rugs, and the period produced it.

The design consists of graceful Persian palmettes, feathery leaves and exquisite cloud-bands, conjoined with realistic Turkish hyacinths, roses, carnations, tulips and iris, intricately interwoven and brilliantly displayed, usually about a resplendent central Persian medallion, quarters of which are repeated in each corner of the field, and with a lace-like border complete a perfect carpet. Usually the pattern is executed in blue, green and gold upon bright crimson ground; blue ground is rare. The color scheme is both Persian and Egyptian, the latter predominant; the knot is Persian-Sehna, and generally the warp is silk after the Persian fashion of the time. The finest weavings, some of large size, are assigned to the sixteenth century; the waning examples, to the seventeenth. The entire work, formerly ascribed to Damascus and sometimes called Hispano-Moresque, is now attributed to Constantinople, where, in Stamboul, the imperial looms were undoubtedly located.

The assumption that the Constantinople looms were established by Selim the Grim, about the year 1518, and brought to perfection of workmanship under Suleyman the Magnificent, rests upon two pedestals: the record that Selim sent to Constantinople from Tabriz a thousand artisans, including weavers, to embellish his capital; and the fatuity of thinking that Suleyman the Magnificent, the most powerful and luxurious monarch of his age, twice personally in possession of Tabriz, first in 1534 and again in 1548, was nevertheless wanting in talented weavers to supply one of his most imperative needs. The first royal Turkish looms were undoubtedly instituted at Brusa, where Josafa Barbaro as much as tells us they were located in his time.

Selim II (1566-1574), son of Suleyman and Roxalana, known as

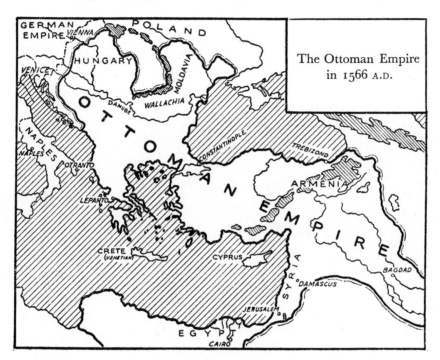

The Ottoman Empire in 1566 A.D.

the Sot and a worthless monarch, lost two hundred and twenty-four ships and thirty thousand men in the great naval battle of Lepanto, fought against Venetians, Spaniards and Knights of Malta, and still was able to consider his loss merely the "shaving of our beard." The galleys were almost replaced the next winter. "When that famous Prince of the Sea, Kilij Ali Pasha, expressed a doubt as to whether he could find the rigging and anchors he needed, the Grand Vizier said to him: 'Lord Admiral, the wealth and power of the empire are such that if it were necessary we could make anchors of silver, cables of silks, and sails of satin.' "*

* Stanley Lane-Poole, *The Story of Turkey*. G. P. Putnam's Sons.

The weavers of Selim undoubtedly continued the creation of the fine rugs of Suleyman the Magnificent, and probably added as a fillip two of the greatest rug novelties, the famous ivory rugs of "bird" and "cloud-globe" pattern. The birds are really leaves or so-called S forms, which with rosettes and other floral items create on an ivory ground a vigorous all-over pattern. Nevertheless the leaves resemble humming-birds with bills inserted in roses. The "cloud and globe" pattern consists of two stripes and three disks, which the textile art of Asia Minor during the sixteenth century constantly displays. The stripes undoubtedly are Chinese cloud forms, and the disks the badge of Tamerlane. In the journal of Ruy Gonzalez de Clavijo, who accompanied the Spanish mission to Samarkand in 1403, is this remark: "The arms of Timur Beg are three circles like O's, drawn in this manner $^{OO}_{O}$, and this is to signify that he is lord of the three parts of the world. He ordered this device to be stamped on the coins and on everything he had."

The ivory grounds of these rugs may have been suggested by similar backgrounds occasionally employed by the Persian weavers of vase carpets. A more likely source is other textile art. Secondary colors principally are red, blue and yellow. Assignment of the weaving to the years between 1550 and 1650 is undoubtedly correct. The cloud-bands employed for border decoration were not used in Turkey, according to present belief, until the middle of the sixteenth century.

Murad III (1574-1595) displaced the drinking vice of his father with the greater sin of political corruption. He allowed sycophants to sell the offices of state to the highest bidder, and for a time kept under his bed the money thus acquired. "The hoard being on an imperial scale, he soon had to sink a well there; and every night he poured in the day's takings until the well held nearly three millions, all in gold coin." His personal affairs were managed by his numerous women, by whom he had a hundred children. He corresponded with Queen

Elizabeth and addressed her as the "most wise governor, cloud of most pleasant rain, and sweetest fountain of nobleness and virtue."

Notwithstanding his uxoriousness, Murad waged a successful war against poor Persia—now a confirmed habit with Turkish Sultans—and by treaty of peace secured Tabriz, for the fourth time a Turkish captive, the Caspian provinces of Persia and the state of Georgia. The result in Turkish rugs was still further diversification of pattern, exhibited in miscellaneous flower, leaf and vase rugs that are the children of the rugs of Tabriz and Herat. Always, however, the style is Turkish, plant form transformed into straight line; curves of sensuous grace made direct and strong. To add still further diversity, in the year 1585, Murad ordered his Bey in Egypt to send eleven carpet masters, with a large quantity of material, to the Imperial Court in Stamboul.

Ahmed I (1603-1617) promptly lost the Persian territory secured by Murad, the Austrian tribute long paid to the Sultans, and the abject obeisance of European sovereigns to the throne of Turkey from the days of the Conqueror. The state was seriously ill and with a Christian kick might easily have expired. Undoubtedly to fortify his national reputation, Ahmed built a beautiful marble mosque and a hundred fountains in Constantinople. Concurrently in the city of Bergama, anciently known as Pergamum, were woven the rugs that appear in the paintings of Thomas de Keyser, now in the London National Gallery, and of Cornelis de Vos in the Brussels Museum. Again Turkish obligation to Persian weaving is obvious. Vases, hanging lamps, treatment of spandrels, use of elongated panels separated by eight-pointed stars in borders, and finally the subdued color schemes of the earlier pieces, are all Persian properties.

Lest the impression be conveyed that the Turk was a mere plagiarist, summary of his splendid contribution to the art of rugs must be attempted. Concerning borrowing, authority says: "We are all whole-

157

sale borrowers in every matter that relates to invention, use, beauty and form." The Persian borrowed from the Chinese; the Turk from the Persian, from the Egyptian, from the Greek, from the Arab and from the Armenian; the Venetian from the Turk, and Europe from the Venetian. Yet, strange as it may seem, each nation in turn was a creator of art new and individual.

The Turk, except in the lifelike flower rugs begun under Suleyman the Magnificent, translated the ornate, complex language of the Persian rug into simple language comprehensible to the average mind. He then turned compositor, typed the composition in Turkish idiom, and locked the frame, so that no letter would move. In a word he simplified and solidified. The dancing grace of the Persian rug he converted into grace statuesque.

Thus to revise Persian art, however, was not enough. The Turk, like all conquerors, must undertake the complete subjugation of art, which is only another sphere. In consequence he acquired and welded together a greater variety of material than an ancient civilization, like Persia or China, would bother with, and created a woven anthology of the rugs of the Orient. In color, his mad love of luxury resulted in effects that no nation, oriental or occidental, ever surpassed. His mastery of red, in all manner of combinations, might be made the thesis for a doctor of philosophy degree; and further degrees could peradventure be acquired by intensive studies of yellow, purple, blue and green. "It hath been an opinion," said Bacon, "that the Spaniards seem wiser than they are." The Turk, in the art of rugs, is wiser than he seems.

Prayer rugs, through consecration to the highest of all services, enjoy in theory an advantage over every other form of weaving. Their motives are ecclesiastical, spiritual and eternal. Secular rugs, even when decorated with the escutcheons of Euclid or the lilies of Linnæus, are but menials in the sanctuary. In the realm of art these relative positions are maintained between prayer rugs and other rugs of ordinary mortals, but not between prayer rugs and palace rugs, which express the divinity of kings. Always, as between these two expressions of deity, the palace rug has the advantage of varied expression and impressive size; the prayer rug the disadvantage of standardized form and small dimension. However, among rugs of small size, prayer rugs undoubtedly display the finest art of their respective periods.

Comparatively, the weavers of Turkey specialized in prayer rugs and produced hundreds of examples as against scores elsewhere created. Contrary to the Persian custom, they felt no compunction about their sale to the unbeliever. They made an artistic beginning in the old Ushaks, reached the summit of their achievement among the weavings of Suleyman the Magnificent, lost beauty but recovered the old strength in the Bergamas, aspired to ethereal realms in the Ghiordes, terminated their power to charm in the Ladiks and Kulas, and created devotional utilities in the Kir Shehrs, Melas and Mujurs. Fortunate is he who owns a good example of almost any one of them, for only rich and well-to-do Turks are so fortunate. The commonalty have no such prayer luxuries, but only decorated cotton cloth and humble mother earth.

Morning, noon, afternoon, evening and night the Mohammedan is enjoined to pray. Tall, gaunt Bilal, negro servant of Mohammed, was first to break the slumber of the faithful with the appointed call:

> "Allah Akbar! God is Great! God is Great!
> There is no God but God, and Mohammed is His Prophet.
> Come to prayer! Come to prayer! Come to salvation."

To which, in the morning, he added the words: "Prayer is better than sleep. Prayer is better than sleep."

Even all-refreshing sleep is to be foregone for prayer: "O thou wrapped up, arise to prayer, and continue therein during the night, except a small part; that is to say, during one-half thereof; or do thou lessen the same a little or add thereto; and repeat the Koran with a distinct and sonorous voice. Verily the rising by night is more efficacious for steadfast continuance in devotion, and more conducive to decent pronunciation; for in the daytime thou hast long employment."

Prayers consist of portions of the Koran, recited from memory, such as the first chapter: "Praise be to God, the Lord of all creatures, the most merciful, the King of the day of judgment. Thee do we worship, and of Thee do we beg assistance. Direct us in the right way, in the way of those to whom Thou hast been gracious; not of those against whom Thou art incensed, nor of those who go astray."

One of the most eloquent of prayers is inscribed on the border of a masterly prayer rug in the Ballard Collection at the Metropolitan Museum of Art: "God! There is no God but He, the Living, the Eternal. Slumber takes Him not, nor sleep. His is what is in the heavens and what is in the earth. Who is he that intercedes with Him save with his permission? He knoweth what is before them and what is behind them, and they comprehend nothing of His knowledge but what He pleases. His throne extends over the heavens and the earth, and it tries Him not to guard them both, for He is high and grand."

Cleanliness and sobriety are requisite to prayer: "Oh true believers, when ye prepare yourselves to pray, wash your faces and your hands unto the elbows; and rub your heads, and your feet unto the ankles. If ye be sick or on a journey, and ye find no water, take fine, clean sand and rub your faces and your hands therewith. God would not put a difficulty upon you; but He desireth to purify you, and to complete His favor upon you, that ye may give thanks." "Come not to prayers when ye are drunk, until ye understand what ye say."

Prayer rugs are characterized by a central panel having a pointed arch (rarely flat) at one end. Occasionally, two or many arches are woven side by side, and sometimes one at each end. Essentially these arched panels are copies and adaptations of the designs of the Mihrabs of the mosques, which are elaborate tile adornments, corresponding to the altars of Christian churches, built into the walls on the side toward Mecca.

"We have seen thee turn about thy face towards heaven with uncertainty, but we will cause thee to turn thyself towards a Kiblah [object of devotion] that will please thee. Turn, therefore, thy face towards the holy temple of Mecca; and wherever ye be, turn your face towards that place." As the worshipper in the mosque prays toward Mecca, when he stands or kneels before the Mihrab, so also when he kneels on a prayer rug at home or on a journey. Only during the first year of the Hegira (622-623), the faithful, by Mohammed's direction, prayed toward Jerusalem.

The source of the Mihrab is important and interesting. Under the arch is a recess into which an idol might fit. Scores of idols filled just such recesses in the sacred building at Mecca before the victory of Mohammed over the defenders of idolatry, in the year 629 A.D. Then the idols were cast out, and the idols worshipped by Buddhists were destroyed in the elaborate temples that came within the purview of the conquering armies of the Prophet. Always, however, the recesses and moldings remained, and on them the Mohammedan, formerly a worshipper of idols, focussed his prayerful attention. Remotely, therefore, prayer-rug designs are the issue of the casements from which the old idols threatened and grinned.

Unless the circumstances of the period are understood, this explanation of the source of the mihrab seems fantastic. The facts show it to be well founded. "Before the advent of the Prophet, Mahāyāna Buddhism, besides converting the Far East, had spread all over Western Asia; and the description given by Arab writers of the Kaaba, the most venerated shrine in Arabia, which was the first model of a

Muhammadan mosque, strongly suggests a Buddhist temple or monastery filled with Mahāyānist images. It had been for all Arabs a place of pilgrimage from a very remote period—Muhammadan tradition says from the time of Abraham. It contained hundreds of images, among them those of Jesus Christ and the Holy Virgin.

"That which happened in later times in every province of India where Muhammadan rule was established must have occurred earlier in Arabia and in Persia, when the war-lords of Islam had few building craftsmen except those they took prisoner or imported from other countries. The Buddhist images were torn from their niches and broken up or melted; the former temple or monastery, if not utterly destroyed, was used as a place of Muhammadan worship, and the empty niches [mihrabs] with their arches—lancetted, trefoiled, or sometimes of the earlier Hīnayāna trefoiled form—remained in the walls. The principal one in the western wall of the converted mosque pointed the direction to which the faithful must turn when saying their prayers, and was called the 'Kiblah'; so the arched niche was retained in every newly-built mosque and became a symbol of the faith.

"In private houses the numerous small niches which formerly had served as shrines for the saints, or household gods, of Mahāyāna Buddhism were also retained; they were useful as cupboards or receptacles for the hookah, rose-water vessel, lamp, or other article of domestic use. The niche with its changed contents became as common a *motif* in the Muhammadan art of Arabia, Persia and India, as it had been when it was the shrine of a Buddhist saint. It followed almost inevitably that the pointed arch was also used structurally for window and door openings."*

The mihrab form, therefore, is secular and promiscuous as well as spiritual and polytheistic; it pervades domes, doorways, façades,

* E. B. Havell, *A Handbook of Indian Art*. E. P. Dutton & Co.

corridors and fountains; and the weavers of prayer rugs created simulations of pretentious doorways, abutted by elaborate columns, pyramided entrances, entire façades of mosques including the planting of the approach, and even a series of landscapes containing the tombs and trees of cemeteries, forcible reminders of the impermanence of temporal existence. Variation in the design is almost literally infinite.

The minutiæ of prayer-rug decoration also runs a wide course of representation. The entire contents of mosques, notably lamps, candlesticks, pulpits and inscriptions are employed to stimulate spiritual emotion. From the apex of the rug niche, lamp, ewer and flower-basket commonly swing into the glowing red or cold blue of central panels. Sometimes a tree of life, copied from mosque tile, is represented, expressing, possibly, the weaver's confidence in or hope of immortality.

The prayer rugs of the sixteenth century formerly attributed to Damascus and now to Constantinople, and hereafter to be associated possibly with the Court of Suleyman the Magnificent, are not only the supreme masterpieces of Turkish religious weaving, but also works of great art. The Ballard Collection in the Metropolitan Museum of Art contains an example infinitely delicate, and the collection of Mrs. William H. Moore a specimen rich and deep. To endeavor to describe them were to create a sure default, because they are things purely poetic, comparable only to the verse which the Turks, avoiding the subjects of war and similar occupations, created out of Persian materials. Flowers, leaves and vines are the counterparts of love, spring and nightingales, which twenty-one out of thirty-four Turkish sultans apostrophized in metric form, after the Persian fashion and often in the Persian language. While the love of art inspires, see at least one of these masterpieces, and in the plumelike border discover the source of the finest Ghiordes borders.

The most archaic character of ornamentation and dryest ancient color is found in the prayer rugs of Ushak, worshipful forms of the famous carpets. These rugs, commonly of the late sixteenth and early seventeenth centuries, are the work perhaps of the descendants of the weavers of Turkomania, and certainly perpetuators of their traditions, whose rugs, Marco Polo said, were "the best and handsomest carpets in the world."

The prayer rugs of Bergama, which anciently was the city of Pergamum, where the apostle Paul established one of the seven churches of Asia, where works of fine art were executed by the Greeks, and where famous professors presided in the colleges and students crowded the libraries, always are numbered among the elect. Ordinarily, to secure symmetry the prayer niche is repeated at the base of the central panel; mosque lamps are suspended from both apexes; and eight-pointed stars alternate with elongated panels in borders. These rugs once were called "Transylvania" (and "Siebenbürgen," meaning "seven mountains"), because many of them were found in Transylvania, Hungary, which was part of the Turkish dominion in the sixteenth century. The period of weaving of museum examples extends from the early seventeenth to the late eighteenth century.

Ghiordes and Kula prayer rugs were made in adjacent cities, and on that account are somewhat arbitrarily differentiated. Custom assigns the finer textures to Ghiordes. As a matter of fact, rich men of both cities indulged in fine texture. Custom asserts that Ghiordes rugs have centres of solid color and three-stripe borders; and Kula rugs ornamented centres and multiple border-stripes. Again, to Ghiordes are assigned rugs containing two cross-panels, one at either end of the field, and to Kula the rugs having one cross-panel.

Always the beauty of the earliest Ghiordes prayer rugs, assigned to the seventeenth century, reflect an apparition of the contemporary Sultan, Ahmet I. "The Padishah was in rich cloth of gold embroidered with pearls and diamonds; his turban covered with fine plumes of black heron's feathers, enriched with great diamonds; and a chain of the same stones hung about the lower part of his turban. On his little finger he had a diamond of large bigness and inestimable price that gave a marvellous great light. He was proudly mounted on a goodly horse richly caparisoned, the saddle embroidered with pearls and diamonds, the stirrup of pure gold and diamonds, and on the horse's mane great tassels of them. Before him on his saddle-bow was a Leopard covered with cloth of gold."* Most museum examples of Ghiordes prayer rugs were woven in the eighteenth century.

Among later weavings Ladik prayer rugs display a versatile art that ranges in architectural pattern from impressive columns to dwarf apexes. The flower of the weaving is the lily that thrives prodigiously, even upside down in some fields, and in border pattern, called Rhodian, where it alternates with the rose. Melas prayer rugs are distinguished by central panels that terminate in diamond-shaped cupolas; and Kir-Shehr, Mujur, Konia and Anatolian prayer rugs by central panels covered by "flight-of-stair roofs."

In the first tale told in the *Arabian Nights' Entertainments*, a merchant ate a date and threw away the stone, which fell upon the Jinn's son and killed him. In the foregoing text the dates of the subject have been eaten; a few stones now remain to be thrown away, if possible without injury to any one. Among Turkish rugs, as among all varieties, are numerous weavings having only minor personality and interest. Merchants secured their names mostly from invoices, rolled them indiscriminately in conversation, as if they were names of importance, and thus created a formidable oriental-rug nomenclature.

In books of by-gone years enough of these stones were piled in the path of the reader to make the journey "from Dan to Beersheba" an easy parasang by comparison. These impediments to traffic include the rugs of Ak Hissar, Demirdji, Kutais, Karaman, Nigde, Tuzla,

* Stanley Lane-Poole, *The Story of Turkey*. G. P. Putnam's Sons.

165

Yuruk, and a vast brood of highway trespassers that answer to the "cluck" of Anatolia. Knowledge of these rugs will not repay the effort to acquire it. Nor will the courses of instruction in the subject, which schools of art are just beginning to offer, deal with them. As instruction in literature is given in Chaucer, Spenser, Shakespeare, Milton and Keats, so cultural training in this art will be concerned with the rugs of Mohammed II, Selim the Grim, Suleyman the Magnificent, Selim the Sot, and Ahmet I.

Modern Turkish rugs are common laborers bearing vast burdens, because they sold their fine inheritance of art for a mess of instant pottage. This metamorphosis is not just another adventure in Turkish rug history, but a calamity wholly new. For when, in the sixteenth century, Turkish taste abdicated to Persian and Egyptian taste, the art of Turkish rugs rose to summits never before attained. When, however, Turkish taste, in the period just before the World War, abdicated to modern Occidental taste in a vast crescendo of commercial effort, the art of Turkish rugs sank into a dark valley from which now it is extricating itself. The explanation of the debacle is a story of bad patronage.

In America, magazines dedicated to houses beautiful, schools of interior decoration and textile manufacturers, had persuaded the American people to use rich, dark rugs, the very antithesis of the long-developed Turkish product. The advice was well-intentioned but the result radical and disastrous. Art was dethroned by harmony, even by mediocre harmony that swaggered like a Barbary pirate. The new vogue instantly threatened the rug dealer; the dealer hurriedly communicated with the wholesale distributor; the wholesaler cabled his eastern agent; the agent instructed the proprietors of factories; buyers, going through the country districts in the spring of the year to gather the rug crop of the winter, shouted the warning at the

The Four Attitudes of Prayer

Mosque Sultan Ahmed, Stamboul

Mihrab, Displaying Niche, Inscription,
Candlesticks and Lamp

Turkish Prayer Rug, Late Sixteenth or
Early Seventeenth Century

Ballard Collection, Metropolitan Museum of
Art

PLATE XLII

Turkish Prayer Rug with Chalice Ornament and
Hebrew inscription, Sixteenth Century

Textile Museum, Washington, D.C.

Ghiordes Prayer Rug, Seventeenth Century

Ballard Collection, Metropolitan Museum of Art

Ushak Prayer Rug, Late Sixteenth Century. Balanced Mihrab variety

Ballard Collection, Metropolitan Museum of Art

Prayer Rug with Balanced Mihrabs and Five
Inscriptions, Late Sixteenth Century

Ballard Collection, Metropolitan Museum of Art

PLATE XLIII

PLATE XLIV.   Fragment Egyptian Rug, Early Sixteenth Century.   Mosque
Pavement Design

James Franklin Ballard Collection, Metropolitan Museum of Art

PLATE XLV. Turkish Carpet, Sixteenth Century. Court
manufactory, probably in Constantinople

Mitchell Samuels Collection

PLATE XLVI. Turkish Prayer Rug, Sixteenth Century. Court
manufactory, probably in Constantinople

James Franklin Ballard Collection, Metropolitan Museum of Art

PLATE XLVII.   Dragon Rug, Caucasus, Early Seventeenth Century.
(Eight dragons, four camels, four elephant heads, and eight birds)
Joseph V. McMullan Collection, Metropolitan Museum of Art

Ladik Prayer Rug, Eighteenth Century.
Design of inverted lily stalks and Rhodian lily border

Typical Mosque Prayer Carpet

Kula Prayer Rug, Eighteenth Century, with "Tomb
and Tree" motive that occasioned the name "Ceme-
tery" carpet

Kir-Shehr Prayer Rug, Eighteenth-Nineteenth Centuries

PLATE XLVIII

Example of design that emphasizes leaf forms, both straight and hooked. Border a descendant of Herat borders

Example of palmette motive expressed in geometric form; and of the leaves of the dragon rug converted into octagonal bands. Border motive became the property of Daghestan and Shirvan rugs

Example of the art of Herat rugs—numerous palmette forms, lancet leaves, small flowers and stems—rendered in the Caucasian manner

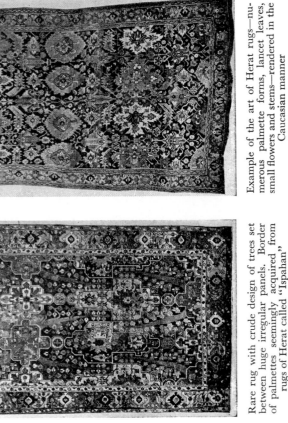

Rare rug with crude design of trees set between huge irregular panels. Border of palmettes seemingly acquired from rugs of Herat called "Ispahan"

Four types of rug art now generally attributed to Kuba. Temporarily the district serves as a cabinet to hold all old Caucasian rugs of vigorous, archaic design. The period of weaving is the seventeenth century (two centre cuts), the sixteenth century (left), and the eighteenth century (right).

PLATE XLIX

Kabistan or Hila. Geometric adaptation of Persion pattern—
rosettes, palmettes, palm-leaves, eight-pointed stars, plus the
famous "eight goose-necks"

Baku. Persian palm-leaves, centre
medallion and corner devices

Shirvan Rug with Caucasian human, animal
and bird forms

PLATE L

Chichi (Tzitzi). A pattern perfected and standardized by continuous, exclusive employment

Semi-antique Prayer, Geometric and Floral Designs

Silé Rug, Showing the last Caucasian Dragons

Verné Animal and Bird Khilim

Soumak Rug from Shemakha or Derbend

PLATE LI

Five Karabagh Rugs

Centre, typical lattice pattern. Right and left, leaf scrolls and flowers adapted from Aubusson carpets

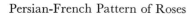

Persian-French Pattern of Roses

Mirror Pattern Containing Rose Bouquets

PLATE LII

Six Turkoman Rugs
Top row: Afghan, Yomut, Akhal Tekke (Katchli)
Prayer Rug. Bottom row: Tekke, Saryk or
Punjdeh Prayer Rug, Beluchistan

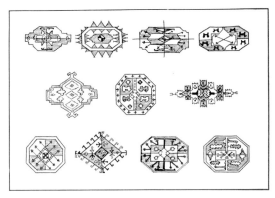

Eleven Turkoman Guls or Tribal Devices
Top row: Tekke, Salor, Tekke, Saryk. Middle
row: Chaudor Yomut, Ersari, Yomut. Bottom
row: Afghan, Yomut, Afghan, Ersari

Salor Jowal or Camel-Bag

PLATE LIII

True Bokhara Carpet. Commonly but erroneously called Beshir. Persian Herati design employed in central field and outer border. Color, terra-cotta red interspersed with Chinese yellow. Web ends, wide selvage and compact Persian knotted weave as in other Turkoman rugs

PLATE LIV

Bokhara Prayer Rug with "Head and Shoulders" Mihrab

Beluchistan Prayer Rug, Picturing Mosque, Inner Court and Numerous Minarets

Beluchistan Prayer Rug with Rectangular Niche and Tree of Life

Bokhara Garden Rug. Compare garden designs in Tekke and Saryk prayer rugs
(Plate LIII)

Yomut Jowal or Camel-Bag, Displaying Caravan; and Yomut Kharjin or "Ass Saddle." Each a half

PLATE LV

Laotsze as God of Longevity

Rug Displaying the Eight Emblems of Taoism

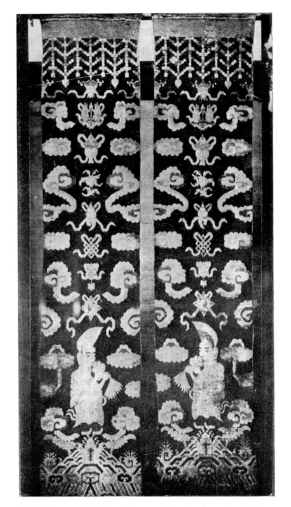

The Buddha, Mathura Museum

Pair Temple Pillar Rugs, Displaying the Eight
Symbols of Buddhism

PLATE LVI

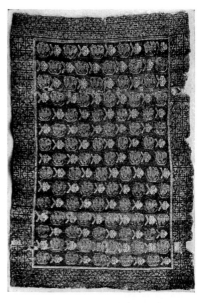

Rug with Alternated Design of Magistrate's Seal and Dragon. Swastika border. Late Ming, 1600

Metropolitan Museum of Art

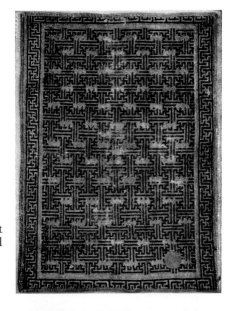

Rug of Swastika and Bat Design. K'ang H'si Period (1661-1723)

Metropolitan Museum of Art

Rug of Fu-Dog Design. Border depicts the animal gods of the Zodiac

Zodiac Rug. The twelve animal deities surround the Tae-Keih

Rug of Aquarium Design

Saddle Rugs. Dragon and cloud design (left) military motive of tiger stripes; traveler's horse beneath tree

PLATE LVII

PLATE LVIII.   Chinese Temple Hanging, Eighteenth Century
Frederick Moore Collection

Temple Hanging. Design of dragon,
clouds, symbols of Buddhism, sacred
mountain and waves of eternity

Chair Back. Design of dragons, phœnix, bats, clouds,
sacred mountain and waves, with peony border

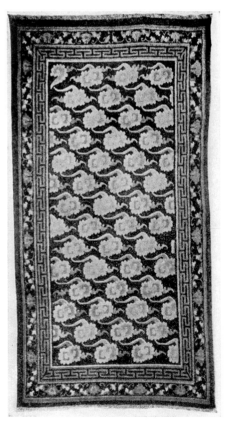

Cumulous Cloud Rug with "T" and
Peony Border Stripes

Eight Horses of the Emperor Mu-W'ang,
a Favorite Subject of Chinese Painters.
"Pearl," "Key," and "T" border stripes

PLATE LIX

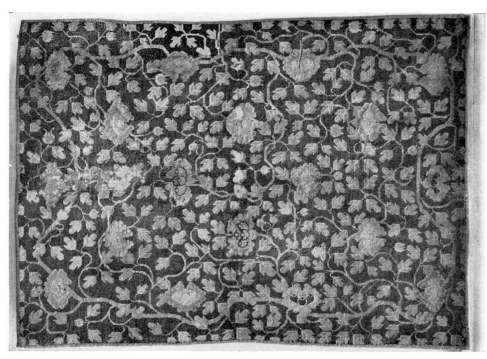

Fragment of Ceremonial Carpet of the K'ang H'si Period (1661-1723), to which is attributed the most artistic and finest woven of extant rugs. Design of peonies, leaves and vines in "all-over" arrangement

Metropolitan Museum of Art

Ceremonial Carpet of the K'ang H'si Period.   Pattern of numerous medallions composed of Ju-i sceptres and lotus flowers

PLATE LX

Three Travel Rugs of "Cart" and "Suit-Case" Varieties. 1. Medallion containing
Kylin, phœnix and sacred pearl surrounded by numerous art objects. 2. Saddled
horse tied to a mountain tree. 3. Crane and stag, both Taoist symbols of long life

Rug Displaying Bats, Symbols of Happiness, Flying about an Octagon which
Contains Design Representing the Philosophic Teaching of Fu H'si. The
centre circle or Tae-Keih (Great All) contains Yin (female) and Yang (male)

PLATE LXI

The Scholar's Rug. The four designs of the scholar, set about the medallion, are:
Chess-board (upper right), box of books (lower right), two rolls of paintings (upper left), and harp (lower left)   Pearl, "T" and peony-shou border stripes

PLATE LXII

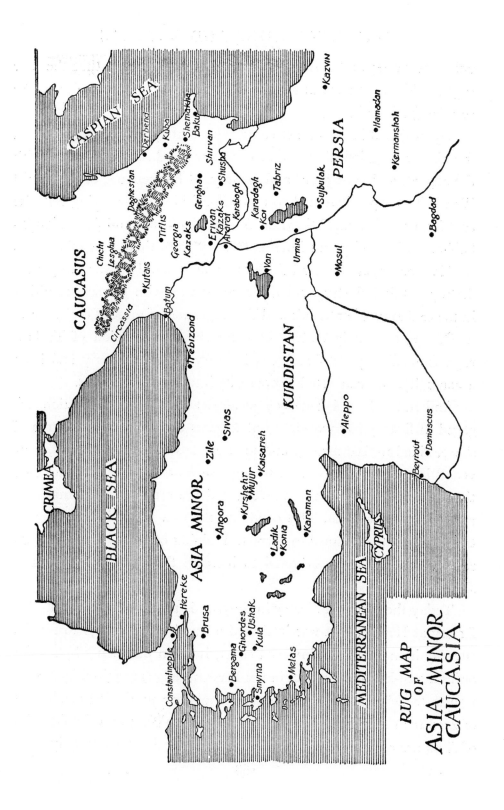

CASPIAN SEA

CAUCASUS

Chichi
Lesgha
Circassia

Derbend
Kuba
Shemakha
Baku
Shirvan
Shusha

Doghestan

Tiflis
Georgia
Kazaks
Erivan
Ararat
Kazaks
Karabagh
Karadagh
Koi
Tabriz
Gengha

Kutais

Batum

Kazvin

Hamadan

Kermanshah

PERSIA
Sujbulak

Bagdad

Van
Urmia
Mosul

Trebizond

KURDISTAN

Aleppo

CRIMEA

BLACK SEA

Hereke

ASIA MINOR

Zile
Sivas
Angora
Kirshehr
Mujur
Kaisarieh
Ladik
Konia
Karaman

Brusa
Bergama
Ghiordes
Ushak
Kula

Smyrna

Melas

Damascus
Beyrout

CYPRUS

MEDITERRANEAN SEA

Constantinople

RUG MAP
OF
ASIA MINOR
CAUCASIA

village weavers; and finally the nomad weavers heard that the new rugs would sell better if afflicted with melancholia. The result was the rug that Jack built.

Upon this ruin of the art came immediately, as if in retribution, the almost complete destruction of the rug industry of Turkey with the advent, and contiguous and subsequent happenings, of the World War. Prior to 1914 Turkey had many flourishing rug-weaving factories centring upon "Infidel" Smyrna. Among the Greek and Armenian inhabitants of the city and interior country were thousands of weavers working for wages paid by British manufacturers. The war completely destroyed this industry, and the ensuing war with Greece, resulting in the exchange of nationals and the migration of most of the weavers to Greece, seemingly ended the commercial production of Turkish rugs. Immediately the Greek rug industry, which formerly had been a nonentity, was converted temporarily into a great business.

And not only did Turkey lose almost her entire population engaged in factory rug weaving, but the loss extended to vast herds of sheep, killed to feed armies, and to enormous quantities of wool, converted into army blankets. Seemingly, all that was left of the art was the slight output of village weavers, and the crude shaggy Anatolian rugs of nomad women. This condition the new Turkish Government took immediate measures to correct. Training of new weavers was instituted, and measures adopted to increase the supply of wool and silk.

Today the factory industry in Smyrna is partly rehabilitated. The factory at Hereke, that was instituted a hundred years ago to fill the rug requirements of the imperial court, is again producing by special order a well-knotted product in the Persian designs required by American taste. The factories in Constantinople are producing small rugs of good texture in imitation of Persian masterpieces; and the factories of Sivas are creating the medallion type of floral rug commonly associated with Kerman and Saruk. In Kaisarieh are woven cheap silk rugs of Ghiordes pattern, on which several thousand weavers are said to labor.

Across the vast land thousands of poor but independent weavers again arduously pursue the ancient winter vocation. Surrounded by snow, they labor upon looms set up in halls and bedrooms of little village houses, and upon looms that sing of luxury within the goat-hair tents of nomad encampments. Only in summer is the labor moderated by other tasks. The problem is not want of weavers or diminution of talent for hard labor, but only indecision as to the character of art to create.

The pendulum of American taste already is swinging away from a too-long-maintained admiration for standardized, meaningless rug art, and moving with the usual rapidity toward a reappreciation of individual beauty. When the movement crystallizes, the weavers of Turkey will meet the demand by the application of an inherited taste equal to the requirement.

CHAPTER VII

RUGS OF THE CAUCASUS

So varied is the topography of the earth that each area indulges a specialization. The specialty of the Caucasus is not ambitious human beings but mountains so obsessed with aspiration to dominate the earth as wholly to relieve man of that necessity. In consequence, man in the Caucasus, including the celebrated individual whose skull established the genus known as the Caucasian race, created not a single great state, and only one small principality of more than temporary importance. Queen Tamara of Georgia and Schamyl, the chieftain, who to the delight of western Europe long impeded Russian sovereignty, are almost the sole Caucasian representatives of the order of superman that all the lesser earth seems able to create in greatest abundance. Instead of producing men and states, Caucasia provided them a refuge. Long before the hordes of Jenghis Khan drove human herds into the mountains, generation after generation of oppressed peoples sought there safe retreat, and in cloistered valleys established an all but impregnable independence. In consequence, the Caucasian people exhibit a diversity of race and a solidity of texture that resemble the strata of which the mountains themselves are composed, one layer of substance deposited against another, each retaining its original character.

RUGS OF THE CAUCASUS

Huge mountains are the epic poems of nature, and poets their natural interpreters. From any one of twelve summits higher than Mount Blanc, Prometheus could have kept his "uncoveted watch o'er the world and the deep." Everywhere about him were "eagle-baffling peaks, black, wintry, dead, unmeasured, without herb, insect or beast or shape or sound of life," "crawling glaciers with the spears of their moon-freezing crystals," and "genii of the storm in loud abysses howling, urging the rage of whirlwind."

The mountains bear a diagonal course across this high bridge between Europe and Asia. On the southwest side, toward Armenia, they incline in terraced plateaus toward hospitality, and on the northeast, sloping toward the Caspian, create for shepherds another pasture for their herds. The vast plains of Daghestan, famous for rugs, are the subject of a fine stanza by the Russian poet Pushkin:

> "Beneath me the clouds in their silentness go,
> The cataracts through them in thunder down-dashing,
> Below them bare peaks in the sunny ray flashing;
> Green moss and dry shrubs I can mark yet below;
> Dark thickets still lower; then valleys green-blooming
> Where the throstle is singing and gentle sheep roaming."

Herodotus writes of the state of affairs there existing in the fifth century before Christ: "On the western shore of the Caspian Sea stretches the Caucasus, which is in extent the largest, and in height the loftiest of all mountains. It contains many and various nations of men, who for the most part live upon the produce of wild fruit-trees. In this country, it is said, there are trees that produce leaves of such a nature that by rubbing them and mixing them with water the people paint figures on their garments. These figures they say do not wash out but grow old with the wool, as if they had been woven in from the first."

Parenthetically, this statement would seem to disprove the con-

171

tention that rug weaving in the Caucasus is a comparatively recent affair. Shepherd people who could weave garments and dye them with fast colors most assuredly produced a comparable art in rugs.

The Caucasus was a wild, worthless dependency of Persia during the centuries before Alexander the Great in 323 B.C. made it the northern wall of his Asiatic estate. In the first century B.C. Armenia annexed the southern area for the ultimate benefit of Rome, the Eastern Empire and Persia, again under the rule of strident kings. Subsequently, Khazar, Huns, Avars and Mongols settled or despoiled it, when Persia and Turkey temporarily forgot their national ambitions there.

Eventually Peter the Great, 1689-1725, decided that the mountains would make an acceptable footstool to the throne of Russia. This decision culminated, during the year 1813, in the cession by Persia to Russia of all her important provinces in the Eastern Caucasus, and in 1828 of the northern edge of the Armenian plateau. Turkey made a similar forced donation of her area in 1829. With clear title, but without possession, Russia then undertook the subjugation of the mountaineers, a task requiring heroic effort for thirty years, due to the obstinacy of the opposition led by the famous Schamyl. Rather than submit, the entire tribe of Circassians, located on the Black Sea frontier, migrated en masse into Anatolia, 1864-1866, and subsequently beggared the streets of Constantinople.

That Russian possession is now complete is proved, among purveyors of rugs, by the embargo which the Soviet has placed, during the past ten years, upon the exportation of Caucasian weavings, and by monopolistic sale of them, bearing labels "Made in Russia," at the recent Russian Art Exhibition held in New York City.

To-day, as in the time of Herodotus, the region is the home of more than seventy distinct primitive races, formerly accounted double that number, each holding its inherited area, perpetuating its customs and languages. The tribe of Dido, consisting of only thirty families, enjoys the luxury of a language wholly unintelligible to its neighbors. The tribe of Chewsurs presents the appearance of a relic of the Middle Ages. "Their coats of mail, helmets, consisting of a concave plate of iron with steel rings, protecting the face and neck; small round shields tipped with iron, their armlets and greaves, recall to mind the heroes of the Crusades." The tribes of Daghestan are accounted "the highest in intelligence, famous for bravery and fidelity; lank figures with sharp-cut features and bold aquiline noses; somewhat savage in disposition, but industrious and efficient in agriculture and home industries, especially weavings, in which they have attained a high degree of perfection. Their villages consist of substantial stone houses."

The business of the people of the cities and towns is petty trade, and of the tribes cattle-breeding, mostly of sheep and goats that constitute their principal wealth. The following picture of Caucasian sheep, extracted from the writing of Rhys Williams, is too fine to be lost in periodical publication.*

"On a clear May morning we started out on the highway that runs east from Tiflis. Behind us lay the strong girdle of the globe—so the Caucasus was known to the ancients—sending its white peaks high up to mingle with the white clouds of the summer sky. Before us in the distance were peculiar clouds of another color. Here and there along the high road they rose in columns, now standing still, now moving slightly toward us—big, billowing clouds of dust.

"It was the spring migration of sheep to the mountains. In hundreds of thousands they came—one, two or three thousand in a flock —headed by a big important buck and assistant he-goats and flanked by weary-eyed dogs and shepherds. Out of the hot, blazing valley they follow this road that leads to the hill trails and up to the cool

*Asia, November, 1926.

173

springs, into rich pasturage, but into no shepherds' paradise. For up there are avalanches, hailstorms and wolves, and worst of all sheep-raiders. It would have been interesting to follow these slow-moving avalanches of wool going up the mountains.

"At dinner I extolled the Georgian cooks for their skill in bringing out the essential flavors of the lamb. 'And you may praise the good grass of the mountain meadows for putting the flavors into it,' said one feaster. 'And the good air,' said another. 'And the good view,' added Arakel quite seriously. This was the first time I had heard that animals were affected by scenery, and I said so. 'Not only lambs,' asseverated Arakel solemnly, 'but all animals. My goats, for example. I just cut through an opening that gives them a wide outlook. At once they show their appreciation.' "*

The bright simplicity of this remark is worth pondering. Art is limited to intellectual attainment; and the mentality of the Caucasian was not ponderous. On his Promethean summits he made no contribution to religion, philosophy, literature or science, and no recognized contribution even to the simple art of living. His ancestors, like the forebears of Turks and Turkomans, were barbarians who mellowed into plain folk, simple, direct, sturdy and generally restrained, compared to the Persian who was destined to brilliance, elegance and refinement.

Comparatively, Persian rugs, elaborate and sumptuous, fluid and sensuous, are the textiles of courts. Turkish rugs are impassive countryman's products that sometimes attain to courtly quality through Persian contact, more often antagonistic than friendly. Caucasian rugs are weavings wholly of tribes that, settling in mountain huts, gravely acknowledged their limitations, and then mingling in towns and cities became ambitious, employed simple Turkish rugs as models, and gathering courage copied rugs of Persian character. Turkoman rugs are

* *Asia*, November, 1926.

the simple products of roaming tribes, still near to the original state of nature.

True as the foregoing generalization is, it lacks emphasis, in the present connection, upon a fact of utmost importance,—namely the propinquity of Persia and the continuous pressure of Persian rug influence upon the Caucasian art, regardless of the national ownership of Caucasian real estate. Shah Abbas built a causeway, called the "Stone Carpet," which traversed the Caucasus from east to west. This causeway, with its network of roads and passes, tied the populous fringe of the country to the Persian system of life. In consequence, the important groups of Persian masterpieces of rug art were known there, as Caucasian copies of Ispahan, vase and medallion rugs abundantly demonstrate. Re-expressions of these rugs display Persian refinement displaced by Caucasian vigor. The quality of archaic virility is the contribution of the weavers of the earliest extant Caucasian rugs to the art.

Sources of exceptional virility are always interesting to trace and discover. This particular source, after much investigation, is now recognized in a group of rugs, woven under Persian sovereignty, but nevertheless paying allegiance to Mongolian art. Its members are known as Armenian dragon rugs, Caucasian animal rugs and Kubas. Befitting a region of mountains, these weavings are textile boulders deposited, in all probability, by some glacial flow of tribes, their large fragments of pattern eventually becoming the motives of Tcherkess, Kazak, Soumak, Karabagh and Karadagh rugs, and their particles the miscellaneous motives of general Caucasian design. No extant rugs of Persia or Turkey present an art so archaic, monolithic and monumental in appearance.

The group derives its fame, which has been both magnified and minimized by mistaken analysis, from the oldest, finest and most interesting examples, which display the forms of numerous dragons, up-

175

right in position, seemingly endeavoring to climb through layers of forms that once must have represented clouds or lightning, as in Chinese silks and paintings, but which here through high conventionalization have the appearance of long, saw-edged leaves, called dentated bands, arranged as a diagonal lattice. Forms of camel, elephant-heads and crude birds sometimes are employed as enlivening secondary decoration. Palmettes and lozenge forms punctuate the points of band intersection. The decoration of dragon rugs, often called "Armenian," is based on earlier Caucasian animal style and floral decoration of Persian origin. The earliest examples are of the sixteenth century and show animal design, such as dragons and phoenixes. Its exact source is unknown. Kuba, along the Caspian coast, has the preference. The city is said to have had, years ago, a large Armenian quarter devoted to rug weaving. This fact seemingly has been overlooked by proponents of the theory that Armenian weavers inaugurated this particular Western adaptation of Chinese art motives.

A second group of these rugs, distinguished by latticed leaf design, entirely discards the dragon forms and in substitution uses numerous eccentrically drawn animals. Colors are lighter and weaving coarser. A third group drops both dragons and animals, shortens the leaves and curves them about enormous egg-shaped palmettes or huge diamond medallions. This is the type on which an Armenian weaver inscribed an unusual confession: "I, Gohar, full of sin and feeble of soul." Both second and third groups probably belong to the late seventeenth and early eighteenth centuries. A fourth and later group, called Kuba, drops the leaves and specializes in large, archaic-looking palmettes. Obviously associated with the earliest of these weavings are rugs displaying primeval trees with heavy, inclined trunks and crude branches, set between huge irregular panels. Theoretically, these tree rugs were inspired by the fine art of trees displayed in Persian rugs during the early years of the sixteenth century.

RUGS OF THE CAUCASUS

The present assignment of the dragon family of rugs to the Caucasus, rather than to Armenia, is based upon considerations of wool, dye, color, design and descent of pattern, first observed and discussed by Mr. Heinrich Jacoby, and proved to be well-founded. The controversy that once raged about them is already historic. Karabacek assigned them to Syria of the thirteenth century. Riegl said they were Turkoman rugs produced under Chinese influence. Doctor Martin maintained that they were weavings of the fourteenth and fifteenth centuries, descendants of the animal rugs of Turkey that now are recorded only in paintings. For a variety of reasons he assigned them to Armenia, and for this opinion obtained a large following. Doctor Bode first assigned them to Syria and then contended that they were "decadent specimens," dating not earlier than the seventeenth century, "their elements of decoration borrowed from the magnificent rugs of the classic period of Persia." The incalculable debt owed to all of these scholars, for infinite unremunerated labor in the interest of rug intelligence, makes these errors of judgment mistakes worthy of gratitude, as steps necessary to all discovery.

Squares, rhomboids, triangles, hexagons, octagons, stars, diamonds and crosses, large and small, heaped and scattered, with here and there a crudely drawn flower, plant, tree, animal or human form to relieve the monotony, are the motives out of which recent and commonly-known Caucasian rug pattern ordinarily is constructed. Only in the settings of jewels and the masterful handling of mosaics are comparable effects secured. Here is real ability in the manipulation of pure ornamental forms, sharp, clear, brilliant and accurate.

To soften the outlines of bold designs an interlocking, shock-absorbing device, known as the latch-hook, probably a sprig of the Chinese fret, is everywhere employed. It probably came into fashion with its appearance in the weaving of Kuba. Noah's-ark animals and men possibly are memorials to the greatest local event in history. Color often is clear and crisp, reflecting a climate that in savage winter ruthlessly destroys life; but color changes with locality. In weaving the work is wholly Turkish, the knot Ghiordes, the materials almost entirely wool, warp and weft usually undyed, the ends webbed and fringed.

Ranged along the Caspian coast, or close to it, is found the one homogeneous group of rugs that begets the general design formula. Its members are known individually as Daghestan, Kabistan, Kuba, Derbend, Lesghian and Shirvan, the names of districts, cities and tribes. All employ the mosaic design, tempered by primitive floral forms, rendered in bright, clear, crisp shades of blue, red, ivory and minor green and yellow. Essentially the distinguishing differences are quality of weave and character of finish. Assign the fine woven examples to Daghestan, the superfine to Kabistan, the coarse to Derbend, the nomadic types with gold and blue color scheme to Lesghia, all the vast residue to Shirvan, and thereby qualify as an authority, and be almost as wise. To substantiate this authority one should know, of course, some distinguishing features of structure, as for example that Kabistan rugs sometimes have cotton weft, warp loops at one end and fringe at the other, which is not common practice. But multiplied data of this character is a madness, indulged fortunately only by books.

There is no such place as Kabistan, which by slip of vowel was created out of Kubistan, meaning the environs of the once important town of Kuba. The name Kuba is applied both to the old weavings, allied to dragon rugs, and to semi-antique rugs of a Kabistan character. But these are minor difficulties. The obstacle to the creation of a dependable terminology is lack of clean-cut demarcation between the species, which constantly overflow and intermingle.

The general appearance of the rug designs of this eastern group resembles aeroplane views of mountain-ranges; battalions of small forms—children's blocks, cones, stars and water motives, garlanded tombstones between trees—often in diagonal formation; and, of special interest, a geometrical device that looks like eight geese conversing in pairs, used in the rugs called Hila. Never to be neglected are the fine prayer-rug patterns, usually a grill or honey-comb.

In addition to the foregoing rugs, three rug types of unmistakable distinction emerge from the Caspian coast, namely Bakus, Chichis and Soumaks. Baku, strident industrial centre of oil-production and anciently the home of fire-worshippers, who still maintain a fire-temple and priest, the latter sent by the Parsee community in India, is the source of the famous cold, light-blue rugs, usually faded and dull, whose chief motive is the Persian palm-leaf, greatly enlarged in size, but delicate with many small flower ornaments, each a jewel set within the leaf form. Usually a stepped, deeply tooled octagon, ornamented with numerous rosettes, constitutes the central medallion, that requires correspondingly decorated corner areas and borders floral and geometric. Design honors obviously go to Persia for the floral forms, wavy stems and single central medallion, which is seldom employed by Caucasian weavers.

Chichi or Tzitzi rugs, coming from the territory north of Lesghia, are instantly distinguished by special border motive. Almost invariably the main border stripe consists of heavy parallel bars, diagonal to the side, separating pointed rosettes. Often too these rugs have a peculiar greenish caste, due to an unusual combination of blue and yellow. Additionally, no jarring note, a nomad mark, ever is seen in this weaving.

Soumak rugs, formerly called Kashmir because of the resemblance of their flat-surface, herring-bone weave and loose-yarn backs to similar work in the shawls of Kashmir, derive their true name from the town of Shemakha, although the principal source of production is Derbend. Once upon a time Shemakha was a place of consequence, as the following letter of Anthony Jenkinson, itinerant Englishman, to the Right Worshipful Societie of the Merchants Adventurers of London, dated 1562, indicates.

"I came to a city called Shamaky, in the country of Shirvan, and there the king hath a faire place, where my lodging being appointed, the goods were discharged; and the next day I was sent for to come to the king, named Obdolowean, who kept his court at that time in the high mountains in tents, distant from Shamaky twentie miles, to avoid the injury of the heat, and the 20th day I came before his presence. This king did sit in a very rich pavillion, wrought with silke and golde. He was a prince of a meane stature and of a fierce countenance, richly apparelled with long garments of silke and cloth of golde embroidered with pearls and stone; all the ground within his pavillion was covered with rich carpets, and under himselfe was spread a square carpet wrought with silver and golde, and thereon was laid two suitable cushions."

King Obdolowean's court was equipped with rugs fabricated elsewhere than in a local courtyard known to us, for only through intoxication of the imagination could Soumak rugs ever be described as rich, or be conceived as inlaid with gold and silver. Rather, fine old examples are dreamy pastels in rose and blue, reminders of old-fashioned New England spinsters, and like them exhibiting amazing strength of character in consequence of angular pattern. Commonly, large jewel-like octagons constitute the decoration. That out of such refined stock should come the wild-eyed, barbarous Soumak rugs of to-day, suitable only to gypsy tents and Russian theatres, is a loss to textile art. That rugs of pile surface also were made in and about Shemakha is affirmed, and one scholar has endeavored to segregate them. If Caucasian rugs generally had only a little more of the quality of inheritance that characterizes Caucasian hats, which in a hundred forms proclaim tribal association, many pile rugs would not become merely a part of the great debated miscellany of weaving harvested by commerce.

With progress toward the west, among the rugs woven on the south and populous side of the mountains, increasing variation in contents and color almost demolishes the group formula. Only through a territory of strong Persian influence and former occupancy does it emerge whole again, this time on an inflated scale, due in part to the Mongolian whirlwinds that blew across this part of the country during the thirteenth and fourteenth centuries. Gross Caucasian design of recent years always hails from the west; only the eastern area practises daintiness.

Most important among the rugs that continuously break the class rules are the superb old weavings of Karabagh, heirloom of once-famous Georgia. So long was this district a province of Persia that the Persian embassy sent to Napoleon during the first Russian campaign extracted a promise that the Czar should be forced to return the country to the Shah. Karabagh means "Black Vineyard," which in turn presages wine, an ingredient both of people and of weavings. If Karabagh rugs fail to feature some of the numerous wine shades, a rich red weft is likely to indicate the presence of the substance in the blood. The patterns of the treasured pieces seem almost equally divided between Caucasian, Persian and European types.

Among the Caucasian examples numerous serrated diamond-shaped medallions, with flower insert, seem the favorite; and among Persian types, the design of Herati, which in the public mind means the design of the weaving of Feraghan. As novelty and extreme rarity attaches to neither, nor to any other of the numerous forms of both varieties, interest centres in the design of roses borrowed from Kerman or France. In this pattern, as in the Aubusson carpet, are roses large with spreading petals, presented *en masse*, sometimes set within ornate frames of golden leaves against a background of richest blue, or allowed to spread afield within a narrow border of undulating vines. Sometimes the gold leaves completely cover the field in vast plume-like swirls, leaving only the least opening for the roses. Too rich a pattern and color scheme for large rugs, none is more engaging and permanently satisfying for rugs of small area, which it must be remembered is the usual Caucasian dimension.

Journeying farther west, through an area of numerous weavings haphazardly assigned, the investigator eventually is confronted with a wild masculinity of rugs that makes all other semi-antique Caucasian weavings seem delicate and feminine, and rugs of such thickness and weight as no amount of battering would seem able to demolish. These weavings, associated, since the migration of the race, with the region about Erivan, are the product of Kazak and Gengha women, lineal descendants of the tribes of barbarians known as Cossacks when they protected the old Russian frontier from invading Caucasians. Extreme length of pile and coarseness of texture, due to the use of numerous weft threads above each row of knots; piebald selvage; and a greatly enlarged scale of draftsmanship, with areas dyed in a single color, give an unmistakable identity. An ancient tawny example may be attributed to one of the old Circassian looms, hundreds of miles to the north, but probably without much justification. The penchant of the Circassian women, before the migration disbanded them, was ambition for marriage with Turkish sultans rather than devotion to the hard art of rugs.

Add to the foregoing recognized weavings at least fifty others bearing locally the hard names of rug-weaving tribes—Grusia, Imeretia, Mingrelis, Swanithia, Tuscha, Pscha, with other final "a's" *ad infinitum*, and the reward is more knowledge of Caucasian rugs than is commonly possessed.

Khilims, the tapestry weavings of all the Near East, are woven everywhere and in great variety. The types known as Silé and Verné, the latter produced near Shusha, are memorable because of fantastic designs of birds and beasts, including the last dragons. "Just needle-work," the commonalty comments and hastens to a glittering textile representing one-tenth the labor and one-hundredth the art.

Border patterns of Caucasian rugs would constitute a valuable kindergarten course in art. Saw-tooth leaf, wine-glass flower, tarantula, crab and serpent forms, counter-change motive that the courtly Polonaise silks employ, telegraphic dots and dashes, posts and bars, ribbon and wave semblances, together with interesting conversions of Kufic writing into hooked latches, are merely the best known of the simple motives of decoration that compose the Caucasian text-book.

Resumed purchase of these rugs, that once possessed a clientele and commanded almost as much attention from the authors of rug books as was accorded to Persian rugs, would re-establish the old salutary variety in floor decoration, to which they greatly contributed. Comparatively, the typical weavings along the Caspian coast are the reed instruments in the symphonic orchestra of oriental rugs. Comparatively, also, the weavers everywhere have adhered commendably to the old tunes.

CHAPTER VIII

WESTERN TURKESTAN, AFGHANISTAN, BELUCHISTAN RUGS

FAR the best understanding of Turkoman, Afghan and Beluchi, whose rug weavings custom and reason associate, is to be acquired from fiction, the branch of literature that, like the oriental rug, glistens with popularity because of constant challenge and conquest of fact and probability. But not all fiction, even oriental, is romantic; part deals with common earth, including the area of Central Asia where Morier and Gobineau located a Main Street more barbarous than our own variety, which is praise enough.

In the *Adventures of Hajji Baba*, Morier records the nature of Turkomans, which is that portion of the Turkish race that still persists in Western Turkestan, members of the vast Turanian family whose eastern quota are known as Mongols. "It is possible," writes the humane historian, "to make a long list of the Turanians, especially as recorded by the Chinese, but the names are unimportant. There was no great difference in the manners and customs of these tribes. As they settled down from time to time, they borrowed much from their civilized neighbors, but their natural manner of life was simple and untrammelled. The glory of all was to die in battle; to die of illness was accounted shameful." With text only slightly modified, Turkomans, Mongols and Tartars are but different editions of the human war treatise perennially issued by Mars, and Morier their translator.

184

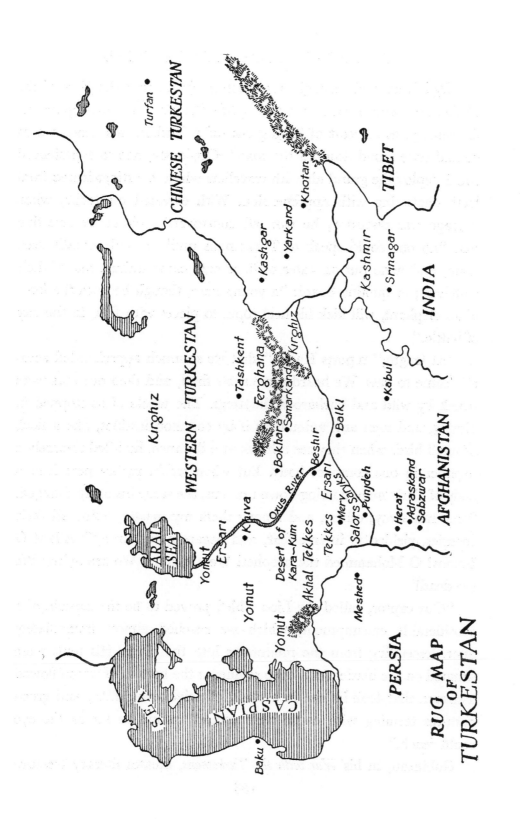

RUG MAP
OF
TURKESTAN

Hajji journeyed through northeastern Persia into the jaws of the Turkomans with a caravan whose guide "enjoyed a great reputation for courage as a result of having cut off a Turkoman's head, whom he had once found dead on the road." Obviously, one so experienced could deploy the grand air with travellers whose boastings issued from teeth chattering with apprehension. With elevated mustache, when courage was discussed, he won all controversies either by asserting that "no one could speak of Turkomans until he had actually seen them, and none but an eater of lions ever came unhurt out of their clutches"; or quoting Saadi: "a young man, though he hath the force of an elephant, will kick his heel ropes to pieces with fear, in the day of battle."

"At length," reports Hajji, "what we so much apprehended actually came to pass. We heard some shots fired, and then our ears were struck by wild and barbarous shoutings. The whole of us stopped in dismay, and men and animals as if by common instinct, like a flock of small birds when they see a hawk at a distance, huddled themselves together in one compact body. But when we in reality perceived a body of Turkomans coming down upon us, the scene instantly changed. Some ran away; others, and among them my master, losing all their energies, yielded to intense fear, and began to exclaim: 'O Allah! O Imams! O Mohammed the prophet! We are gone! We are dying! We are dead!'

"Our captor, called the Lion Chief, proved to be the captain of a considerable encampment, which we reached almost immediately after descending from the mountains into the plain. His tents were situated on the borders of a deep ravine, at the bottom of which flowed a stream that took its rise in a chain of neighboring hills; and green pastures teeming with cattle were spread around as far as the eye could reach."

Gobineau, in his *War with the Turkomans*, creates literary treasure out of the same material. His hero, Aga, meaning "My Lord," but in station only a common soldier in a theoretically powerful Persian force sent to teach the Turkoman rascals the advantages of international comity, recounts the will of Allah as he personally experienced it:

"Our generals remained at Meshed. It seems to be absolutely necessary that it should be so, because they can direct better from a distance. The colonels imitated the generals, probably for the same reason. In short, we had very few officers above the rank of captain, and it was just as well, for officers are not made to fight, but to receive the soldiers' pay. I do not speak of my gun. In the first place, it had no trigger, and in the next place, the barrel was split. But it was a very good weapon, notwithstanding. The question of powder was difficult. They had not given us any on our departure from Meshed. The generals had sold it."*

Aga, captured and made a slave, was taken by his master into a tent "made with walls and partitions of plaited osier covered with thick felt; the floor was of wood and carpeted; there were three or four chests painted all sort of colors, and a large bed with cushions. In this charming habitation was a young woman, who, I learned afterwards, was one of the beauties of the country. I would not have doubted it at the first view. She resembled a street poster of Tabreez. She had large and flat shoulders, a big head, little eyes, prominent cheek bones, and a mouth like a baker's oven, and upon her chest two mountains. I have seen yet worse-looking ones. She made a sign to me which I did not understand, and without explaining anything, she took a stick and hit me over the head. 'Are not you people of Iran more stupid than our horses?' she asked. 'Yes, mistress,' I replied with humility; 'it is very true; Allah has ordered it so.' 'The Turkomans,' she continued, 'rob you, steal you, carry you off and sell you to whom they will, and you can find no means of preventing

* Joseph Arthur Comte de Gobineau, *Five Oriental Tales*. The Viking Press.

them.' 'It is true, mistress,' I replied again; 'but it is because the Turkomans are brilliant people, and we Persians are asses.' "*

Turkomans and Mongolians consider the American Indians one of their lost tribes. Shown pictures of red men, they immediately call them cousins, and tell the story of two brothers who were separated by a bolt of lightning. Rather, they were separated by the explosion of a vast human volcano.

According to tradition the oldest of the Turkoman tribes, known as Salor, migrated from the region north of Kashgar, westward into the region north of Samarkand, thousands of years before the Christian era. According to conjecture, the original molecules of the American Sioux tribe moved, during the same indefinite period, from approximately the same territory, into Virginia and South Carolina. Subsequently the Salors migrated to Merv, and the Sioux from Virginia to the basin of the Missouri and upper Mississippi Rivers, both in the process splitting into fragments, creating tribal branches. Both tribes were bloodthirsty savages living a nomadic existence in tents, and consorting with animals, which only the Turkomans extensively domesticated and utilized in the production of floor coverings of uncontestable art.

That the Turanians should produce rugs vastly superior to those created by the Indians was due to an environment of culture—particularly that eventually attained by the satanic Mongols, who in the thirteenth century moved westward on a squib of rover's philosophy: "Profitless 'tis in this world to build the strong castle or palace; ruins they are in the end, and profitless too to build cities." Then outgrowing their season of wild oats, the Mongols built gardens about palaces, and palace rugs later to be acclaimed under the name of Timurid. But as with all Turanians, the palace began as a tent.

The wheel-equipped home of Jenghis Khan, the Cyrus the Great

* Joseph Arthur Comte de Gobineau, *Five Oriental Tales*. The Viking Press.

of these fluid nations, was a "tent made of felt stretched over a frame-work of wattled rods with an aperture at the top to let out the smoke. This was covered with white lime and ornamented with pictures. A peculiar kind of tent, however, this yurt that wandered all over the prairies, mounted on a cart drawn by a dozen or more oxen. In it was kept the family treasure—carpets from Bokhara or Kabul, looted probably from some caravan; chests filled with women's gear, silk garments bartered from a shrewd Arab trader, and inlaid silver. More important were the weapons that hung on the walls, short Turkish scimitars, spears, ivory or bamboo bow-cases, arrows of dif-ferent lengths and weights, and perhaps a round shield of tanned leather. All were looted or purchased, passing from hand to hand with the fortunes of war.

"While visiting the yurt of a khan supposedly friendly, Jenghis discovered that a pit had been dug under an innocent-looking carpet upon which he had been invited to sit."*

Friar John of Pian de Carpini records in his travel journal, 1245–1247, that the tent of the Regent Empress Turakina was "so great that more than two thousand men might stand within it"; and that the tent in which Kuyuk was placed upon the imperial throne "was erected upon pillars which were covered with plates of gold and joined to other timber with golden nails. It was covered inside with baldskin cloth, but there was other cloth spread over it on the out-side. Among the abundance of gifts presented to him by the ambas-sadors, there was a certain small tent which was to be carried over the emperor's head, and this was set full of precious stones." When the great prince Batu rides "there is a small tent carried over his head upon the point of a pole; and so do all the great princes of the Tartars, and their wives also."

Mongolian indulgence in gold nails and imperial canopies set

* Harold Lamb, *Genghis Khan, Emperor of All Men*. Robert McBride & Co.

with precious stones, which the Turkomans never achieved, clearly indicates the divergent paths which the two great branches of the Turanian race were to follow in subsequent history. Simplicity of life, to which both originally were as much addicted as were their horses, sheep and goats, was maintained to the end only by the Turkomans. Contacts with settled, civilized people, which their continuous raiding effected, eventually drugged the Mongols into acceptance of the rampant faith of Mohammed, into serious flirtation with pacificism, and finally into the erection of courts, mosques and colleges in many cities, particularly in Samarkand, Bokhara and Tashkent. For a time the rulers, notably Tamerlane, were the masters of the active world, and their intellectuals the equals in ability of the scholars, theologians and scientists of other peoples. Then, almost as suddenly as it took form, this dazzling accomplishment went to its tomb.

To-day "no astronomers study the sky from the tops of minarets; scholars waste their time on puerile scholasticism; priests, no longer followed by the people, thirst for personal enrichment. The wealthier inhabitants of the cities are grossly sensual. Only the agricultural laborer has preserved the uprightness, diligence and sobriety which characterized the Turkish peasant." This agricultural laborer is to-day engaged in the cultivation of over eight and one quarter million acres of irrigated land, half devoted to the raising of cotton, the "white gold" of the region. The Soviet is the ruler, Western Turkestan the outpost of Bolshevism in Asia, and old Tashkent a rebuilt city with fine boulevards proclaiming the new and firm Russian purpose.

Western Turkestan as Russian territory is summarized in the following contemporary report. "In the vast hinterland beyond the railways live a variety of native peoples, deposited by successive waves of invasion, speaking different languages, with cultures of their own, which although devoid of sanitation or general literacy, yet have produced a land-irrigating technique, cotton growing, famous vineyards, rug weaving and embroidery, architecture of some magnificence and many kindred arts. All, being Moslems, have the usual Islamic social system: women veiled and confined to the women's quarters, court procedure based on the Koran, schools devoted to reciting it. But the Bolshevists make no effort to preserve former customs. They pass laws against polygamy, declare that marriage by purchase is a form of prostitution, fix the marriageable age of girls at sixteen, organize farm-hands and tenants against landowners, and confiscate lands and re-distribute them to landless laborers. In a decade of rule they have attempted more drastic reforms than the British have tried in several generations of government in India."

In the year 1924 the Soviet organized republics based on nation-ality all over Western Turkestan, and theoretically gave each absolute equality with the great Russian SFSR and the Ukranian SSR. The most important division is Uzbekistan, which includes all the prin-cipal cities, Tashkent, Samarkand, Bokhara and Ferghana, and nearly all the valuable irrigated regions, the total area comprehending a population of four million Uzbeks and a million nondescripts.

The second great republic is Turkmenistan, a seemingly endless earth of steppes and deserts centring on the Kara Kum Sands, lying east of the Caspian, north and east of Persia, a country too dry for easy agriculture, too cold for comfort, always by nature a place of de-parture and never of settled abode. The comrades of Turkmenistan are a million illiterate tent-dwelling, rug-weaving, sheep and cattle-raising nomads, now existing in comparative peace and wondering what all the ancient excitement was about. Rugs adapted wholly to tents and treking, a double requirement that results in small rugs, many of odd and interesting shape, are their chief product and pride.

The tents of circular, domed shape belong to the "merry-go-round" variety. Approximately they have a diameter of fifteen feet, a height of eleven feet at the centre, and of six feet at the perimeter.

Materials consist of numerous wooden rods, something more than an inch in diameter, used for framework; dried sheep-gut and camel-hair rope used for binding; and thick felt and reed matting used for cover. The framework consists of four diagonal lattice arcs set end to end, for walls; a six-foot wheel, with central smoke-hole, for dome; and finally rods inserted between the walls and the wheel to create the sloping roof. Around the outside of the walls are sheets of felt bound by reed matting. Over the top is a felt cover with vent-cap operated by cords. Ropes over the roof and stakes driven into the ground about the walls secure this "bird-cage," which requires only an hour to erect or dismantle. Men are the carpenters of the frame-work, which lasts indefinitely; women the camp-makers, and camels the transportation force.

A fireplace occupies the centre of the tent, the kitchen and wood-shed the entrance area, and the living- and sleeping-quarters the space at the rear, which is carpeted with felt overlaid with rugs.

Interior walls are decorated with camel bags, called Jowals, which are four and five feet long and approximately three and a half feet deep, woven separately in pairs, joined together, and flung one on each side of a camel to serve as "suit-cases" during periods of migra-tion. On the walls, Jowals are still receptacles for all manner of articles. Only the Yomut tribes weave them in irregular forms, sometimes with five, six or seven sides. Other wall rugs consist of donkey saddle-bags, called Kharjin, woven as a single piece and converted into bags by folding the ends toward the centre, binding the sides, and fastening the openings with two lines of goat-hair loops. Khilims, which are tapestry weavings, are equally serviceable as hangings and as wrap-pings to bundles. A pillow rug, called Torba, approximately one by two feet or slightly larger, is usually found in place at the end of a floor rug. Torbas and Jowals, which are to contain the wealth that goes with the daughter at marriage, usually are woven in the most expert manner and of the finest materials. The girls themselves prove their talent in the smaller fabrics.

Doorways are hung with rug valances a foot or more wide, designed often from the borders of rugs and ornamented with extra trapping of wool fringe and cords. About the tent, below the roof-line on the outside, weavings known as tent-bands, often more than forty feet long by a foot and a half wide, are run and fastened for decoration.

All materials are the appropriated clothing of sheep, goats and camels, for which the country is famous. Nowhere is the wool of sheep finer and more luxuriant; the fleece of lambs, known as Pashm, more silk-like; the wool vests of goats and Bactrian camels so soft, ample and durable—qualities that result from the severity of the climate, the sturdiness of the stock, and the abundance and excellence of the food-supply along the water-courses.

Sometimes, small quantities of these materials are used in natural color—white from sheep, black and gray from goats, and tan and chestnut from camels. Wild silk, dyed magenta, is used a pinch at a time, occasionally, in choice small rugs. Cotton, with which the country adjacent abounds, and which in most countries is an important rug ingredient, is here without recognition and employment.

The principal color is the glorious Turanian red, obtained from madder-root, cochineal insects and now sometimes from synthetic dye, that still suggests the ancient struggle for existence, the human and animal butchery of thousands of years. The shades range from "light meat" to "dark liver," which accounts for the designation of the rugs as "the Rembrandts of weaving."

Friar William of Rubruck, envoy of Louis IX of France to the Turanians during the years 1253–1255, recounts a tale of this color that, true or false, is interesting. "One day a priest of Cathay came and sat by me, and he was clothed in a red cloth of a most beautiful color, and I asked him from where such a color was got. He told me that in the east of Cathay there are very high rocks where live certain creatures who have the form of a human being, except they cannot bend knees. Also they move about, I do not know just how, but by jumping. They are not more than a cubit tall and their body is covered with hair. These beings live in inaccessible caverns. The hunters bring them mead to get them drunk; they make holes in the rocks in the form of vases, and pour the mead in them.

"Then these hunters hide themselves and the jumping creatures come out of their caves, taste their mead, and cry: 'Chin, Chin.' It is because of this cry that they got their name, for they are called 'Chin Chin.' They assemble in crowds, gorging their drink, and becoming drunk they fall asleep on these rocks. Then the hunters approach and bind the hands and feet of these sleepers. After that, they open a vein in their necks, draw three or four drops of blood, and then send them back free. This blood, according to the priest of Cathay, is excellent for coloring purple or scarlet."

During the period when Turkoman red was creating its dynasty, that was to become more autocratic even than Imperial Yellow in China or authoritative blue in Persia, design set up a triumvirate that no plot or revolt ever was able to overthrow. Only with the consent of the Octagon, Diamond and Tree of Life, the immortal Octavius, Antony and Lepidus of Turkoman rugs, did any other motive dare raise its head. In consequence, only as modest subordinate forms, atoms of experience and solemn learning, appear arrows and arrowheads, clubs, hooks, prongs, dogs, camels, scorpions, tarantulas, serpents (S forms), swastikas (double S forms), fish and birds (the latter usually only head and neck), pears, gourds, eight-petalled flowers and eight-pointed stars, ancient seals and combs, all rendered in the native language of art, and consequently often needing interpretation.

As ruling and subject forms were employed in diverse shapes and sizes, surprising variety characterizes the art and furnishes the key to the cross-word puzzle of identification. Comparison of octagons reveals approximately a dozen varieties, each an established tribal device. Diamond-forms and trees of life likewise assumed tribal shapes. These individual "brands" the Turkoman calls "guls," which means "flowers of ornament." Guls and textures proclaim the source of the weaving.

Bokhara and rugs have long been associated. When Mansur II occupied the throne of Bokhara, almost exactly a thousand years ago, courtiers, mortified by his plebeian clothes, and restive for lack of courtly distractions, asked him some personal questions. His reply in verse was unanswerable:

> "They ask me why fine robes I do not wear,
> Nor covet stately tent with carpets rare.
> 'Midst clash of arms, what boots the minstrel's power?
> 'Midst rush of steeds, what place for rose-girt bower?"

At the outset of the survey of the rugs of Western Turkestan, begun years ago, Bokhara, Merv, Beshir, Khiva, Balkh and Adraskand were the driven stakes, the prospectors' camps, in the vast expanse. Tribes that practised the art within the confines of the province of Bokhara could roam over eighty-five thousand square miles of territory without going out of bounds. Merv, at the heart of so fertile an oasis that its oriental name was Paradise, was the centre of a vast region occupied by three important rug-weaving tribes—Salors, Saryks and Tekkes. Beshir, a dot in the landscape greatly aggrandized by rug association, was almost in the middle of the Ersari country. Khiva, on the River Oxus, was in the midst of the northern branch of the Yomut family. Balkl, located in northern Afghanistan, had for neighbors the Turkoman tribes that weave the rugs called Afghans. Finally, Adraskand in western Afghanistan was within the ring of the rugs that are known in America only as Beluchistans.

But assignment of wandering rugs to stationary cities is no longer warranted. People even in Turkestan are of more consequence than places, that like rugs are either created or inherited, and tribal names of more significance than the names of rug marts.

Unfortunately for the cause of accuracy in rug nomenclature, the name Bokhara, like the name Ispahan, cannot at this late date be dethroned in public usage. The attempt even to correct its faults is probably doomed to failure. Nevertheless, the so-called "Royal Bokhara" rugs of the market are the product of the Tekke tribes which impinge, not on Bokhara, but on Merv; and real Bokhara weavings, product of tribes located in the southwestern corner of the Khanate of Bokhara, are not true Turkoman weavings at all. They are rugs woven in miscellaneous design acquired from Persia, Caucasia, Samarkand and Mongolia, rendered in a composite of the colors of these sources.

The representative type of true Bokhara, now sold in America as Beshir, is a large, long, stout and comparatively coarse rug of all-over Persian Herati design, or other floral motive, rendered in stiff, rectilinear fashion, surrounded by borders of Caucasian and Mongolian character, the entire composition executed in colors more salient and advancing than are commonly used in Turkoman weavings. Yellow, influence of Samarkand, mixed with red, produces a terra-cotta tone which is not a true Turkoman color; and clear yellow guard stripes are a still further departure from standard type. Bokhara, cosmopolitan city of Moslem theology, Asiatic learning, silk and cotton fabrication, caravan trade, point of infinite human contact, conflict and compromise, is the source of the mixed blood in genuine Bokhara weavings.

False or "Royal Bokharas," creation of the powerful and savage Tekkes, display for compoundment of their fault of name true Turkoman design and color. The identifying ornament or "gul" is a narrow, flattened octagon, called "camel-foot," indented on all four sides, quartered and decorated with hooks and trefoils. Design consists of three or four rows of these octagons, arranged commonly eight to a row, both with and without the "telephone connection" or checkerboard outline.

The Tekke "gul" has so long been called a camel-foot that the interpretation must probably be accepted. Nevertheless, the feeling that the early weavers were endeavoring to represent a tribal encampment, rather than a camel-trodden oasis, has both practical and artistic justification. Numerous tents create similar design. That the pattern is meaningless is equally reasonable and tenable. The Salor tribes employed it as a secondary motive. If, as is believed, the Salors taught the art of weaving to the Tekkes, the latter may have appropriated it, capriciously, as an emblem.

Tekke mastery of the dyer's art is exhibited in reds that the Persians never surpassed even in the famous Ispahans, in dark blues of brilliant lustre, and in orange, yellow, mauve and deep green shades that glow. When the texture is climaxed to the impenetrable density of four hundred knots to the square inch, as sometimes happens, recognition of technical supremacy, too, must be accorded the weavers of the rugs that are neither Royal nor Bokhara, but nevertheless a feat of art of which the entire group might well be proud.

Against this credit to the account of the tribe of Tekke must be placed a huge debit in the virtual extinction of the fine rug weavings formerly executed by the tribe of Salor. By merciless and unrelenting war the Tekkes, in the year 1856, dispossessed the Salors of their fertile homestead north of Merv and drove them into the northeast horn of Persia, where the Khans rifled them of their superb rugs also, and made further weaving occasion for further despoilment.

The "gul" of the Salors is a picketed octagon with approximately thirty-two triangular barbs, counting both outer and inner sides of the perimeter. Seemingly it represents a fortification protecting a central camp, which has the form of a quartered octagon of indented contour. Certainly no design could better represent the needs of a tribe that vainly fought itself out against a younger and more vigorous generation. Usually twelve picketed octagons, always whole and never quartered, six in each of two rows, are employed in the complete composition. The texture of the rare old examples is a superior accomplishment, sometimes, through the use of the finest materials, attaining a density of four hundred and fifty knots to the square inch. The ground color is the nearest to plum found in any of this group of weavings.

East of the present Salor territory is located the tribe of Saryk, whose "gul" is an elongated camel-foot octagon, distinguished by eight varsity "H" letters. This motive is asserted to be an idealized drawing of a sheep-dog, who, because he needs them, is given two heads. Color is invariably rich, and texture fine and velvety.

The camel-foot of the Tekkes, fort of the Salors, and dogs of the Saryks, real or fancied, are the A B C's of Turkoman rug design. Excessive simplicity, however, always is suspect. Dog pattern, for example, is not a device used exclusively by the Saryks. The tribe of Ersari, neighbors on the northeast along the Oxus River, use an octagon containing both four and eight dogs, and also an octagon decorated with arrow-heads and hooked clubs, both plagiarisms, the latter from the Afghan Turkomans living on their southern exposure.

For tribal distinction in Ersari pattern recourse must be made to the earliest extant weavings of the group, rugs approximately two hundred years old, that display a broad trellis of diamond-shaped panels, somewhat resembling the Gordon and MacGregor tartans of Scotland, decorated with octagons, eight-pointed stars and crudely indented leaves. Commonly, rugs of this motive are assigned to the weavers of Beshir, an attribution far too narrow for a tribe so far-flung.

WESTERN TURKESTAN RUGS

In color, Ersari rugs display considerable Bokhara and Samarkand yellow. Materials always are good, but texture only mediocre. Size varies from average dimension, in a tendency to much greater length in proportion to width, and in the production of a greater number of carpets. It follows that except rarely Ersari rugs are not collectors' trophies.

The diamond trellis of the old Ersari rugs is a device common to Caucasian rugs, notably to Shirvans. Interestingly, the old home-ground of the Ersari tribe was the eastern coast of the Caspian Sea, only a few days' sail from the Shirvan shore, and immediately north of the country occupied by the great body of the tribe of Yomut, whose rug brand is a diamond with serrated or latch-hooked edges, also a common Caucasian motive. The Caspian coast, east and west, is the ancient repository of the diamond pattern. From this area the Turkoman tribes carried the motive into western Afghanistan, and the Kashgai tribes into the region about Shiraz.

Yomut diamond motives, with slightly heightened color from the use of fine turquoise blue and rich green, another Caucasian importation, are arranged in regular diagonal rows. They are both regular and irregular in outline, hooked and toothed, but always unmistakable in their red velvet setting.

As boundaries of countries mean nothing to Turkomans, their presence in northern Afghanistan, weaving rugs that we, in Persian fashion, name according to place and call Afghan, occasions no surprise. In common with the weavers of the Salor, Saryk and Tekke tribes, Afghan Turkomans employ the octagon, but distinguish their rugs by being emphatic about it. The result is the Fil-Pa, meaning "elephant-foot" octagon, used in quantities of twenty-one or twenty-four, always in compact arrangement and usually in three parallel perpendicular rows. These large "prints" are quartered in the native fashion, decorated with trefoils and eight-pointed stars about a squared centre, and colored blue and orange, with less white than most Turkomans employ.

Woven of wool of iron constitution, frequently installed on a gray goat-hair warp, Afghan rugs bear an enormous burden of labor both at home and abroad, partly through extra length of pile. Their large size, usually nine to eleven feet in length, has been an important factor in their sale, which, however, like the Western sale of all Turkoman rugs, has been decidedly on the wane.

The name Beluchistan as applied to rugs is to-day as wide of the mark and as misleading as the name Bokhara. It is bestowed promiscuously on the large rug product that grows profusely over the mountainous country of southwestern Afghanistan, and eastern Persia, the province of Herat at the centre. No one seems to know why the country of Beluchistan, with its little output of rugs, should have been given the credit for so vast a weaving. Possibly the Eastern name for the group, "Siyah-kar," meaning "dark-work," recalled the prayer of the Arab poet:

> "O Allah, seeing Thou hast created Beluchistan,
> What need was there of conceiving Hell?"

Beluch-Afghan rugs revel in the sombre heavyweights of color—dull reds, blue toning to purple, dark browns and greens, that sometimes raise a cheer with tans derived from natural camel-hair. No simple "gul" is employed, but rather a style of ornamentation that greatly resembles the Caucasian. Here are repeated designs of diamonds, eight-petalled rosettes, latch-hooks, trefoils, octagonal discs, crude trees of life, uncertain sprawling geometric inventions, and all manner of angular detritus to fill every natural design declivity.

Two subdivisions now emerging from the group are the rugs woven in the neighborhood of Adraskand, which are esteemed the finest, and the rugs created in the province of Sabzwar, which, meaning "green-colored," has attributed to it all rugs having a quantity of this color. Dealers classify the strictly commercial product as Meshed, Sistan and India Beluch, and esteem it in that order, holding the southern product of least account.

The most interesting rugs of Turkestan, Afghanistan and Beluchistan, and many of the finest, are inspired by religion, as the evangelist would assert, and devoted to the function of prayer. The most common pattern is an oblong field divided into four equal oblong panels by two intersecting bands resembling a cross. Obviously this design, called Katchli, meaning "cross," is the nomad interpretation of the garden rugs of Persia. In the glorious original the bands represent intersecting paths, and the four oblong areas garden-plots. Reminiscent of the Persian pattern also are many miniature plant forms that frequently are misidentified as candles.

Above this field is either one large prayer niche (called a mihrab), shaped like a tent, or a row of many miniature prayer niches. The single niche prevails among the rugs of the western or Akhal Tekkes; the multiple pattern, commonly called Punjdeh (Pinde), meaning rugs woven in the district of that name, at the junction of Turkestan, Afghanistan and Persia, is the work of Salor, Saryk and Yomut artists.

A third common prayer-rug type is created by the Afghan weavers of Beluchistan rugs. A single, narrow central panel commonly is decorated with a tree of life that extends its crown into a deep rectangular prayer niche, on either side of which are special tree-decorated panels for the placement of hands.

Additional distinctive prayer rugs, not exactly rare but uncommon, are produced by the Bokhara and Ersari tribes. The former use an elongated "head-and-shoulders" mihrab, resembling somewhat the prayer pattern of Melas rugs; the latter, a broad, double or triple roof niche that looks like an attempt to represent a large ridge-pole tent.

Both types are decorated with trees of life and floral ornaments executed in angular manner. Always the tree of life dominates the prayer rugs, the octagon the secular rugs of the heart of the country, and the diamond the rugs of the east and west fringes of this no-man's land.

In the journal of Friar John of Pian de Carpini, heretofore mentioned, is to be found a Turanian admonition widely applicable and particularly appropriate to the pursuit of rug knowledge: "Take heed that you understand all things thoroughly, for if you should not understand the whole matter, it might breed some inconvenience." How the old cut-throat author of this sage counsel would chuckle, forgetful of the torments of seven centuries of the nether world, if our appreciation of his word "inconvenience" were communicated to him.

CHAPTER IX

CHINESE RUGS

TWELVE hundred years ago, during the T'ang dynasty (618-906 A.D.), the Golden Age of Art and Learning, there lived in China three great poets, Tu Fu, Li Po, and Po Chu-I, whose works are so highly esteemed that no library is thought complete which lacks them. Po Chu-I entitled one of his poems "The Big Rug." It has the merit of novelty and brevity:

> "That so many of the poor should suffer from cold
> What can we do to prevent?
> To bring warmth to a single body is not much use.
> I wish I had a big rug ten thousand feet long,
> Which at one time could cover up every inch of the city."*

The northern Chinese of the T'ang period used rugs both as blankets and mattresses, as all northern Asiatic peoples have done from the beginning. In a poem entitled "Being Visited by a Friend During Illness," Po Chu-I mentions the use of a rug in a manner customary with us:

> "I have been ill so long that I do not count the days.
> At the southern window, evening and again evening.
> They took my couch and placed it in the setting sun;
> They spread my rug and I leaned on the balcony pillar."*

* Arthur Waley, *170 Chinese Poems*. Alfred A. Knopf.

ORIENTAL RUGS AND CARPETS

In the Shosoin Imperial Treasury at Nara, Japan, are fragments of T'ang dynasty rugs whose designs of lotus, flower-sprays, rosettes, birds, clouds and crags, woven mostly in blue on a dark yellow ground, prove that the Chinese art of rug weaving had even then attained maturity.

Six hundred and fifty years ago youthful Marco Polo with his father and uncle made the arduous, dangerous journey from Venice to the court of Kublai Khan, Mongolian ruler of China, in the year 1280. In the incomparable *Travels*, Polo recounts how Nayan, a chief and kinsman of Kublai Khan, revolted, and how he was put to death "by being enclosed between two carpets which were violently shaken until the spirit had departed from the body. The motive for this peculiar sentence was that the sun and air should not witness the shedding of the blood of one who belonged to the imperial family."

Chinese rug weaving, therefore, is not the wholly modern art that many people conceive it to be. It is an art that has been practised in Kansu, Shansi, Shensi and Chili, the four northern provinces of China, for more than twelve centuries; and there are reasons for believing that it was practised centuries earlier by the Chinese peoples of Turkestan.

Nor are Chinese rugs, by any impartial standard of judgment, the rug family of least art and consequence, as recent and belated recognition might imply. The fact that fantastically interpreted religious motives, amusing illustrations of myth and fable, and exaggerated nature forms are included among its thousands of designs in no way impairs merit. These incidentals add to the gaiety of nations. At their best, which is marvellously good, Chinese rugs are formidable contestants for unqualified esteem.

However venerable the practice of Chinese rug weaving, many designs and color schemes are at least two thousand years older, their source the cradle of Chinese philosophy, religion and practice of life. To understand them requires no little retrospection.

CHINESE RUGS

The Chinese have two great native schools of thought, one founded by Confucius, the other by Laotsze. Confucius, man of the world of 551 B.C., taught the merit of personal dignity, mutual respect, reverence for parents, seniors and ancestors, devotion to ceremony, and service to the State. "The highest ideal in life is to be noble and to create a noble state. The noble sort of man pays special attention to nine points. He is anxious to see clearly, to hear distinctly, to be kindly in his looks, respectful in his demeanor, conscientious in his speech, earnest in his affairs. When in doubt, he is careful to inquire; when in anger, he thinks of the consequences; when offered an opportunity for gain, he thinks only of his duty."

Confucius, in a period of riotous social upheaval not unlike that of the present day, made forceful and permanently impressive exhortation for the maintenance of the highest traditions of Chinese life. For over a thousand years before his time, ceremony of most precise character had been a Chinese institution. So rigid were the ceremonies of the court that the days of the Emperor were entirely without leisure, and a similar condition of ceremonial servitude governed all important family life. That this tradition of manners, which Confucius summarized, permeates old Chinese rugs is indisputable. Comparatively few examples are wanting in fine personality. Symbols of this teaching are lacking only because nobility is impossible to symbolize.

The second great teacher of the Chinese was Laotsze, a mystic, whose "Tao" or "Way" was "a great square with no angles, a great vessel which takes long to complete, a great sound which cannot be heard, a great image with no form." Laotsze said: "A man may know the world without leaving the shelter of his roof. Through his own windows he may see the Supreme Tao. The further afield he goes, the less likely is he to find it. The Sage knows things without travelling, names things without having seen them, and performs everything without action." The Taoist Song by Chi K'ang (A.D. 223-262) is to be commended for at least two good lines about fishing:

"I will cast out Wisdom and reject Learning.
My thoughts shall wander in the Great Void.
Always repenting of wrongs done
Will never bring my heart to rest.
I cast my hook in a single stream,
But my joy is as though I possessed a King.
I loose my hair and go singing:
To the four frontiers men join in my refrain.
This is the purport of my song:
'My thoughts shall wander in the Great Void.' "*

Indifference to the pleasures and powers of the world, and a return to the imaginary simple life of the past, is the substance of Taoism. The reward of adherence to the faith is long life, and after death the enjoyment of a Paradise in which eight Immortals, representing successful practitioners from the various trades, each designated by an emblem, wander in fields of bliss, sit about in social groups, and receive messages from earth conveyed by storks. The emblems of Taoism, continuously employed in Chinese rug design, are a basket of flowers, belonging to the patron of gardeners; a flute, property of the patron of musicians; a lotus flower, worn by the virgin patron of "housewifery"; castanets or bamboo clappers, manipulated by the patron of actors; bamboo tubes and rods, pertaining to the patron of artists and scholars; a pilgrim's magic gourd and iron staff, used by the patron of astrologers and magicians; a sword of supernatural power, brandished not by the despised military classes, but by barbers; and lastly a fan, that an undesignated individual used to revive the souls of the dead.

To these two great native religions was added in the year 67 A.D.

* Arthur Waley, *170 Chinese Poems*. Alfred A. Knopf.

the religion of Buddhism, instituted in India by Gautama, contemporary of Confucius and Laotsze, and in China by the Emperor Ming Ti, who saw in a vision a gold image which bade him send to the western countries for truth, books and idols. The return of his envoys was celebrated by the erection of the famous White Horse Temple.

Gautama, the reflective one, conceived the way to heaven as an eightfold path consisting of Right Views, Right Aspirations, Right Speech, Right Conduct, Right Livelihood, Right Effort, Right Mindfulness and Right Rapture. The result of acceptance was the peace of self-forgetfulness. Buddhism is represented in Chinese rugs by eight symbols: the canopy, symbol of sovereignty; two fish, symbol of married happiness; covered vase, a receptacle for relics; lotus, emblem of purity; conch shell, emblem of victory and safe voyage for the mariner; state umbrella, emblem of official authority; endless knot, symbol of long duration; the bell used in temple service to secure the attention of the gods, or more commonly the ever-revolving wheel of the law, probably a symbol of the prayer wheel.

Common employment of these motives to-day has shorn away most of their religious character. They are properties of art and expressions of national consciousness, rather than testaments of religious conviction.

Only rarely do Chinese rug weavers attempt to depict the features and attitudes of the important deities of the Taoist and Buddhist faiths; rug portraiture is too exacting. Nevertheless Hsi Wang Mu, ruler of the Taoist paradise in the K'un-lun mountains, "where the peach-tree of longevity grows," and Kwan-Yin, Buddhist Goddess of Mercy, have been recognizably represented; and also Manjusri, Buddhist God of Wisdom, armed with a fly-brush, made to ride a fabulous lion controlled by a rope attached to a ring in his nose.

Mohammed, "Allah-Breathing Lord," only faintly influenced Chinese rug design. His followers, penetrating China after the eleventh century, carried with them the pattern of the Islam prayer rug; but Chinese weavers rarely employ it.

The use of rugs in temples is a practice that is to be inferred from the continuous weaving of religious motives. Temple rugs consist of wall, pillar and doorway hangings in the designs of the dragon, symbol of God, Nature and Emperor, combined with the symbols of the faiths of Laotsze and Buddha. Only the long, narrow Chinese prayer rugs, consisting of small squares just large enough for a single worshipper to stand or sit upon, are used on the floors. Symbols of several religions sometimes appear on a single rug, for the Chinese are tolerant.

The Chinese dragon, unlike the European specimen that engaged the attention of St. George, is a beneficent creature. In religion, it represents the Deity, powerful and merciful; in its own right, it is the sovereign of the forces of nature; it became the symbol of the Emperor when Tao Ts'ou in the year 206 B.C. established the divinity of kings. Imperial dragons have five toes; dragons that have lost one or more toes represent lesser grades of monarchical blood. Sky dragons keep the heavens from sinking; earth dragons trace the course of rivers; spiritual dragons rule storm-clouds and winds; and sentry dragons guard hidden treasure. Six dragons once a day draw the chariot of the sun, and one transports a philosopher to Paradise.

But only the oriental can summarize the talent of the dragon, a feat which Okakura Kakuzo achieves in the ensuing revelation: "The Eastern dragon is not the gruesome monster of mediæval imagination, but the genius of strength and goodness. He is the spirit of change, therefore of life itself. We associate him with the supreme power or with that sovereign cause which pervades everything, taking new forms according to surroundings, yet never seen in a final shape. The dragon is the great mystery itself. Hidden in the caverns of inaccessible mountains, or coiled in the unfathomed depth of the sea, he awaits the time of activity. He unfolds himself in the storm-clouds; he washes his mane in the blackness of the seething whirlpools. His claws are in the fork of the lightning; his scales glisten in the bark of rain-swept pine-trees. His voice is heard in the hurricane, which, scattering the withered leaves of the forest, quickens a new Spring. The dragon reveals himself only to vanish. He is a glorious symbolic image of that elasticity of organism which shakes off the inert mass of exhausted matter. Coiling again and again on his strength, he sheds his crusted skin amid the battle of elements, and for an instant stands half-revealed by the brilliant shimmer of his scales."

The poet also does well in dragon epitome:

"When the dragon comes, ah!
The wind stirs and sighs,
Paper money thrown, ah!
Silk umbrellas waved.
When the dragon goes, ah!
The wind also—still.
Incense fire dies, ah!
Cups and vessels cold."*

In rug design the dragon is used single, in pairs, and sometimes in groups of five. Usually, within its coils, is a disk grooved by a tongue of fire. This is the "Pearl of the Dragon," symbol of thunder and lightning, and source of both.

Closely associated and often depicted with the dragon is the phœnix or love-pheasant, emblem of the Chinese Empress and sometimes of brides. It is described as having the head of a pheasant, the beak of a swallow, long neck, gorgeous plumage, flowing peacock tail, and claws pointing backward as it flies. Its five colors symbolize the five cardinal virtues. Phœnix and dragon together represent happiness. An equally companionable pair are the crane and stag, both Taoist

* Arthur Waley, *170 Chinese Poems*. Alfred A. Knopf.

209

symbols of long life. Stag and dragon are combined in the kylin, a fabulous creature with the body, legs and hoofs of the stag, the head of the dragon, a bushy tail, and flaming shoulders that indicate supernatural source. The kylin is the noblest of beasts; it treads so lightly that insects are unharmed; it lives a thousand years and appears at the birth of sages.

The popular animal among rug weavers, if test of popularity is extensive representation, is the lion. Like the dragon, phœnix, kylin and unicorn, the lion is a docile creature despite an equipment of flaming mane, tail and joints. He is defender of law and protector of sacred buildings, and his syllable "shih" means "teacher." The male lion is represented by a ball in the claw; the female by a litter of cubs. A lesser lion is the "fu" or "happy dog" to which is assigned the task of guarding the doorways of temples and houses against the attacks of evil spirits.

It is a proper question how the Chinese came to imagine and create such fantastic creatures. The explanation is simple and reasonable. The early Chinese were agriculturists, dependent upon the forces of nature. As a consequence, they visualized in smiling and threatening clouds the forms of animals, and assigned to the firmament and zodiac twelve animal deities: horse, dog, bullock, monkey, serpent, dragon, rabbit, rat, tiger, hare, fowl and boar, which symbolize, also, the twelve months of the year.

Older even than the designs derived from religious and mythologic sources are the many simple geometric motives that so highly individualize Chinese rug borders. Patterns of "T," "Key," "Latch-Hook," "Swastika," "Thunder Line," and "Pearl" are the hieroglyphics of Chinese infancy. Other primitive motives are squares called Dice; circles called Coin; male and female forms called Yin and Yang; fortune-telling trigrams called Pa-Kua; and a sceptre for the Supreme Deity of Heaven.

CHINESE RUGS

Yin-Yang and Pa-Kua are combined in the design that represents the philosophic teaching of Fu Hsi, reputed creator of the six classes of written Chinese characters. Yin, the dark female, and Yang, the light male, are the source of the universe, the peace of which depends upon their exact equality. The universe itself consists of male and female elements, expressed respectively by solid and broken lines in the Pa-Kua. The elements are heaven, earth, fire, water, mist, mountains, thunder and wind. Whether seriously or with humor, Fu Hsi represents thunder as two-thirds female, and wind as two-thirds male.

Modern rug weavers who employ these geometric patterns perpetuate the earliest forms of Chinese art. Bronzes of 1000 B.C. are ornamented with the same lines and scrolls. "It has been the genius of the Chinese people to preserve unchanged the same art spirit from generation to generation. The same art motives which flourished in the earliest dynasties stirred the artists of the later dynasties. There has never been a dread of reproduction or copying, for the reason that copying has never been with them a slavish exercise. The shapes of early bronzes were reproduced in pottery and later in porcelains; the crude drawings of dragon and phœnix were beautified in painting and rugs."*

Numerous rug designs have their source in other Chinese art. Among the common subjects of Chinese painting are the eight horses of the Emperor Mu Wang (985 B.C.), whose reputation as a sportsman and lover was greatly abetted by his marvellous steeds. The rug designs that display these horses are taken from paintings. From the same source come the effective rug motives of birds and flowers, and landscape patterns of mountains, valleys, rocks and trees.

Porcelain decoration often displays the assemblage of art objects called the "Hundred Antiques." These heirlooms include gongs, bells, harps, flutes and tabors, incense-burners, boxes of books, potted

* Ferguson, John C. *Outlines of Chinese Art*, University of Chicago Press.

plants, glass flowers, jade pendants, tasselled swords, decorated screens, delicate taborets, writing equipment, chess-boards and rolls of paintings. These motives, continuously employed in Chinese rugs, old and new, add much to their interest and beauty.

When four of these designs—harp, chess-board, rolls of paintings and box of books—are used together and apart from the others, the rug which they decorate is reputed a scholar's rug, for the scholar is the man most proficient in music, games, art and literature. "The scholar's harp has a clear note."

The flower of flowers in Chinese rug decoration, and for that matter in all design, is the lotus. It is the symbol of purity because it rises bright and spotless from the "caldron of the elements," and of immortality and regeneration because it launches young flowers fully mature on life's waters. Lotus is also the special flower of the gods. Sitting or standing upon some one of its variously colored forms are the figures of Vishnu, Brahma, Buddha, Maya, mother of Buddha, and Kwan Yin.

Whether its use in art spread from Egypt to Assyria and then into Greece, and from Greece to Persia and China, or whether the Chinese forms are native or solely of Buddhistic and Indian origin cannot profitably be discussed. Its forms are natural and conventional, circular and profile, and its appearances resemble a sceptre, wand, wheel, star, medallion, and a flower with many-pointed petals—eight, for Buddha. Seed and leaf forms add other appearances and meanings.

The peony bears the same relation to the lotus that the "phœnix" bears to the dragon. In the Ch'ien L'ung period (1736-1795) it duplicated the popularity which the lotus enjoyed during the Ming period (1368-1644). Its petals are curved and its sepals pointed, which is the reverse of the lotus representation. Its meaning is wealth and respectability.

CHINESE RUGS

"In the Royal City spring is almost over;
  Tinkle, tinkle, the coaches and horsemen pass.
  We tell each other 'This is the peony season,'
  And follow with the crowd that goes to the Flower Market.
  'Cheap and dear—no uniform price.
  The cost of the plant depends on the number of blossoms.
  For the fine flower—a hundred pieces of damask:
  For the cheap flower—five bits of silk.' "*
                    —"The Flower Market," by Po Chu-I.

The flowers of the four seasons used in rug decoration are peach-blossom, emblem of spring; lotus, emblem of summer; chrysanthemum, emblem of autumn; and narcissus, emblem of winter. Other commonly employed flowers are prunus or plum-blossoms, symbols of beauty; bamboo, symbol of long life; orchid, cherry-blossom, magnolia, mallow, gardenia and poppy. The fruits that contribute to pattern are the peach, which is the "fruit of life" and of the eight Taoist immortals; the pomegranate, which signifies progeny; cherry, pear, plum and citron. The flower of the citron, a popular motive, has petals that resemble the classic position of Buddha's hand.

The strained and sometimes senseless meaning of some of the objects of Chinese decoration has its origin in similarity of sounds. The bat is the symbol of happiness because "fu," meaning "happiness," is the last syllable of the word for bat. Butterfly and great age, vase and peace, fish and abundance, jade bell and blessing are similar confusions.

As Chinese art is primarily narrative, the designs of rugs continuously reflect the rank of rugs.

"We go to the Golden Palace,
  We set out the jade cups.
  We summon the honored guests
  To enter at the Golden Gate
  And go to the Golden Hall."*

* Arthur Waley, *170 Chinese Poems*. Alfred A. Knopf.

ORIENTAL RUGS AND CARPETS

The rugs of the Golden Hall, specially woven in many shapes and sizes, contain appropriately the designs of dragon and love-pheasant, official tablets, seals and general insignia of government.

Ceremonial and kong rugs are the two important types pertaining to the houses of the wealthy classes. Ceremonial rugs are large weavings, sometimes fifteen or even eighteen feet square, which on grand occasions, such as New Year's Day, weddings, and grandfathers' anniversaries, are used to cover the stone pavements of the large central courts about which the houses are arranged, where a temporary canopy is built over them. On these special days they are used also on the floors of reception-rooms, which ordinarily are bare.

The kong is the elevated section of the Chinese reception-room, six or seven feet wide and the length of the wall, where the Chinese sit, entertain and sleep. It is an enormous couch or divan, built of brick or tile, and warmed by wood-fires kindled beneath. Père Huc describes the kong of the Tartar-Chinese inns as a "sort of furnace on which the guests eat, drink, smoke, gamble, dispute and fight." Kong rugs are four to six feet wide and seven to eleven feet long. Usually they are padded and the pads are removed when the rugs are exported.

Other rugs are covers for tables, seats and backs of chairs, which are large or small as the owner is important or of inconspicuous station. Be it understood that, in the decoration of Chinese stone monuments, earthenware, pottery and porcelain, "a servant is always smaller in size than the master, an animal smaller than a human being. This is the artists' tribute to the idealistic spirit which placed moral considerations on a higher plane than visible effects."

Every important house is equipped with travel rugs, and whatever contributes to mitigate the discomforts of travel is of consequence. Travel rugs consist of cart rugs, saddle rugs and "suit-case" rugs, all small in size but of much interest in design. Here are employed the

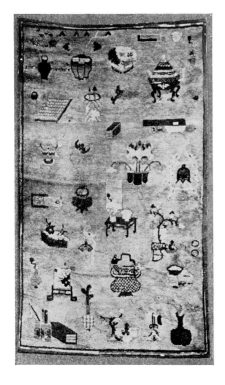

Vase and Two Rugs Decorated with the Numerous Objects of Art and Utility that Collectively Are Known as the "Hundred Antiques"

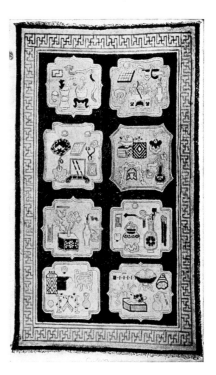

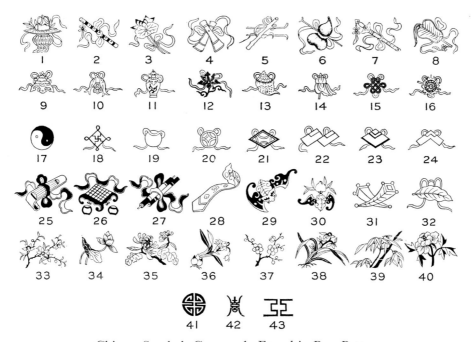

Chinese Symbols Commonly Found in Rug Patterns

Nos. 1-8. Eight Symbols of Taoism: 1. Flower Basket. 2. Flute. 3. Lotus. 4. Bamboo Clappers. 5. Bamboo Tube and Rods. 6. Crutch and Gourd. 7. Sword. 8. Fan.

Nos. 9-16. Eight Symbols of Buddhism: 9. Canopy. 10. Two Fish. 11. Urn. 12. Lotus. 13. Conch. 14. Umbrella. 15. Knot of Destiny. 16. Wheel of the Law.

Nos. 17-43. Common Symbols: 17. Tae-Keih. 18. Swastika. 19. Pearl. 20. Money. 21. Victory. 22. Books. 23. Lozenge (Painting). 24. Stone Gong. 25. Harp. 26. Chessboard. 27. Rolls of Paintings. 28. Sceptre. 29. Bat. 30. Peach and Bat. 31. Drinking Horns. 32. Artemisia Leaf. 33. Peach. 34. Lotus. 35. Chrysanthemum. 36. Narcissus. 37. Plum. 38. Orchid. 39. Bamboo. 40. Peony. 41. Shou. 42. Long Shou. 43. Fu Luck Sign.

PLATE LXIII

Ceremonial Carpet, Ch'ien L'ung Period (1736-1795). Peony pattern, employed in medallions and corner ornaments, supplemented by the flowers of the four seasons, fruit sprays and butterflies

PLATE LXIV

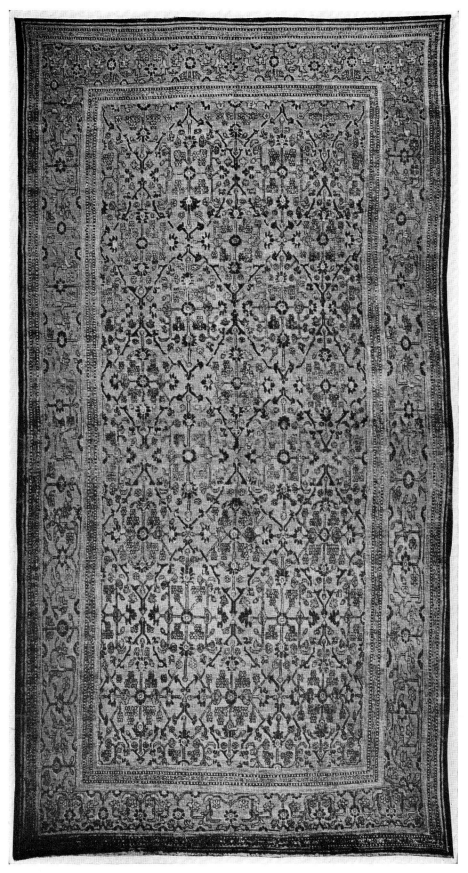

Khotan (Mongolian) Silk and Metal Rug,
Eighteenth Century

PLATE LXV

Khotan Wool Rug,
Vase-Wave Design

Khotan Wool Rug, Mountain-Disc
Pattern

Kashgar, Disc-Star-Seal
Pattern

Kashgar Mohammedan Prayer Carpet

Kashgar; Octagons, Rosettes, Scrolls

Rugs illustrated in the upper
row reflect the style of Chinese rugs during the Ch'ien
L'ung period (1736-1795).
Those below display the
geometric style of the late
Ming and early K'ang H'si
periods (1600-1700)

Kashgar; Scrolled Lattice
Pattern

PLATE LXVI

PLATE LXVII.   Incomplete Rug with Coats of Arms, Letur(?), Early Fifteenth Century

PLATE LXVIII. Rug with Wreath Pattern, Cuenca(?), Middle of
the Sixteenth Century

PLATE LXIX. Fragment with Wreath Pattern, Alcaraz,
Early Sixteenth Century

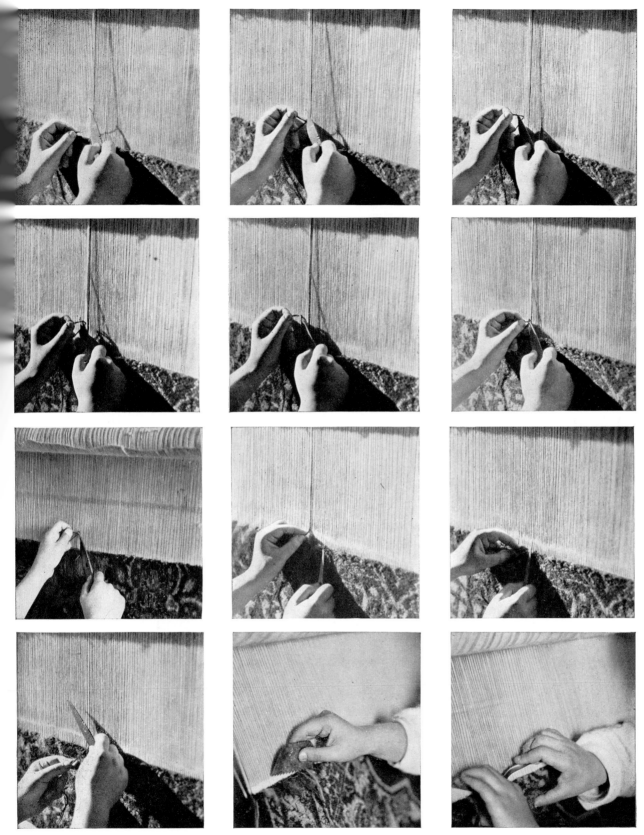

Weaving as Practised at Tabriz, Persia

(Reading left to right):

1. Lifting first warp with hooked knife for insertion of yarn.
2. Yarn inserted. End held between thumb and first finger.
3. Hook inserted below yarn end in going after second warp.
4. Raising second warp. 5. Hooking end of yarn to pull under second warp. 6. End of yarn again between thumb and first finger after passed under second warp. 7. Knot finished. 8. Knot being drawn down into place. 9. Knot in place and in line. 10. Yarn about to be cut with knife. 11. Combing out yarn ends before shearing. 12. Shearing off the nap.

PLATE LXX

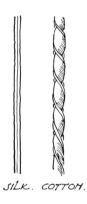

The nature of rug materials is quickly understood from visual illustration. Maximum curl and scale makes wool easiest to spin and dye. Twist and fibre tentacles serve effectively in cotton. Because of poverty of scale, hair ordinarily is used in natural color. Fineness of fibre is the success and failure of silk

HAIR. WOOL.

SILK. COTTON.

Dye Processes in the Rug Industry of India

PLATE LXXI

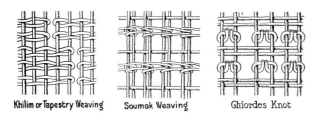

Khilim or Tapestry Weaving

Soumak Weaving

Ghiordes Knot

Right-hand Sehna Knot

Left-hand Sehna Knot

Four Varieties of Weaving. Two create a flat surface, and two a pile surface. Additionally, the Sehna knot is tied in two ways

Top row: Other aspects of Ghiordes and Sehna knots. Bottom row: Appearance of selvage and weft. Left side: Important angles of knots. Right side: Three of many variations in the appearance of knots as seen on the under side

Enlarged Paper Sketch of Design, Ruled into Minute Squares, Each Square Colored to Indicate the Color of the Knot to be Tied

Boy Weavers at Tabriz Employing Colored Paper Sketches

PLATE LXXII

Design or Talim-Writers in India

Reader, Design Sheet in Hand, Droning Instructions to Weavers

Rug Designers in India

TALIM SHEET.

The Writers' Work. Design sheet or code of instructions for the color of every knot. Executed in hieroglyphics to frustrate theft

PLATE LXXIII

Knot Counting in Persia. Computed by linear ponza, which is 2¾ inches. Maximum speed of weaving about nine hundred knots an hour, which produces nine thousand in a ten-hour day. Few weavers accomplish this result

PLATE LXXIV

Khorassan Triclinium (Three Couches). The carpet consists of three "couches"—the head and two side rugs—woven as the borders of a centre rug. Ordinarily the four rugs are woven separately, and laid side by side in similar position

PLATE LXXV

patterns of swastika, bat and shou, characters of good fortune, and the forms of animals and trees to be seen along the road. The contours of saddle rugs are irregular and their colors yellow, tan, blue and ivory, according to their period. The red military saddle cloth is decorated with "tiger" stripes, each representing, it is said, a wish for a year of good fortune to the great commander. The city of Ninghsiafu on the Huangho River is famous for saddle rugs that are a fine art. The "suit-case" rug is lined with huge pockets for extra raiment. When walking, the traveller throws it over his shoulder; when riding, over the back of his mule. At night it is a pillow.

Chinese rug design of the last three centuries is derived largely from the arts of bronze, sculpture, jade, porcelain, painting, lacquerware, embroidery, tapestry, brocade and court costume, and only negligibly from new inventive genius. Like all design, it displays, over so long a period, many styles, which means not only varied forms but varied expressions of form. These styles are composites that blend and defy scientific classification. Nevertheless, careful observation of hundreds of Chinese rugs, seemingly covering all the existing types, reveals four chief decorative modes.

The earliest styles, attributed to the years immediately succeeding 1600 and called Ming, because an earlier dating of antique rugs generally is unwarranted, consists of patterns made up of archaic and geometric forms, and of patterns that employ lotus flowers, which were in special favor. The former is the style of greatest simplicity, strength and restraint; the latter a sophisticated performance that harks back to the rugs of the T'ang dynasty. Neither type ever is assigned with authoritative confidence.

The style of 1700, called K'ang H'si, displays an unmistakable striving after beauty in the perfection of floral decoration. The flowers are highly conventionalized forms of lotus and peony, often arranged in rows—studiously correct, uncompromisingly formal, the acme of gentility and good breeding. Frequently the border is a wide, plain band of brown. Usually the texture is the finest that the Chinese thought needful in rug weaving. Unquestionably it is adequate to every requirement of the art.

The style of 1775, called Ch'ien L'ung, is the grand opulent realistic style. Here is an array of flowers that can be called by name—peach and prunus blossom, orchid, chrysanthemum, narcissus, lotus, peony, the tall stalks of bamboo and the flowers of the four seasons. Here are the magnificent disks of gorgeous bouquets and exquisite butterflies, symbols of happiness. Here are mild animals, fairy buildings and poetic landscapes. It is this realistic style, most ornate and brilliant, running a wide range of silk colors, that living weavers have simplified for modern use.

The lack of city, town, district and tribal names for these distinctive styles and equally varying weavings is due to lack of knowledge concerning the early centres of production. We know that rugs were never woven or used in the hot southern districts. Good grounds exist for believing that certain primitive types, often attributed to North China, were woven in Manchuria and Mongolia, exactly as rugs of Chinese character were and are woven in Tibet, Khotan, Kashgar, Yarkand, Turfan and generally throughout Central Asia. In all probability the old Chinese rug district was a homogeneous unit compared to the rug-weaving districts of the rest of Asia; and Chinese rug decoration a replica of cosmopolitan style, rather than a reflection of local fashion. The centres of modern rug weaving are Tientsin, Pekin, Kalgan and Chin-chou Fu in Manchuria.

Commercially, to-day, modern Chinese rugs occupy second position in the American market, crowd the manufacturers of Persia for first place, and so far distance the imports of all other varieties as to embarrass their proponents. Artistically, at their best, they satisfy the American requirement of simple beauty in floor coverings. At their worst, when simplicity has been lost and the use of American, Persian and Japanese design has resulted in the creation of more mongrel art than oriental rugs have ever hitherto exhibited, they are an abomination. When, however, one stops to consider that the new weaving is an infant in arms, it must be acknowledged a prodigy, competent to great feats and usefulness.

The advent of Chinese rugs in America was as dramatic as was their quick capture of popular approbation. As if the art had arrived from another planet, the American Art Association announced the first sale of it in 1908. One rug of rare beauty in ordinary size sold for eighteen thousand dollars. Rugs not much larger than handkerchiefs brought hundreds of dollars each. As a result of this reception, due to colors of silk, simplicity, dignity and rarity, importers immediately undertook the modern weaving.

It is no exaggeration to assert that if modern Chinese rugs had been available twenty years ago they would have commanded astonishing prices. The explanation of the collapse of prices is merely that the old Chinese rugs were as limited in number as they are exquisite in character; whereas new rugs are a voluminous competitive product. That prices are exceedingly moderate is the inevitable deduction of all who consider that Chinese weavers, working of course by hand, produce on a single loom barely three nine-by-twelve rugs a year.

The materials of Chinese rugs are the materials of all oriental rugs. Essentially they consist of the wool of sheep, hand-knotted on a foundation of strong cotton yarn. The essential dyes are the old vegetable pigments derived from indigo (blue), madder root (red), sumach (yellow), gall-nuts and acorns (brown). Modern synthetic dyes, now used advantageously for special shades of color, will soon wholly displace the vegetable pigment, unless all portents fail.

The weaving of Chinese rugs is identical in essential character with the best weaving of Persia, India and Central Asia. The knot employed is the "Persian" knot, which divides the yarn into two equal tufts and inclines it right or left. The fact that the rugs of China are not as finely woven as the rug masterpieces of Persia has nothing like the importance that is attached to it. Superfine texture, like all fine quality, has its afflictions. The Chinese have never underestimated the value of fine technique, when occasion demands it; always, however, they have had the wisdom to hold special dexterity in rug weaving to be of less account than fine artistic expression.

The fact that Chinese rugs, old and new, are in manner of construction identical with the rugs of Central Asia, and unlike the weaving of Western Asia, is proof added to the proof supplied by the poets of 800 A.D. that the Chinese did not acquire the art from the Mohammedans who appeared in China in the twelfth century.

Only two peculiarities of the weaving require special comment. The rugs are woven, not by the "ta'lem" and "vagireh" methods of Indian, Persian and Turkish rug weavers, which means vocal direction and the copying of samples, but from outlines made in ink on the strung warp and from complete paper models, the size of the rug to be woven, set up beside and behind the looms. The second peculiarity is the engraving or embossing of the design by short clipping of the yarn along the contours of the patterns. This custom secures immediately firm design outlines, which usually are desirable, and which are obtained in the other families of rugs by strong and numerous color contrasts, by shading, and in the course of time by unequal corrosion of materials.

Chinese art is at once the most provincial and most universal art, the invaluable inheritance of all races because it expresses a truly great culture. Distributed broadcast from earliest times by trade, travel, migration and particularly by the Mongolian conquest and domination of Asia in the thirteenth and fourteenth centuries, it influenced beneficently the art of all Asia. Culturally, it converted the inhabitants of Tibet and East Turkestan into subject peoples. It contributed immeasurably to the rug art of Persia, found copyists among the weavers of Turkey, and journeyed into Spain on the rugs of the Moors.

SYMBOLIC DESIGNS IN CHINESE RUGS

Religious Designs:

Dragon—Symbol of God.

Kwan-Yin—Goddess or God of Mercy (Buddhist).

Eight Symbols of Buddhism—Lotus Flower, Covered Vase, Conch Shell, Two Fish, Umbrella, Canopy, Bell or Wheel of the Law, Endless Knot.

Seven Gems of the Universal Monarch (Buddha)—White Elephant, Bundle of Jewel Rods, Treasurer, Gold Wheel, General, Lovely Women, Horse.

Eight Symbols of the Taoist Immortals—Crutch and Gourd, Bamboo Clappers, Fan, Sword, Flower Basket, Flute, Lotus Seed-Pod, Bamboo Tube and Rods.

Sacred Mountain—First Manifestation of Life.

Waves of Eternity.

Cloud-Bands—Symbol of Deity.

Sceptre of Supreme Deity—"Good Wishes."

Philosophic Designs:

Tae-Keih or Yang and Yin—Male and Female, two curved cells within a circle.

Eight Trigrams—Heaven, Earth, Fire, Water, Mist, Mountain, Thunder and Wind.

Mythologic Designs:

Animal Gods of the Zodiac, and Symbols of the Twelve Months: Tiger, Rabbit, Dragon, Serpent, Horse, Hare, Monkey, Fowl, Dog, Wild Boar, Rat, Bullock. Occasional substitutes: Elephant, Bull, Cow, Mule, Sheep.

Ky-lin—Fabulous animal of good omen, partly deer and partly dragon. Appears on the birth of sages.

Lion—Authority.

Fu-Dog—Happy Lion-Dog.

Horse—Nobility, Strength.

Carp—Perseverance.

Fish—Abundance.

Imperial Designs:

Dragon—Symbol of the Emperor.

Canopy—Symbol of Sovereignty.

"Phœnix" or Love-Pheasant—Symbol of the Empress. "Goodness."

Tablets—Oblong with square corners.

Seals—Jade with dragon handle.

Umbrella—Official authority.

Art Designs:

Hundred Antiques:

    Furniture—Tables, Stools, Screens, Baskets, Books; Art Objects—Vases,

Jades, Glassware, Rolls of Paintings; Musical Instruments—Bell, String and Wind varieties.

Arms—Swords, Spears, Axes.

Writing Equipments—Brushes, Ink-Cake, Stand, Slab.

Incense-Burning Sets—Vase, Rods, Burner, Cup.

Eight Precious Things:

Pearl—Charm against Fire and Flood.

Rhombus—Symbol of Victory.

Lozenge—Representation of Painting.

Coin—Wealth.

Artemesia Leaf—Dignity.

Pair Horn Cups—Disclose Poison.

Jade Gong—Rung by Those Desiring Justice.

Two Books—Learning.

Scholars' Designs:

"Four Fine Arts"—

Harp.

Chess-Board.

Box of Books.

Rolls of Paintings.

Other Literary Designs:

Cups for Chessmen.

Box of Dominoes.

Snuff-Bottle.

Flower Designs:

Flowers of the Twelve Months: Prunus, Peach-Blossom, Tree Peony, Double Cherry-Blossom, Magnolia, Pomegranate, Lotus, Pear, Mallow, Chrysanthemum, Gardenia and Poppy.

Flowers of the Four Seasons: Peony—Spring; Lotus—Summer; Chrysanthemum—Autumn; Narcissus or Prunus, called "Hawthorn"—Winter.

Fragrant Fingers of Buddha: Finger of citron-flower. The petals resemble Buddha's hand with index and little finger pointing upward.

Lotus—Purity.

Peony—Riches and Prosperity.

Peach-Blossom—Illicit Love and Ill Success.

Chrysanthemum—Fidelity and Constancy.

Good Fortune Designs:

Swastika—Ten Thousand Ages of Good Luck.

Coin—Wealth.

Bat—Happiness.

Fu—Happiness.

Five Bats—Five Blessings: Happiness, Riches, Peace, Offspring, Long Life.

Sceptre, Bar of Silver, Writing-Brush—Success.

CHINESE RUGS

Fragrant Fingers of Buddha, Peach and Pomegranate—Happiness, Long Life, Male Issue.

Butterfly—Happiness and Love.

Two Fish—Married Happiness.

Mandarin Ducks—Conjugal Fidelity.

Conch Shell—Safe Ocean Voyage.

Shou
Crane
Stag
Pine } Longevity.
Peach
Peach-Tree
Three Plums

Mushroom—Immortality.

Stream of Water—Eternity.

Note: Sacred Objects are bound with ribbons.

CHINESE DYNASTIES

Shang Dynasty	1766-1122 B.C.
Chou Dynasty—Bronze Period	1122-255 B.C.
Chin Dynasty	255-206 B.C.
Han Dynasty—Sculpture Period	206 B.C.-220 A.D.
Wei Dynasty	220-265 A.D.
The Six Dynasties—Dark Ages	265-618 A.D.
T'ang Dynasty—Poetry Period	618-906 A.D.
The Five Dynasties—Culture Period	906-960 A.D.
Sung Dynasty—Finest Paintings	960-1280 A.D.
Yuan Dynasty (Mongolian)	1280-1368 A.D.
Ming Dynasty—Period of Reproduction	1368-1644 A.D.
Ch'ing Dynasty (Manchu)—Rugs and Porcelains	1644-1911 A.D.
K'ang H'si	1661-1723 A.D.
Yung Ch'eng	1723-1736 A.D.
Ch'ien L'ung	1736-1795 A.D.
Chia Ch'ing	1795-1820 A.D.
Tao Kuang	1820-1850 A.D.
Hsien Feng	1850-1862 A.D.
T'ung Chih	1862-1875 A.D.
Kuang Hsu	1875-1909 A.D.
Shin Tung	1909-1912 A.D.

Note: The T'ang dynasty was the period of earliest known rugs. Existing rugs date from the Ming dynasty.

CHAPTER X

CHINESE TURKESTAN RUGS

CHINESE Turkestan rugs are the weavings of the cities of Khotan, Kashgar, Yarkand, Turfan, and of the nomad tribes of Kirghiz, and not the weavings of the world-famous Samarkand, as they have so long been called. The latter dazzling name came probably to be applied to them quite as the name Bokhara to the rugs of Western Turkestan, because of overtowering fame. After Tamurlane had completed his private collection of twenty-seven pilfered crowns, the court and the rich inhabitants of Samarkand possessed together probably an unsurpassable rug collection. So far as present knowledge reaches, the entire art has been lost, and with its going Samarkand turned its interest wholly to quantity production of muslin and silk.

Chinese Turkestan is located on one of the lower terraces of the great central plateau northwest of Tibet. This territory, administered by Chinese officials from a capital twenty-two hundred miles west of Pekin, has been a possession of China for over two thousand years. The people inhabiting the eastern section are pure Chinese. The northern stock is Mongolian, the western Turkish, the southwestern Aryan, and the southern Tibetan. The universal language is Jagatai Turkish.

222

CHINESE TURKESTAN RUGS

As a group, the people are tame and submissive. "Down any bazaar in Kashgar, Yarkand, and Khotan, you and I, each armed with but a shillalah, might victoriously drive the herded, happy people, provided always that there chanced not to be within the herd some Kirghiz, mountain Afghan or nomad Turkoman." "Apathetic oasis dwellers," they have been called, "without taste for hard labor or mental discipline." Their good qualities are hospitality, love of home and of festivals. Originally worshippers of idols, and then ardent Buddhists, they became Sunni Mohammedans in the tenth century, and builders of mosques on the sites of old Buddhist shrines.

The population of one and one-half million people is both settled and nomad. The former occupy such ancient mud-walled cities as Kashgar, Yarkand, Khotan and Turfan, each containing from fifty to one hundred and fifty thousand people. In addition to rugs, Kashgar and Turfan produce cotton fabrics, Yarkand and Khotan silks and felts, and Khotan important jade. Each city is the centre of an oasis containing fine orchards and districts of rich cultivation. The leading nomads are the Kirghiz, fifty thousand in number, who regard themselves as the eastern branch of the Kazak tribes of the southern Caucasus. One hundred thousand shepherds, more or less, raise and tend sheep and goats beyond number.

Presumably from these cities, plains and deserts, at a very early time, the nomad process of rug weaving was transported to China. At some later period, as if in payment of the indebtedness, China sent her art of design and color into Turkestan. How well the province invested the patrimony is obvious; for "Samarkand" rugs follow like children the Chinese art of rug decoration. They repeat the primitive geometric designs with secondary decoration of flowers. They progress by natural stages to design of conventionalized flowers and fruits, all very artificial and formal. Finally, at the stage of profuseness, they appropriate the designs of realism—vases, flowers of the seasons, fruits of meaning, butterflies and ornate medallions. This progression is Ming, K'ang H'si and Ch'ien L'ung, in Chinese rugs. Naturally, the proximity of Persia tended to stimulate the production of more ornate rugs. Six border stripes, which is double the Chinese number, are not uncommon. But the stolid conservatism of the weavers was not greatly impressed by the elaborating disposition of the talented western neighbor.

Specifically the rugs of Chinese Turkestan, now seldom encountered in our markets and rarely mentioned by travellers, are much harder to describe and classify than their creators, "The Maids of Turkestan":

> "Straight and slender-waisted are the maids of Kashgar.
> Short, with sack-like figures, are the maids of Yangi Hissar.
> A goitre above and fat below are the maids of Yarkand.
> Arranging apples on saucers are the maids of Khotan-Ilchi."

Kashgar and Yarkand rugs, like the rugs of the neighbor cities of Ghiordes and Kula in Asia Minor, are attributed more or less arbitrarily. Rugs showing most Persian character are assigned to Kashgar because Yarkand comparatively is an aloof city on the caravan way to India. Rugs of both cities use for color Chinese red, blue and yellow, in strong contrast. Probably five out of ten examples are dominantly red, two blue, one yellow and one ivory. The most popular design consists of three blue medallions, ornamented with stiff flowers, woven tandem on a plain red field. Corner areas are commonly latch-hook; borders consist of wave, mountain and cloud motives separated by T, key and swastika stripes. Occasionally a prayer rug of Mohammedan design is secured in these cities, but, correctly or otherwise, the reputation for prayer rugs is monopolized by Lhassa.

Khotan rugs of the ancient vintage, with geometric blocked design, numerous borders, half-Chinese and half-Persian, often executed in silk and metal thread, are the outstanding jewels of the Chinese Turkestan family. According to Chinese tradition, they were woven for the Imperial Palace in Pekin. That their creation was inspired by the silk and metal rugs of Persia, now called Polonaise, seems obvious. Fame of Khotan, however, attaches mostly to jade and silk. Here, according to legend, two Persian monks in the employ of Justinian, *Basileus* of the Byzantine Empire, secured and carried away in hollow bamboo staffs, at the risk of their lives, the precious eggs of the silkworm which gave birth to the silk industry in Europe.

"Khotan silk rugs," writes Miss Ella Sykes, in *Through Deserts and Oases of Central Asia*, "are highly prized and very difficult to obtain. One belonging to our host had pale yellow coloring. The best wool rug that I inspected had a pattern consisting of a series of panels each containing Chinese vases and swastikas. The favorite design consists of rows of pots with stiffly protruding flowers. Chinese Turkestan has evolved no art of its own. Its art is Chinese, Indian and Persian."

Mr. C. P. Skrine, British Consul-General in Chinese Turkestan 1922-1924, places us under deep obligation for two intelligent paragraphs about rugs, contained in *Chinese Central Asia*: "It must be confessed that Chinese Turkestan is poor in arts and crafts compared to Persia, Turkey and Kashmir. The reason is not far to seek. In these latter countries the progressive decay of taste and craftsmanship which marked the nineteenth century has been delayed and in some cases arrested by the commercial enterprise of the West. No such force has acted in Chinese Turkestan, with the result that the carpet-weaving industry of Yurungkash, Lop and other villages in the Khotan district is hopelessly debased. Not only are the natural dyes, used until thirty years ago, forgotten, but the beautiful old flower patterns are seldom used, being replaced by unspeakably hideous modern Chinese designs of mauve tigers and magenta tea-pots.

"Ninety-five per cent of the specimens brought us were in bad condition, the pile in many places worn right away, and we acquired only three of the genuine old Khotan flower-pattern rugs. The best example, which measures eight feet by five feet, is a fine specimen of the work of a hundred years or more ago. Its design is a most interesting mixture of Persia and China. The whole treatment, conventional flowers symmetrically arranged on a monochrome ground and enclosed in a broad-banded border, is unmistakably Persian; and the five-rose *motif*, consisting of a straight stalk with three roses on one side and two on the other, though not, so far as I know of, found in Persian or Turkish carpets, still belongs to the same genre. But many of the details are Chinese, such as the wave and key patterns in the border, and the fleur-de-lis interspersed in symmetrical groups of four among the roses. There could be no more striking illustration of the cultural mingling of East and West."

Khotan silk rugs have a superior archaic character of pattern and a mellow scheme of color that makes them enviable possessions. They are silk rugs of strength when compared with Polonaise rugs, which are silk rugs of utmost sweetness.

Kirghiz rugs, the Kazak rugs of Chinese Turkestan, are country-bred, vigorous and coarse. Their dominant color is Chinese red, relieved by blue and yellow. The design in greatest favor is an obvious simplification of the Persian-garden pattern, four or more plots or panels each decorated with highly conventionalized flower motives. The finest examples are said to come from the regions about Karshi and Tchardjui, south of Samarkand, which is the western terminus of Kirghiz wanderings.

Kirghiz means forty maidens "who dipped their fingers in a foaming river and gave birth to the nation." In addition to rugs the descendants of these maidens fabricate quantities of muslin and silk velvets. "Certainly a good wife must be above rubies to a Kirghiz. She looks after the flocks, herds, does all the milking, makes cream, curds, cheese and koumiss, the fermented milk of mares, cools the food, fashions clothes for herself and her family and rears the children. Besides all this she is skilled in weaving felts, embroideries and coarse but pleasing carpets."

CHAPTER XI

RUGS OF SPAIN

BY MAURICE S. DIMAND

WITH the conquest of Spain in 710 Muslim civilization obtained a strong foothold in Western Europe. When the Umayyad rulers of the Near East were defeated by their enemies, the Abbasids, Abd al-Rahman fled to Spain, where he founded the Western Caliphate. The city of Cordova, chosen the capital and residence of the Spanish Umayyads, rivaled Bagdad, the eastern city of the caliphs. In 786 Abd al-Rahman began the construction of the Great Mosque, with its forest of pillars and splendid interior decoration. It was further embellished by Hisham I, who completed the mosque and built a minaret. The mosque was greatly enlarged under the learned and scholarly caliph al-Hakim II—Mustansir (961–976), the son of Abd al-Rahman III (912–961). This ruler erected also a magnificent palace at Madinat al-Zahra, near Cordova.

Both the mosque of Cordova and the palace were richly decorated with cut-marble slabs. The ornament, which consists chiefly of semifloral scrolls, differs radically from contemporary Abbasid ornament of the Muslim East. The beautiful marble plaques of the Cordova mosque, preserved at each side of the mihrab (prayer niche), are decorated with palmette scrolls and trees of life. These masterpieces of Hispano-Moresque sculpture show several characteristic features, among them the absence of solid surfaces. The motives are dissected into small thin scrolls and palmettes, which together form a lace-like pattern.

In the eleventh century Muslim Spain was ruled by a number of petty Berber dynasties, known as *Reyes de Taifas*, "Party Kings." Although Cordova remained the chief art center, some of the provincial cities had a prominent part in the development of Hispano-Moresque art. An important monument of the eleventh century is the palace of Aljaferia at Saragossa erected by the ruler Abu Ja'far Muktadir (1046–81). The palace had a rich stone and stucco decoration, based on the Cordova style, but showing new stylistic features developed in Muslim Spain. Palmettes have now entirely replaced acanthus motives and are stylized in a manner peculiar to Spain. The carving is more deeply undercut than in the tenth century, exaggerating the decorative effect of light and dark.

In 1090 under the Berber dynasty of Almoravides, Muslim Spain was combined with Morocco into one empire. In the twelfth century the civilization and arts of Andalusia invaded the Maghrib (Moorish North Africa) where, in such cities as Marrakesh (the capital of the empire), Fez and Tlemcen, splendid monuments were erected. In the second half of the twelfth century, the Almohades favored a comparatively simple style of architecture and in decoration, preferred the East Islamic arabesques to the exuberant floral scrollwork of Spain.

The political decline of Western Islam began about 1235 with the gradual reconquest of Spain by the Christians. The only great dynasty able to hold out against the Christians was that of the Nasrids of Granada, who revived the old splendor of Muslim Spain. The most magnificent example of fourteenth-century Moorish of Spain is the Alhambra at Granada. Here a rich and elaborate stucco decoration covers the walls and arches of the rooms and courts. The principal ornament consists of geometrical interlacings and arabesques of both the Spanish and the Moorish type. The intricacy of the ornament is further enhanced by the rich polychromy of white, blue, red and gold. This type of painted stucco decoration spread to other parts of Spain and is characteristic of the so-called Mudejar style. It appears in the Alcazar of Seville, the Mudejar chapel of the Cordova mosque and several buildings of Toledo.

Under the Umayyad rulers of Spain, arts and crafts achieved a high degree of perfection. Famous are the carved ivory boxes, round or rectangular, often inscribed with the names of the rulers or their court officials. The main decoration consists of palmette scrolls into which occasionally animals and birds are introduced. Some of the boxes, such as the one in the Louvre dated 968, and another in the Victoria and Albert Museum dated 970, are decorated with court scenes with entertainers and hunters, derived from the Fatimid art of Egypt. In the eleventh century the Umayyad style of ivory carving became even more elaborate, and the compositions frequently overcrowded. Among the famous eleventh-century pieces is the jewel casket of the queen Blanca, dated 1004/5, and preserved in the cathedral of Pamplona.

The development of the ceramic art of Spain is based to a great extent on the achievements of the potters of Syria and Mesopotamia. The Arabs introduced into Spain important ceramic techniques, such as luster painting, invented in Mesopotamia in the eighth or ninth century. Ceramics of the tenth century produced at Cordova have either a painted polychrome decoration of birds and floral motives or a lustered decoration.

An important ceramic center of Moorish Spain during the thirteenth and fourteenth centuries was Paterna, near Valencia. The typical Paterna ware has a painted decoration of animals, birds and human figures in green and brown, or purple manganese on a white ground. In the fourteenth and the beginning of the fifteenth century, the potters of Malaga and Granada excelled in the production of large vases, tiles and bowls with a very fine decoration in gold luster often combined with blue. Well known are the ovoid "Alhambra vases" with wing handles, decorated with arabesques, Arabic inscriptions and stylized animals.

Another important ceramic center of Spain from the fourteenth through the sixteenth century was Manises in the province of Valencia. To the beginning of the fifteenth century we can assign lusterware which perpetuates the traditions of the Malaga school. Albarelli, plates and vases are decorated with arabesques, palmettes and geometrical interlacings in brown luster and blue. This type of lusterware was made also for Christian families, as several pieces bear coats of arms.

During the first half of the fifteenth century Gothic elements were gradually introduced into patterns of the Valencia lusterware. A popular type shows a design of an over-all pattern of rosette blossoms on a dotted background upon which are frequently placed stylized animals and Gothic inscriptions in blue. To the period between 1450 and 1465 can be attributed a group of lustered plates and bowls with a large and bold design of animals and birds on a background of scrollwork and large palmettes. In the second half of the fifteenth century lustered plates and vases are usually decorated with Gothic vine scrolls and European coats of arms.

In the sixteenth century the manufacture of ceramics at Manises passed gradually into Christian hands. The traditional Moorish design degenerated into a crude pattern frequently showing European influence.

The Arab conquest of Spain introduced the art of weaving fine silk fabrics. Spanish textiles were mentioned in papal inventories as early as the ninth century. Idrizi, the Arab historian (1099–1154) recorded that there were eight hundred looms at Almeria in Andalusia for the weaving of costly silk stuffs. Fine textiles were also woven in

Murcia, Seville, Granada and Malaga. A fabric in the Royal Academy of History at Madrid, decorated with a tapestry-woven band with octagons containing geometrically stylized animals, birds and human figures in blue and red, shows the influence of Arabic textiles of Egypt. It is inscribed with the name of Hisham II, Caliph of Cordova (976–1009).

An important group of Andalusian textiles of the eleventh to the twelfth century is characterized by a bold pattern of figures, birds and animals, usually in red, green and gold. Some of them show the legendary lion-strangler or pair of sphinxes, which are represented in various collections of Spain, Europe and America. Fine brocades were made in the twelfth and thirteenth centuries. In this group we find pairs of griffins or birds in circular medallions, usually in red brown, cream white and gold. Another type of thirteenth-century brocade has a geometrical pattern, in which gold threads are profusely used. Some of these come from the cope of Don Felipe (d. 1274), now in the Archaeological Museum of Madrid, while other gold brocades belonged to the cope of Saint Valerius, preserved in the cathedral at Lérida.

Fourteenth- and fifteenth-century textiles of Spain, probably woven in Granada, are decorated in the so-called Alhambra style. The rich ornament consists of interlaced bands, polygons, arabesques and inscriptions in vivid colors. This Hispano-Moresque style continued until well into the sixteenth century and was copied by weavers of Morocco.

The rug industry of Spain goes back to an early period. According to literary sources, twelfth-century rugs, woven in Chinchilla (Tantaliya), province of Murcia, were exported to foreign countries, including Egypt. Technically, Spanish rugs differ from those of the Near East. While the Persian Sehna and the Turkish Ghiordes knots are tied over two warps, the Spanish knot is tied on a single warp. The Spanish knot is also found in a number of rug fragments found in Central Asia which are dated from about the second to the sixth century of our era. A number of fragments found in Egypt at Fustat, the old Cairo, show not only the Spanish knot but also ornamental features which point to Spain as the country of origin. Some fragments in the Textile Museum in Washington, D. C., the Metropolitan Museum of Art and the Arab Museum, Cairo, are decorated with Kufic inscriptions, which recall early Saljuk rugs from Konia in Asia Minor.

As to the origin of Spanish rugs, opinions are divided. It is probable that they were introduced from the Near East, possibly via Egypt, where a modified version of pile rugs was produced in the Coptic era. The knots of these "Coptic" rugs were not tied individually but, as stated previously, produced by cutting of loops. The rug industry of Spain was a flourishing industry even before the twelfth century. In the thirteenth century it was in full swing and we have a report from the year 1255 which tells us that, at the wedding of Doña Leonor of Castille to King Edward I, a great display of Spanish carpets was evident in the streets of London.

From the second half of the thirteenth century Christian rule was gradually established in Spain. Moorish craftsmen continued to work for their Christian masters, producing fine carpets. This work, which is typical of Spain, is generally known as Mudejar, in which Moorish and Western elements are often combined into a new style. Besides looms already known, such as Chinchilla, new weaving centers were established under the Christian rule. One of them was Litur or Letur; the other, even more famous, was the city of Alcaraz. Letur is usually identified as the production center of heraldic rugs with coats of arms, which go back to the middle of the fourteenth century. We have literary evidence that Pope John XXII (1315–1334) bought rugs with coats of arms for his palace at Avignon. Judging from a fresco in the Avignon palace, there were also carpets without coats of arms, showing an over-all pattern of small octagons, containing stars and other motives. To the fourteenth century can be attributed the famous synagogue carpet in Berlin, decorated with an elaborate candelabrum whose arms end in "Thora" shrines. The border of pseudo-Kufic writing recalls some of the Saljuk rugs from Konia. Such decorative Kufic borders are a characteristic feature of fifteenth-century heraldic rugs of Spain.

Spanish rugs with coats of arms form an important group of Mudejar rugs, which were made to the order of the Royal House or prominent Spanish families such as that of Admiral Enriquez. The coats of arms are placed upon a field ornamented with a repeat pattern of small octagons enclosing geometrical motives, birds, animals and human figures, angular in design and knotted in vivid colors. The borders are divided into several bands of geometrical design, Kufic inscriptions, sometimes legible, and stylized figures. Some of the rugs show the coat of arms of Castille and Aragon. They were probably ordered by Maria de Castilla, who married Alfonso of Aragon in 1415 and became Queen in 1416. Three of these rugs, in the Hispanic Society of America, Detroit Institute of Art and the Textile Museum at Washington, D. C., come from the convent of Santa Isabel de Los Reyes at Toledo.

Another group of heraldic rugs bears the coat of arms of Admiral Enriquez and comes from the convent of Santa Clara at Palencia. To this group belong rugs in Berlin, the Williams collection in Philadelphia, the Hispanic Society and the Metropolitan Museum of Art. We have records that Juana de Mendoza left to the monastery at Palencia two large rugs with her coat of arms and those of her husband, Alfonso Enriquez.

A typical Moorish group of Spanish rugs shows a colorful pattern of rectangular fields with many pointed stars within octagons. These rugs are usually attributed to the looms of Alcaraz, which are often mentioned in literary sources. There is a letter of Queen Isabel of

234

RUGS OF SPAIN

Castille to the city of Alcaraz, thanking for a gift of "alfombras," which indicates that its rug industry was fully developed in the second half of the fifteenth century. The rugs with the star pattern are probably contemporary with the heraldic rugs and may be dated to the first half of the fifteenth century.

The patterns of this group of rugs with rectangular fields were well known in the Near East since earliest times, and were derived from mosaic and stone pavement of the Byzantine period. The rectangular division of the field was common in early Anatolian rugs and fifteenth-century Timurid rugs of Persia. There is no doubt that they served as prototypes for the geometrical Spanish rugs made in Alcaraz. This is particularly evident in the second variety of rugs with octagonal patterns in which the star motive was replaced by octagons with eight palmettes and a small central star. The pattern of these rugs, particularly of the one in the Count Welczek collection, is related to the Turkish Holbein rugs, which were imported into Spain. These Spanish rugs vary in size from three rectangles to eighteen, as in the rug of the Cleveland Museum. The latter, together with several others, came from the convent of Santa Ursula at Guadalajara, and could be dated to about the middle of the fifteenth century.

As in other Spanish arts and crafts, Gothic elements were introduced by Moorish rug weavers of the second half of the fifteenth century. An interesting group of Mudejar rugs, made probably in Alcaraz, shows a mixture of Gothic and Moorish ornament. The red field of these rugs, as the one in the Textile Museum in Washington, D. C., has an over-all pattern of large ogivals enclosing large dark blue palmettes with inner small dark-green palmettes. In the dark blue border we see degenerated Kufic letters with angular lions and tree motives in various colors.

In the sixteenth century the Moorish weavers continued to work for their Christian masters, introducing Renaissance ornament or

235

copying the design of Turkish carpets. Alcaraz continued to be a center of importance but in addition other places, particularly Cuenca, became famous for its carpets. An interesting design of sixteenth-century Spanish rugs shows a wreath pattern with "Renaissance" arabesques in the field. A characteristic feature of these rugs is the use of two colors only, such as blue-green on tan, dark green on light green, or green on a red ground. In several rugs of this group, the Renaissance character of the decoration, particularly in the border, is quite apparent. The design of these borders, as seen in a rug of the Ballard collection of the Metropolitan Museum, shows a "Renaissance" arabesque combined with bodies of phoenixes and ending in dragons' heads. Such rugs show very little of their Moorish origin and it is probable that Christian weavers of Cuenca were responsible for the production of this type of Spanish rugs. Sometimes true rug patterns were abandoned by Spanish weavers in favor of textile design. A number of such sixteenth-century rugs show an over-all pattern in two colors derived from Italian velvets and brocades, chiefly of the Venetian variety.

During the sixteenth and seventeenth centuries, oriental rugs, particularly Turkish ones of the Ushak variety, were imported to Europe in quantities. Ushak rugs were quite popular in Spain and influenced the design of rugs produced by weavers of Cuenca. The so-called Lotto rugs with angular arabesques in yellow on red ground were most frequently imitated by Spanish weavers, who, however, changed the color scheme, preferring blue arabesques on a golden-yellow ground. Such rugs, which can be seen in Spanish and American collections, are usually dated to the middle of the seventeenth century.

Some of the Spanish rugs of the seventeenth and eighteenth centuries adopted not only the Turkish design but also the Turkish Ghiordes knot. The rugs made in Cuenca and Valencia during the eighteenth century (there are several dated examples), follow either the oriental or Western tradition. The design, however, is inferior to that of sixteenth- and seventeenth-century rugs.

In the nineteenth century, rugs were made in the district of Alpujarra, south of Granada. These rugs, which were imported to America, are not knotted but show a looped surface known from the textiles of the Coptic period. The floral and animal design, often in bright colors, is based on traditional motives but treated broadly in conformity with the folk character of these rugs.

CHAPTER XII

FIBRES AND DYES

ACCORDING to the highest authority, the substance of things hoped for is faith. Not wool, nor hair, nor cotton, nor silk, but faith, therefore, is the substance of oriental rugs for such as desire them. The Mohammedan chuckles and quotes a proverb: "Have faith in Allah, but when the wind becomes a tempest, cast anchors astern." In the tempest of oriental-rug temptations that continually beset us, let us with the Mohammedan retain our faith, but add understanding; for knowledge of materials is essential to good judgment in rugs.

The only material essential to the creation of oriental rugs is wool, product of the great Asiatic wool-belt that extends from Smyrna to Pekin, along the fortieth degree of latitude. Mountains rising to vast heights, above and below this latitude, notably in the Caucasus and in Persia, greatly increase the width of the belt and improve the quality of the wool product, for mountain wool is best. High altitude means fine wool and inferior art; low altitude inferior wool and the superior art of cities. Only high and low, the old extremes, combined, produce rug masterpieces, and only transportation of wool by caravan, motor and ship extends the region of rug weaving beyond the confines of the wool-belt.

Wool, that millions of people wear and tread without contingent enlightenment, is a member of the Hair Family, from which it is

238

estranged by unsocial refinement of character. To be sure, wool maintains a speaking acquaintance with fine varieties of hair, some of which slightly resemble it; but with coarse hairs, such as the bristles of swine and the spines of hedgehog, it has nothing in common. The coarsest fibres of wool indulge a waist-line of only one two-hundred-and-seventy-fifth part of an inch, which permits some six thousand members of the class to stand with comfort in every square inch of surface, both of sheep and of rugs. This, be it understood, is a gathering of common wool fibre, on common sheep and in common rugs. When the assembly consists wholly of refined members, each with girth of only one three-thousandth part of an inch, one hundred thousand occupy the space that can be covered by the thumb.

Extreme refinement almost invariably indulges in furbelows. In this instance curls and plaits, the latter always called scales, which magnified resemble the rough bark of trees, constitute the proof of worldliness. Fondness for curls sometimes carries wool's indulgence to an enviable thirty kinks to the inch, and propensity for plaits or scales to the almost incredible grandeur of three thousand to the same measure.

Curl here serves for once a practical purpose. It so far facilitates spinning as almost to beget yarn without manual aid, and in becoming the amalgam of yarn, it attains its highest ambition. Plait or scale renders an equally valuable service in making room and accommodation for neighbor fibre, which results in matting and compactness, and in giving access to dye, which otherwise would find no entrance. Because of lack of curl and scale, to an amount worthy of mention, hair is not easy to spin and is difficult to dye. As a result, practically all hair used in oriental rugs is used as nature dyed it.

Truly, while it lasts, it is a fine life that wool leads, its tiny cells dependent for existence upon a coat of fat, and its fat-coat for protection upon a thin skin, called yolk, that peels off at the slightest touch of tepid water. Still, what amazing desire to live delicate wool displays, that withstands hammering thrusts which only granite and concrete find supportable, and then amazingly belies its reputation by melting away, seemingly without provocation, because of mistreatment or poverty. Next to art, the most important ingredient of oriental rugs, infinitely outranking dye and weaving, is wool.

Quality depends upon many factors. Sheep differ greatly in variety, age, health and cleanliness; and areas of the earth's surface from which they derive their subsistence differ in altitude, climate, seasonal changes and pasturage; all of which creates vast differences in the wool of rugs. Even the section of the body from which the wool is derived means much to the rug purchaser. The finest wool is obtained from face, shoulders and sides, where the flesh is richest. Generally two hundred grades are considered sufficient to measure ordinary wool differences, but no less than three hundred grades meet the requirements of scientific accuracy, as tested and proved by the chemist.

Ancestry and variety of oriental sheep are seemingly unexplored subjects. Neither Herodotus, the earliest authority, nor modern naturalists dispense much information. Wild sheep with coats of hair and short tails are only presumed to be the ancestors of the almost infinite varieties of domesticated sheep, and wool and long tails to be the results of taming. Herodotus says: "There are two kinds of sheep worthy of admiration, which are seen only in Asia. One kind has tails not less than three cubits in length [four and one-half feet] which, if suffered to trail, would ulcerate by the tails rubbing on the ground. But every shepherd knows enough of the carpenter's art to prevent this, for they make little carts and fasten them under the tails, binding the tail of each separate sheep to a separate cart. The other kinds of sheep have broad tails, even to a cubit in breadth [one and one-half feet]."

Marco Polo saw sheep on the plains between Kerman and the Persian Gulf "equal to the ass in size, with long and thick tails, weighing thirty pounds and upwards, which are fat and excellent to eat." Three hundred years ago, Adam Olearius remarked that "Persian sheep are but lean because the tail draws all the fat out of them. It hangs in great gobbets like locks of wool, which much hinders them from running and leaping." He observed also that "the sheep of the Tartars of Usbeque have a grayish long wool, curling at the ends into little white and close knots like pearls, which make a pretty show, whence it comes that their fleece is more esteemed than their flesh, inasmuch as this kind of fur is the most precious of any used in Persia next to sables. They are very tenderly kept and for the most part in the shade; and when they are obliged to bring them abroad, they cover them as they do horses. These sheep have as little tails as ours."

Fat-tail sheep are the physical ancestors of oriental rugs, and extra long and short tail varieties inconsequential relatives. The most acclaimed Persian sheep, all or nearly all broadtails, are the breeds known as Bakhtiari, Kurd and Khorassan. The first are large, big-eyed, bony-faced animals, covered with wool of excellent quality. Their wool is less esteemed, however, than that from the slightly smaller animal of the Kurds. Compared to these varieties, Khorassan sheep are pigmies, and their clip far less durable, largely because, until recently, it has been sheared twice a year and in consequence lacks sufficient length of fibre to create strong yarn. Fat-tail sheep are the dominant rug variety also of India, Turkey and Turkestan. The tail is considered a great table delicacy, comparison being continually made to oysters and bacon.

Age means as much to wool quality as variety. Extremely fine wool, commonly called lamb's wool, is sheared at the eighth month. Wool unshorn until the twelfth or fourteenth month is, on the basis of age, the next finest grade. Subsequent shearings produce poorer and poorer grades, until the end is reached in the fleece of dead sheep, which is known as slaughter-house wool.

ORIENTAL RUGS AND CARPETS

Although the chemist is the sole master of wool grades, finger-tips applied lightly to the ends of rug fibre will register pronounced differences in substance. The pile of an old Tekka or Kurd rug creates the sensation of needles having considerable sharpness, if the pile is short. This is superlatively fine rug wool, expensive and infinitely enduring through sturdiness of individual member. By comparison, the fibre of many old Turkish and Chinese rugs evokes a mushy, spongy sensation. Resistance to wear is here attained by compensatory matting of fibre.

But surely experts do not judge wool quality through the fingers, as the blind read? No, except as confirmation of facts learned from instruction and experience. They ask always the source of wool, about which they are most particular, and then ask about clips and tests. In examining a rug they do not err through the assumption that each one is woven of wool of a single grade. Each rug, old and new alike, contains many grades, which for the best factory products are carefully selected: one for length, another for strength, another for brilliance and softness, all carefully blended into the yarn, which is doubled, tripled and quadrupled.

Of the three million seven hundred and fifty thousand pounds of wool produced annually in Persia, according to consular report, "one-third is used for knitted socks, saddle-bags, animal blankets and similar articles; another third for the production of rugs for domestic use; and the final third for the weaving of rugs for export to Europe and America." On the basis of known sales of wool and rugs this estimate should be doubled. Russia buys annually Khorassan wool to the value of two million dollars, and the United States annually about eight million dollars' worth of rugs, foreign valuation. Forty per cent of the latter, or more than three million dollars, is the estimated cost of the wool; ten per cent, the cost of the cotton; and fifty per cent, the cost of labor.

FIBRES AND DYES

Because Persia produces this ample supply it is not to be assumed that the peoples of rug-producing countries are clothed and carpeted with wool. On the river at Shanghai a tourist observed "a barge loaded with wool, with one leaking bale. Little handfuls of the precious commodity began to dot the crowded waters, and instantly half a dozen small boats, poled by women and girls, screaming with excitement, shot skilfully between the houseboats, and gave chase to desirable bits. Small children with long picks fished the trove treasure from the water, swearing volubly as other boats and other treasure seekers intercepted a desirable morsel. The water carefully squeezed out, the flotsam and jetsam were laid out to dry on little decks. Each of these women and children had risked life in this frenzied dart among the steam-craft after a few cents' worth of wool." Mighty is Asia in poverty.

Nevertheless, Asia is the mother of sheep and shepherds, and her flocks are numberless. "When the sun is half an hour high," writes Doughty, "the shepherd casts his mantle upon his shoulder, calls to the flock, and steps forth; and they, getting upon their knees and feet, troop out after him to the pasture. The goats and sheep feed forward with their loitering herdsman till toward noon. Then he calls in his scattered flocks, and if it be not the watering day, he leads them to shadow of rocks or some desert thorn; and there he milks a goat to his breakfast. The sheep hang their heads together, in the breathless heat; the goats couch by themselves; the herdsman stretches his idle length upon the soil to take his noonday slumber until the sunny hours be gone round to the half afternoon; then rising, he leads forth again to the pasture, till the going down of the sun, when he calls them and they follow.

"To every head of cattle the nomad give a certain name, and in every great mixed flock, if their herdsman, whose voice they know, call to any beast by name, it will look up. We sat one evening by Hamdy's fire, and Rubba, the sick shepherd, told me over the names

243

of the sheep and goats that stood by, or lay chawing their cuds about us. The droves when mingled at the drinking-places may be in this wise separated; the herdsmen, leading up from the water, call out their own by their names."*

The goats of Kashmir, Angora and Bokhara, famous the world over, also provide rug materials. The soft vest of the fleece is wool; the shaggy coat, hair. The wool is obtained by combing in the early spring, and the hair by shearing. The rugs of "Bokhara," so generally and correctly admired, contain both. The hair used for foundations and binding is unmistakable. Hair, however, is the essential material not of rugs but of tents.

Camel wool and hair range in color from light chestnut to chocolate, according to the age and breed of the animal from which it is procured. In hot countries the camel competes with the human native in nakedness, but in the high regions of Turkestan and China some ten pounds of fleece is obtained yearly from each beast. It ranks high among rug materials, and is growing scarce, partly because of change of fashion in rugs—the browns going into the discard—and partly because of the substitution of automobiles for the ancient "ship of the desert," in the area of former production.

Camels, goats and sheep together provide an astonishing supply of wool and hair having natural color suitable to the weaver's palette. Nomad weavers utilize this bounty to the utmost, and in natural shades of rufous, brown and gray create effects that win applause for genius unpossessed in the art of dyeing. Natural black, obtained from the despised black sheep, that for permanence no dye-master has ever equalled, is an illustration of nature's tantalizing superiority.

After wool and hair, the next most important substance in oriental rugs is cotton, which seems to have been cultivated first by the people of India. Herodotus says: "The extreme parts of the inhabited world

---

* C. M. Doughty, *Travels in Arabia Deserta*. Horace Liveright.

somehow possess the most excellent and wonderful products. In India certain wild trees bear wool instead of fruit, that in beauty and quality excels that of sheep; and the people make their clothing from these trees." Persia has cultivated cotton for centuries. The Moors are credited with carrying it into Spain. Thereafter, all Europe raised it.

Cotton fibre consists of innumerable vegetable hairs that under the microscope have the appearance of a twisted fire-hose. The twist is of utmost importance because, like the curl of wool, it facilitates spinning and multiplies strength. Length varies from half an inch to three inches, which necessitates blending, commonly six or eight of the thirteen grades being spun together. Much cotton spun by machinery in England has lately displaced hand-spun cotton in oriental rug weaving, and not disadvantageously. Because of its rough, hairy surface, cotton is easily dyed. But since it discards dye, when not adroitly handled, as readily as it absorbs it, and is lustreless compared with wool, its serviceability in rugs is confined almost wholly to use as warp and weft. When used undyed in rug surface, which is rare, it creates sharp contrast.

The erstwhile American impression that cotton is an inferior substitute in rugs, employed to save more valuable wool and hair, is contrary to fact. Equal in strength to wool of comparable grade, it has for use as foundation the great superiority that it neither shrinks nor expands with atmospheric change, and consequently keeps a flat rug surface. To distinguish between wool and cotton, if in doubt, apply a lighted match. Burnt wool creates an odor and leaves a deposit of carbon-beads. Cotton burns with a flash without odor or remaining ash.

Silk is the fairy thread that some post-diluvian Chinaman first, of all men, observed as an essence of substance suitable to the adornment of his lady. It is not a negligible fibre in oriental rugs, despite its insignificant quantity. It constitutes the cobweb foundation of an occasional wool-pile masterpiece, and is the surface material of the de luxe editions of rugs, which include those that Shah Abbas (Persia, 1600) had woven for the aggrandizement of his state, and for presentation, as special tokens of his favor, to European monarchs.

The story of silk and its dissemination is capably summarized by Gibbon: "I need not explain that silk is originally spun from the bowels of a caterpillar, and that it composes the golden tomb from whence a worm emerges in the form of a butterfly. Till the reign of Justinian, the silk-worms which feed on the leaves of the white mulberry-tree were confined to China; those of the pine, the oak and the ash were common in the forests, both of Asia and Europe; but as their education is more difficult, and their produce more uncertain, they were generally neglected. As silk became of indispensable use, the Emperor Justinian saw with concern that the Persians had occupied by land and sea the monopoly of this important supply, and that the wealth of his subjects was continually drained by a nation of enemies and idolaters.

"But two Persian monks had long resided in China, perhaps in the royal city of Nankin. Amidst their pious occupations, they viewed with a curious eye the common dress of the Chinese, the manufacture of silk, and the myriads of silk-worms, whose education, either on trees or in houses, had once been considered as the labor of queens. They soon discovered that it was impracticable to transport the short-lived insect, but that in the eggs a numerous progeny might be preserved and multiplied in a distant climate. Religion or interest had more power over the Persian monks than love of their country. After a long journey, they arrived at Constantinople, imparted their project to the Emperor, and were liberally encouraged by the gifts and promises of Justinian. They again entered China, deceived a jealous people by concealing the eggs of the silk-worm in a hollow cane, and returned in triumph with the spoils of the East. Under their direction, the eggs were hatched at the proper season by the artificial heat of dung; the worms were fed with mulberry leaves; they lived and labored in a foreign climate; a sufficient number of butterflies was saved to propagate the race, and trees were planted to supply the nourishment of the rising generation."

Silk is not a fibre of uniform grade, as people thrown off balance by a fine silk rug are wont to suppose, but a fibre of many grades. Wild and domesticated silk constitute the two grand divisions. Both bifurcate indefinitely and create so many qualities that the best silk rugs of Persia and China have little in common with their weedy relatives, and nothing but lustre in common with rugs composed of artificial silk and mercerized cotton.

In its natural state the fibre of the best silk is said to have strength equal to wire of similar diameter. Manipulation in spinning, dyeing and weaving probably reduces this strength by half; but half is strong enough for moderate service. Silk rugs are limited in usefulness chiefly by their inappropriateness for all but the most sumptuous purposes.

Mineral fibres are rare rug materials. During the sixteenth and seventeenth centuries, gold and silver thread was indispensable Asiatic fashion in clothing, trappings, hangings and floor coverings. It appears in silk and tapestry rugs of those eras. At an earlier period, jewels were woven into rugs for display of even greater wealth.

The labor of producing and collecting rug materials is followed by back- and arm-breaking processes in adapting them to use. The first is washing, which for fine results requires water of the utmost purity, such as is found in meadow-streams. Villages in Persia are famous for water that creates in wool softness like down; and other villages are infamous because of water full of alkali. Combined with washing is the task of removing burrs and other adhesions. Drying, often effected on a flat house-top, requires continuous attention—turning, opening, and careful timing of exposure—to avoid hardness. Then follows sorting for colors and qualities, and combining or carding the materials, or "testing" them with the cord of a heavy bow, into orderly arrangement for spinning. The primitive bows, mallets and combs used in these labors are heirlooms of awesome antiquity.

Spinning many fibres into thread is done by rolling them between thumb and fingers, between the palms of the hands, and between the palm of one hand and the thigh. To facilitate the latter process, fibres are attached to one end of a stick, considerably larger than a pencil, called a spindle, which is rolled between the thigh and the right palm until the twist is sufficient, when the thread is wound about the stick and the process repeated. Some spindles are weighted with a ball of clay, so they can be twirled; and others, among nomad tribes, consist of a suitable stone at the end of a strip of linen. The spindle antedates Homer.

No one knows when or where some rare oriental mechanical genius, tired of much rubbing and twisting, contrived the wheel and belt to turn the omnipresent spindle, plus a staff or distaff to hold the loose fibres. This simple tool, the spinning-wheel, which came from Asia into Europe about the time that Columbus discovered America, and subsequently migrated to New England, is the sole machine used in oriental rug manufacture, and not much used.

The last and only ubiquitous substance of oriental rugs is dye, a fascinating subject of interesting history. Pertinent to a comprehension of its importance are the following instructions given in the year 1579 by M. Richard Hackluit of the Middle Temple, London, to M. Morgan Hubblethorne, "Dier," sent into Persia by the Right Worshipfull Societie of Merchant Adventurers:

"For that England hath the best wool and cloth of the world, and for that the clothes of the realme have no good vent [sale], if good dying be not added; therefore it is much to be wished that the dying of forren countreyes were seene, to the end that art of dying may be brought into the Realme in greatest excellency.

"In Persia you shall finde carpets of course thrummed wooll, the best of the world, and escellently colored; these cities and towns you must repaire to, and you must use meanes to learne all the order of the dying of these thrummes, which are so dead [fast] as neither raine, wine nor yet vinegar can staine; and if you may attain to that cunning, you shall not need to feare dying of cloth.

"If any Dier of China, or of the East parts of the world, is to be found in Persia, acquaint yourselfe with him, and learne what you may of him.

"Returne home with you all the materials and substances that they die with all in Persia, that your company may see all. In some little pot in your lodging, I wish you to make daily trials in your arte, as you shall from time to time learne ought among them. Set down in writing whatsoever you shall learne from day to day, lest you should forget, or lest God should call you to his mercy; and by ech returne I wish you to send in writing whatsoever you have learned, or at least keep the same safe in your coffer, that come death or life your company may enjoy the things that you goe for, and not lose the charge and travel bestowed in this case.

"If before you returne you should procure a singular good workeman in the arte of carpet making, you should bring the arte into this Realme, and also thereby increase worke to your company."

The eminence of dye among the amenities of ancient life may be inferred from the value attached to the famous Tyrian purple pigment of the third century A.D., that had its source in shell-fish, and its use in coloring the robes of emperors, kings and chief magistrates. It sold for the equivalent of five thousand dollars per pound.

Dyeing, the chief source of rug beauty and of its fellowship with painting, is the process of subtracting color from one thing and adding it to another. It is color divorce and remarriage brought about by a liquid, usually just water. The water wins the dye away from the substance that contains it, and bestows it on the fibre that is to be made beautiful. The art of dyeing, consequently, is the art of color affinity.

To know color affinities the dyer must know the chemical substance of textile fibres; wool, cotton and silk require very different dyes and treatment. A dye that produces a rich color in wool will frequently only tint cotton; and incredible color variations result often from quality variations. For example, wool of different clips, dyed in the same pot, without alteration of the dye substance, will produce distinct bands of color in a rug in which the material is used separately. The resulting effect, called "Abrash," is highly esteemed by lovers of the beautiful, and equally contemned by patrons of uniformity. Exquisite shades of color are the results of infinitely blended dyes and specially created conditions.

Fastness of color depends upon strength of affinity. Oriental rug dyes are made fast, or as fast as talent can contrive, against the numerous chemicals contained in dust and mud, against the lime, sulphur and iron contained in water and soap, against humidity, and finally against light, all of which endeavor strenuously to induce the dye to elope. High humidity and strong sunlight that prevail in American store-windows, during summer months, are the greatest ravishers. Dampness infinitely magnifies the pull of light, and soon renders null and void the power of alum, sulphate of iron and tin, dates, raisins, tamarind, mango and pomegranate-rind to anchor color, that would stand like Gibraltar in dry Persia and India.

The dyes of oriental rugs, like the materials, are obtained from all kingdoms. The chief animal dyes are insect juices and sheep's blood. "The female members of the insect cochineal," says the oriental, "are gathered out of oak-trees, killed and dried to the number of fifty thousand to produce a pound of red dye." However wildly incredible, this is true. The female *Coccus cacti* is twice the size of the male and outnumbers him two hundred to one, which creates a "bag" ration of four hundred to one.

Vegetable dyes are obtained from the roots, bark, leaves, flowers and seeds of innumerable plants and trees, and even from the skins of fruits. The most important are indigo, whose juicy five-foot leaves are the chief source of blue; madder, whose roots are the origin of many reds; and the leaves of sumach and the stigmas of saffron that yield yellow.

The personal experience of a Persian boy with a Persian dyer on his native heath will disclose the practice that produced the famous colors of Persian rugs and took Dyer Hubblethorne, Englishman, to Persia in 1579:

"Austa Iskender, or Master Iskender, made dyeing a trade. He was skilled in the painstaking art, which demanded for the best results faultless vision, taste and a nicely timed immersion of the wool into the dye-pots. The house of the master dyer was easily distinguished in late summer and autumn; for many colored yarns would be hung out to dry on his roof in the clear sunlight. The hands of the austa himself were likewise an advertisement of his trade, since they were deeply stained with dyes of all colors. The small boys of the village, and I among them, used to watch him at work in his yard. Propped on big stones, between which the fire crackled, his great dye-pots bubbled merrily, and into the pots the austa dipped his yarns, watching them anxiously all the while. He would let us have the scraps with which he tested the dyes, and we used them for slings.

"In the springtime the austa gathered the herbs and plants to make his precious dyes. Often we little boys trudged at his heels over the hillside and along the river-bank. He gathered the buckthorn berries, which yielded a clear green dye, and the saffron-plant for its yellow color, and the leaves of the thorny henna-tree for deeper shades of orange. He dug the roots of the madder-plant, which made all shades of red and pink and, mixed with green walnut-hulls, produced brown shades. The wild indigo-plant gave blue dyes. In the very early spring the austa would search for a peculiar insect, a species of cochineal, that feeds on the oak-tree at that season, and from this he made a crimson dye.

"But the master dyer would not let us watch him when he prepared his dyes. That was his secret, how to mix the plant juices, the dried bodies of insects, the juices of tree bark, the blood of animals and the crushed petals and leaves of flowers to obtain his marvellous colors. His secrets had been handed down to him by generations of master dyers, and they were jealously guarded." *

It is astonishing how the modern magic called science provides equivalents for almost everything, including the old oriental dyes. Almost exactly one hundred years ago a German chemist, experimenting with coal-tar, obtained a product that gave a bright blue coloration under the influence of bleaching powder. Neglected for twenty-two years, this discovery became of practical value in 1856 when Sir W. H. Perkin produced the first dye of science. Thereafter the whole gamut of "synthetic dyes" was developed in rapid succession. Thick black coal-tar, secured by the distillation of bituminous coal in the production of illuminating-gas, is the Pandora box of modern dyestuffs.

The materials of all antique oriental rugs are dyed with vegetable pigments. The materials of all new oriental rugs, except those employed by isolated weavers, eventually, in all probability, will be dyed with the new alizarin. Is this a calamity or a blessing? The impartial and authoritative opinion of Mr. A. F. Kendrick, keeper of the De-

* Y. B. Mirza, *Asia Magazine*, December, 1929.

partment of Textiles at The Victoria and Albert Museum, London, expressed in his excellent work, *Handwoven Carpets, Oriental and European*, is as follows:

"The worthlessness of the early aniline dyes for producing permanent colors led to a prejudice against all synthetic dyes, of which the aniline colors are but one small branch,—a prejudice which is very slow to disappear. Yet the chemists have made immense strides. The chemical nature of many of the vegetable dyestuffs, including indigo and madder, has been discovered. It is now possible to make them synthetically on a commercial scale, and the product is every bit as good as the original. Most important is the fact that new dyes are being discovered which surpass the older ones in point of resistance to light and other disintegrating influences. In spite of these facts, possibly in ignorance of them, it is very common still for writers to use the arguments levelled against the aniline dyes of more than forty years ago.

"It would be hard," Mr. Kendrick continues, "to point out any great branch of the artistic handicrafts now practised in the East with better results than are obtained in oriental rugs. It may be justly claimed that surprisingly beautiful modern carpets may still be bought at trifling cost."

In an important matter, such as this, numerous expert witnesses may be necessary to establish the truth of an opinion; but for most persons the foregoing statement should close the discussion. The new dye wins because it is the chemical equivalent of the old, possessed of the incalculable advantage of seven-league boots. Instantly it is in the dyer's hand, and vast labors and areas devoted to the cultivation of dye substances are released to other purpose. Interestingly enough, a very similar transition occurred years ago in the art of painting. Leonardo da Vinci ground and mixed his own pigments; Whistler and Sargent squeezed tubes.

ORIENTAL RUGS AND CARPETS

Can the same favorable report be made of the chemical treatment of oriental rugs, attendant feature of this dye revolution, by which positively homely new rugs are magically provided with angelic countenances? In place of "yes" or "no," let us consider the facts.

Doubtless a few superb rugs—the very great—were born beautiful; beyond a doubt, most attained beauty. Beauty of rug color is, to an extent far beyond public belief, the product of faded dyes. Seemingly, rugs positively hate ugly color. Not scores but hundreds of thousands of rugs make daily progress toward "the mellow beauty of ground in the woods this Autumn afternoon." Chemical washing of rugs is a series of processes that facilitates this transformation. A bandit rug by conversion becomes a saintly adornment, free from natural odor, germs, larvæ; immune from moths; all of which is salutary. The high sheen so offensive to delicate sensibilities is not of long duration; wear and dust soon destroy it.

Born in a small tub in the basement of a rug-store on lower Broadway, New York, approximately thirty years ago, this innovation has become an American institution employing hundreds of workers. The little tub, filled with chlorine solution, soon was superseded by many large tubs, supplemented by rinsing-drums using thousands of gallons of water, drying-wheels and drying-rooms, cylindrical combing-machines, and finally by employees applying to weak spots and improvable areas alizarin pigments, only one of which, the blue, is ordinarily subject to disturbance by water, air or saliva. Experience proves that chemically treated rugs give general satisfaction. Nevertheless, there is a shadow in the life of instant beauty.

The shadow does not greatly trouble, because through recurring similar experience the American is almost impervious to it. It is added cost, observed by the observing in increased expenditure and reduced service. Making rugs beautiful adds about twenty per cent to initial outlay, and impairs endurance in about the same proportion. The processes of nature are leisurely, and the works of nature marvellously enduring. Impatient man always pays for his expedition; and it is fair to add that he should.

Any assumption that the chemical washing of new oriental rugs is now a fixed process, a cosmetic forever to be applied to the face of the art, is mistaken. Every year reveals a little more natural beauty and a little less of the artificial variety. Constant experiment, more exacting requirements and closer supervision in the East have, it is claimed, recently created rugs that require only plain water-washing with a special oil soap, to be charming. Relentless pressure to reduce cost favors the return to natural effects.

Change of dye and cosmetic treatment of the youth of rugs, covering a period of forty years, is the greatest physical change that has taken place in the oriental rug industry in its entire history. Revolutionary as it appears, it is but the appointment of a Western member to the Cabinet of rugs compared to the change in the Presidency of the art that gradual replacement of oriental by occidental patronage, over a period of three hundred years, has effected.

If Maksoud of Kashan were to-day to return to Persia, an oriental Rip Van Winkle, he would refuse to believe his senses. In his day, rugs were a monarchical art of the highest importance, rug artists honored decorators to a brilliant court, rug dyers superior persons constituting a class apart, and rug patrons among the upper classes were people of refined and exacting taste with inherited rug knowledge. In our day, Persia and the other rug-weaving nations of Asia export only the scant remains of great art and new decorative accessories to Western art; and all the important buyers are Westerners humanly wanting the best that can be produced, but too often lacking the trained taste, knowledge and experience to demand and secure it.

When, as should happen through long-continued patronage, the present deficiencies of the Western patron are made up, and converted into a virtuosity equal to his vast material resources and expenditure, another great change will occur; namely, the re-creation of rugs that are genuine works of art. The event is reasonable. Having saved to the East the practice of rugs, which he found dying on its feet; having added to its resources a new dye and other improvements still to be reported; and having by enthusiastic patronage assumed virtually the entire direction of production, there is every reason to believe that the new patron will carry through, and that rug art worthy of the best traditions of the East and of the high aspirations of the West will result.

Obstacles to the attainment of this goal and to the creation of thoroughly commendable rugs of little cost, an equally worthy ambition, are both numerous and formidable. As they are discussed at length in an appendix to the *Quarterly Report of the Administrator General of the Finances of Persia*, 1926, and are matters far better revealed and repaired than concealed and condoned, only good can issue from further open conference.

Listed first is the use, too frequently, of wool that is known as "dead," removed from slaughtered animals by the application of labor-saving lime, which closes the scales of the wool and renders it brittle and insusceptible to the absorption of dye. The result is lustreless, antique-looking new rugs, and rugs containing streaks of color which can be obliterated only by chemical washing and the application of new pigment. Streaks result also from the practice of mixing worsted with wool, from compounding wools of different ages and colors, from urine-stains and even from knots in skeins. The importance of streaks as a detriment to art is here assumed to be acknowledged. Actually, the effect of streaks must be individually estimated. Streaks can be artistic and are so esteemed when created by the weavers of Kurdistan. Want of streaks and flat uniformity of background is one of the symptoms of the living death that besets machine-made rugs. Concerning the use of dead wool and lime, however, there can be but one opinion.

The practice of chopping wool into short lengths to facilitate spinning is next brought under indictment as creating loss of weight in washing and loss of years in rug service. Already this practice, which prevailed mostly in the Meshed district, has been discontinued by the Western manufacturers, whose example will eventually be followed, however reluctantly, by native weavers. If not, Western publicity will discourage the practice.

Concerning dyes, the Report says: "The demand is for carpets in fast half-tones and soft blends. To meet this requirement the American manufacturers in Persia are using the best and most expensive dyes in order to obtain these soft colors and thus obviate the expenditure involved in washing and painting the carpets in America." This sentence might advantageously be re-read. Recommendation is made, however, for government installation of steam-dyeing plants in important rug centres, in order that independent weavers may be able readily to secure good dyeing at low cost. Exclusive use of India-stone indigo for blue, and of madder-root not less than three years old for red, is insisted upon. Comparatively, over the years, cheap modern blue dye is considered fugitive, and red obtained from juvenile madder-root is placed in the same category.

Important as these matters are, they are minor and remediable compared to the task involved in bringing order out of the chaos into which the primitive contract system of home weaving has precipitated the industry. But again this is another story.

CHAPTER XIII

THE WEAVER'S WORK

"I hear the weaving of a hidden loom.
  I see the weaver! Fair and lightly made,
  Like a young ash-tree in a garden dim.
  She sets the threads with hands, oh, little hands
  That are more deft than spiders when they spin."

In the essay "On the Pleasures of Painting," Hazlitt remarks that painting requires not strong, but continued and steady, exertion of muscular power; that painting for a whole morning gives one as excellent an appetite for one's dinner as old Abraham Tucker acquired for his by riding over Banstead Downs. The kind of painting referred to is not laborious white-washing, such as Tom Sawyer shrewdly capitalized, but the delicate, fine art of painting, which many people think the product of retirement and relaxation.

Hard, sustained physical effort is the silent unnamed partner in every accomplishment of fine art, and in none more than in oriental rugs, which are labor personified. Sometimes it is carried on from sunrise till long after sunset, even to fifteen and sixteen hours a day, and from childhood to feeblest old age. Always it is the labor of Hercules performed by women and girls, sometimes by boys and men, with little respite and absolutely no complaint, in order that life, which each accounts a blessing, may be sustained. American labor, by com-

258

parison, knows nothing whatever either of labor or poverty, but enjoys the luxury of oriental monarchs. Fortunate America, that acquires everything, and in the acquisition of oriental rugs often provides the bread that sustains hopeful oriental life!

The labor of oriental rugs is performed on huge "embroidery" frames called looms. Personally, I think of looms as harps, because they are strung like harps, and when the taut strings are released by the strong fingers of vigorous weavers, they sing the joy of release.

The loom consists of two upright timbers, set four to twenty or more feet apart, according to the width of the rug to be woven, joined top and bottom by rigid or rollable cross-timbers. This frame is set upright in the ground, leaned against a wall, or infrequently laid flat on the earth. In the case of a rigid upright loom the weavers work from a scaffolding, on which they ascend sometimes twenty and even thirty feet. Usually, however, the cross-timbers are rollers, and the line of work is lowered to the level of the hands of the weaver, who sits upon a bench; and the completed weaving is wound upon the lower timber.

The first labor of weaving is the stringing of the loom with strands of cotton yarn, wool, hair or silk. A harp has nineteen strings to each foot of width. A loom is laced with ninety-six to seven hundred and twenty strings to each foot of width, or from nine hundred to six thousand five hundred strings to the usual width of nine feet. The length of this vast skein, in a rug measuring nine by fifteen feet, is never less than two and one-half miles, and may be twenty miles; in common quality it is eight miles. Sometimes the skein is arranged and counted on bamboo poles, and subsequently slipped upon the loom. Frequently it is wound upon the loom from spools, which are raised and lowered times beyond number. The weaving is done on this yarn, which is now called warp, and the manner of it depends on the kind of weaving which is undertaken.

ORIENTAL RUGS AND CARPETS

The earliest kind of oriental rug weaving, known as khilim and tapestry, is still much in vogue in the Orient because of useful and decorative qualities, small bulk and light weight. Essentially, it is a bedspread, used over thin cotton mattresses. It is also a travel weaving, used for the hanging and furnishing of tents, and for the bundling of every manner of personal possession. To make it, the weaver inserts strands of dyed yarn crosswise through the warp, with change of color to effect a design. The result is a rug of flat surface, front and back alike, ordinarily shot with narrow openings where the colors break, although sometimes compact and almost water-proof, the various colors woven separately in narrow parallel bands.

The finest khilims are woven to a density of one hundred cross-yarns or shoots to the perpendicular inch, which means seven thousand two hundred of them to the common length of six feet. Prayer rugs of this exquisite fineness often contain a considerable quantity of gold and silver thread. The rugs of Babylon and Persepolis are their remote great-grandparents and all European tapestries their first cousins.

The second type of weaving, sometimes called Kashmir, is personally associated with a travelled American. "I have just returned from Kashmir," he said, "and now appreciate my old Kashmir rug." He thought rug names and places of origin synonymous terms, which commonly is not so. Kashmir, in this instance, means not *place* of weaving, but *similar manner* of weaving. The dyed yarn is run above four warp strings, back under two, over four and back under two, twenty or more to the vertical inch, with binding weft between each pair. The surface thus created is flat, as in a khilim, but gross and grained, and the under-surface is a mass of loose yarn ends that act as a pad.

Excellently woven in engaging mosaic design and years ago in beautiful colors, but lacking sheen and brilliance, which are peremptory American requirements, this weaving is now out of fashion

—a striking example of unappreciated merit. Its source is the Caucasus, and its proper name Soumak, an abbreviation of Shemakha, which is one of the several towns, including Derbend, in which it is woven.

The third and final form of weaving is the rug of pile surface, the lustrous rug of the market. The pile or nap is the product ordinarily of wool yarn, hand-knotted literally millions of times into miles of warp. The surface of a common-grade Persian rug, ten feet wide by fifteen feet long, is composed of yarn that rises from one and a half million knots. The luxuriant pile of an average quality Kerman rug of the same dimension is rooted in approximately five million knots; and modern Kashan rugs of this dimension embody eight million knots. If, as is commonly remarked, a million of anything transcends human comprehension, the five hundred million to one or more billion knots, that compose the surface of the oriental rugs in a typical stock, represent surely a body of work that rivals the miracle of the pyramids.

To tie a knot a weaver, quicker than it can be told, passes an end of dyed yarn between two adjacent warp strings, around one and over and under the other, snaps the two loops into the line of weaving, and severs the projecting yarn with the stroke of a knife; or passes the yarn end between two warp, around one and merely under the other. This operation is repeated by exceedingly expert and ambitious weavers as many as twelve thousand times a day. Maximum speed is approximately fifteen knots a minute, which sustained is nine hundred knots an hour.

Knots are tied in rows, one to each pair of strings, and bound in horizontal ranks by a cross yarn, called weft, which is run through the warp strings above each row of knots. Compactness is attained by hammering down the rows as each is completed. Infrequently, four to six rows of knots will be tied before a weft is inserted, and again as many as six wefts will be used to each row of knots. The former procedure sacrifices strength to fineness, the latter fineness to strength.

The knots are of two kinds, single and double, the former called Persian or Sehna, and the latter Turkish or Ghiordes. Unfortunately these names are misleading and inadequate. They are misleading because they create the impression that Persian rugs are woven in the Persian knot, which is true and false. Of fifty-seven varieties, more or less, varying with the decades, only eight are now woven in the Persian knot, namely: Saruk, Saraband, Sehna, Shiraz, Kashan, Kerman, Khorassan, Feraghan. Key them "SKF," an abbreviation of Sehna (Persian) Knots Finest. With rare exceptions all other Persian varieties, approximately fifty in number, are tied in the "Turkish" knot. The names are inadequate because they leave out of account the character of the knotting practised in the other rug-weaving countries.

The Turkish or Ghiordes knot is the Near East Knot, the custom and practice of weavers west of the Caspian Sea. The Persian or Sehna knot, similarly, is the Far East Knot, because it is the knot used by weavers east of the Caspian. The weavers of Persia, midway between, practise both knots. Speculation as to the ancient source of these knots, and as to how the cleavage of Asia by them came about, is instantly enveloped in utter darkness.

Theoretically, the identification of these two knots should be about as simple as the recognition of four-in-hand and cross-bow ties. Seemingly, the only requirement is a modicum of haberdashery intelligence. In practice, however, the knotting is often so fine as to baffle the eye, and make necessary the use of magnifying-glass, pincers and patience. As lack of knot-acquaintance has cost occasional monetary loss through purchase of machine-made copies, attention to the following explanation may not be without future compensation.

The knot of an oriental rug "goes through." To prove this, locate a lonely point of color on the face of a rug and then find its base immediately beneath on the back. Additionally, the appearance of the knot on the back resembles two miniature rings or collars unless, as in rugs of exceeding fineness, one is tucked beneath the other. This statement applies equally to Near East and Far East knots, because both are tied on a pair of strings. Identification of knot must be made from the face of the weaving.

If this is sought, open the pile along any line of knots, and explore the depths for collars; for identification is a game of "Collar, collar, what kind of collar, large or small?" The collar of the Near East knot covers two strings, and therefore is wide, and should be easily seen. The collar of the Far East knot encircles only one string, is half-size and, in fine weaving, is buried from sight. A row of Near East collars usually presents the appearance of a solid chain of uniform links; a similar row of Far East collars, that of a chain with every other link omitted. Also an exposed warp string, in the latter weaving, is identifying.

Because most finely woven rugs are produced in the Far East or "Persian" knot, amateurs assume that the "Turkish" or Near East knot is inferior. It is inferior if fineness is the end and aim of weaving, in which case we are using some of our fine rugs wrong side up. It is not inferior if comparison is made with the "Persian" knot employed in China, which is coarse. The truth is that fineness of weave is largely the product of fineness of materials; that rug masterpieces are produced in both knots; and that the buyer who knows discriminates against neither.

Commonly the number of knots varies from sixty-four to four hundred in every square inch of rug surface. To compute them, lay a ruler along a line of weaving, count the "collars" within the space of an inch, and multiply the number counted by the number of lines of weaving in a vertical inch. Knots that are wider than they are high are most numerous in the vertical inch, and create borders wider at the sides than at the ends. Average weaving ranges from sixty-four to one hundred knots to the square inch; fine weaving from one hundred and forty-four to two hundred and twenty-five knots. Rarely is any advantage gained, artistic or otherwise, by increasing the knotting to four hundred and sixty to the square inch, which is the fineness of some modern Kashans.

Theoretically the backs of rugs, consisting only of warp, weft and loops of knots, the latter unaltered in appearance by variation of kind, should look much alike. In reality, there is a possible total of some ten thousand different effects, as a little computation will prove. The number of warp to the inch commonly varies from eight to forty, making a possible difference of thirty-two. The position of warp may be flat, double or intermediate; total difference, three. The number of weft to the inch varies from four to forty, making a possible difference of thirty-six. The position of weft, depending on tension, is straight, circular and semi-circular; total difference, three. Actually, there are not ten thousand or even one thousand variations in the surfaces of the backs; and of whatever number there is, the "rug man" uses for identification only a few dozen.

Surface yarn inclines toward the bottom of the weaving because the yarn of both knots rises to the surface below the collars. When the "Persian" knot is used, the yarn inclines also toward the right or left side—toward the right when the knot is tied on the left warp, and toward the left when tied on the right warp. One should be wary, however, of naming the knot solely from the inclination of the pile, for the pile of the "Turkish" knot also slopes sidewise when the warp is crowded.

This flow of surface material occasions the surprising variations of tint and shade with every change of angle at which oriental rugs are seen. One way, light is absorbed; the other way, reflected. There is no correct way to lay a rug, except the way it looks best; and usually it looks better one way than the other; and better at night than during the day, or the reverse.

The "miracle" of oriental weaving, however, is not the hand-tying of millions of knots, as is commonly asserted, but the expression of a masterly design through the medium of millions of knots. Any one can sit on a piano keyboard and create a sensation, but few can strike a million notes in such succession and accord as to produce a sonata.

One of five methods is employed to translate a small colored rug sketch into a rug of much greater dimension. The Persian method is to make a large drawing of a small section of an accepted pattern, rule it into squares each representing a square foot of the finished weaving, subdivide each square into one hundred and forty-four squares, each representing a square inch, and these again into sixty or four hundred squares, each colored to represent a particular knot. This herculean task of draftsmanship the weavers follow with pains-taking care. Chess, played on sixty-four squares, suggests a kinder-garten pastime, compared with a game that has been played, in a single rug, on thirty-five million squares. The Persians also create small sample weavings, approximately three by five feet in size, called "vagirehs," for the weavers to copy. "Vagirehs" are common prac-tice for intricate corners and oft-repeated sections. To copy a rug, weavers everywhere follow the knotting of the original as revealed on the underside.

The India method of design translation is to employ "ta'lem" or design-writers and readers. The "ta'lem" writer is the unfortunate scribe who must determine the color of each and every knot required in each and every line of weaving, and write it all down for the reader to communicate to the weavers. Usually, too, the writing must be done in hieroglyphics, as a protection against theft. Consider the task involved in indicating on paper the color of even the million knots

265

that constitute the workmanship of a common nine-by-twelve rug. Consider also the reading of the foregoing composition to four and twenty weavers sitting at a loom. It is an astonishing performance.

The Chinese method is either to create a full-size paper model of the intended rug for the weavers to copy, or to trace the design with colored crayons on the set-up warp. This latter method is practicable for rugs of large pattern and open areas.

Rough shearing of the surface of all rugs proceeds apace with the weaving, but always final clipping is left for shearers seated at a bench. It was the fashion of manufacturers until recently to trim the pile short, even on coarse rugs, which need long overlapping yarn. Short pile clarifies the design and gives to the uninitiated the impression of fine texture. Unfortunately it is unenduring under rough usage, and lustreless in appearance. To-day durability is a most important consideration, and medium-brilliant pile the vogue.

It is unfortunate that the oriental shears that so evenly trim the surface of rugs cannot also remove undesired lengths and widths, so that every oriental rug might magically fit whatever place it magically transforms through its art; for original fitness in size is an obstinate American requirement, its roots fast in the belief that the alteration of hand-made things is a matter of doubtful and immoral accomplishment. Yet every oriental rug size can be altered, and the alteration made without injury to appearance or impairment of strength. Every knot is independent of every other knot, firm on its own private foundation. To reduce size is merely to sever and rebind elements as independent as the leaves of a book.

Only time, the universal reaper, is a ruthless rug-surgeon. Still, its abrasions, cuts and holes the rug-doctor can heal. Appraisal of damage is best made on the underside. Holes are due mostly to accidental perforation, only occasionally to rotting of warp and weft from long-continued dampness. They are local defects, not difficult to remedy, or defects indicative of serious structural weakness. The exact state of affairs is determined by grasping the back with two hands, as one grasps a stick, and endeavoring to fracture it. If warp and weft are everywhere easily broken, the foundation obviously is rotten, unless the severity of the strain is disproportionate to the natural and required strength of the material. Delicate foundations of one or two ply yarn are not to be expected to withstand equal strain with heavy multiple-strand yarn. Even weak foundations hold indefinitely when undisturbed, and break mostly in cleaning.

Niccolæ Manucci, the Venetian, travelling through Persia during the reign of Shah Abbas, 1586–1629, records in an interesting tale how this great monarch cleverly solved the mystery of papers abstracted from a bag which some one had cut open and rewoven without obvious repair. "Secretly he burnt a hole in a carpet which he prized so much that he seldom used it to sit upon. The employee who had charge of it, discovering the burn, was in great fear lest the king might order his hand to be cut off for taking so little care of so precious an article. Taking possession of the carpet, he removed it in secret to his own house, and diligently searched for a workman who could mend it so perfectly that no one could see that it had been repaired. Through God's will it so happened that he got hold of the very workman who had rewoven the bag.

"After some days the king asked for his favorite carpet. When it was brought and spread out, the king took his seat upon it, and without attracting attention searched for anything in the nature of a darn. In spite of its having been repaired, he could not find the place. Thereupon the king ordered the employee to produce in his presence the workman who had darned the hole; and the man being produced the king asked: 'How much did you get for mending this bag?' "

The mending of holes calls either for the re-establishment of warp and the tying of new knots, or the insertion of patches, which often are so well chosen and so finely mortised as to escape further attention and regret. Cuts often are sewn to twice their original strength, never again to be observed. Cut and abrasion of the under loops of knots, due to moths and washing treatments, can be serious matters. Nevertheless, knots wholly eaten away below have long remained otherwise intact, even under hard service, because of compactness.

Careful examination of the surface of oriental rugs discloses variations from a perfect level, like valleys rising to undulations of hilly country. As a rule, new rugs have smooth, baby faces, and old rugs scarred, characterful faces. The latter are the product both of wear and of dye-corrosion. Some dyes, in the course of time, cut the pile of rugs as naturally and effectively as men carve wood and chisel stone. Secondary greens, browns and blacks, raising reds, blues and yellows to brilliant eminence upon their shoulders, seem actually to possess artistic intelligence. Whether or not clever dye-masters intentionally created this faculty and result, the effects are magnificent, except to the uninitiated who rate only newness grand.

At what point does uneven surface impair value? At the point where the fine old color begins to disappear in areas too large to be restored. Sometimes wear is obvious and value not only unimpaired but increased by other considerations. Rugs that display "grain" or pebble effect should be provided with buffers, thick but inexpensive pads now at last extensively advertised, or used for beauty of color on plain carpeting. With such assistance, they will give joy and service to further generations.

The factors that contribute to wear are traffic, dirt, moths, dye-corrosion and accidental injuries. Except in public places, under desks and dining-tables, traffic corrosion is far overestimated. To be sure, shoes exert more thrust than bare feet and slippers. Nevertheless, a machine ingeniously contrived to record foot-pounds punishment registered two hundred thousand blows without producing apparent wear on an uncushioned carpet, and six hundred thousand blows without obvious wear on a cushioned carpet.

The great factors in rug destruction are the twin house-wreckers, dirt and dust, that both lodge and board free of charge in rug-wool's millions of scales. Dirt eats wool more deliberately but as certainly as a saw eats wood, and during damp seasons makes an accomplice of mold, that given sufficient time completes the wreck. That wool wilfully should attract and, if permitted, contentedly live with such company is the chief defect of its character. Hard snow is a magnificent cleanser, and a bath each alternate spring a sure riddance of defilement.

Moths, the "tailor's only friends," are heartless rakers of oriental rugs. By comparison, the scythe of time is a zephyr, soothing and considerate. Only silk rugs and rugs chemically treated are immune, and only soap-washing dislodges eggs and larvæ. The cost of boarding moths is high, at fifty to sixty dollars per week for repairs. Whether knowledge of this increased cost prompted our scientists in the Department of Agriculture to discover a new fumigant five times more poisonous to the pest than any hitherto known is not asserted. We are told only that three parts by volume of ethylene dichloride and one part carbon tetrachloride, exposed in liquid form in a dish, set in closets or tight containers for a few days, will positively terminate the lives of the festive revellers assembled there.

Physical imperfections in oriental rugs, requiring repair, and lack of suitable dimensions in particular rugs, requiring alteration in size, have been amazingly well tolerated by Western buyers accustomed to the physical perfection of products created by machines. Certainly this phenomenon is a compliment to American intelligence, a proof of innate taste for art. For hand-labor, no matter how efficient, is not the major key to oriental rugs; nor is the true value of its product determined by turning over a rug corner and heralding the result with expressions of astonishment. True value depends not upon display of craftsmanship, but upon display of art.

The rule by which to measure craftsmanship was recorded by Sir John Chardin about the year 1675: "The Persian Rule to know good carpets and to Rate them by, is to lay their Thumb on the edge of the carpet and to tell the Threads in a Thumb's breadth, for the more there are, the dearer the Work is. The most Threads there are, commonly, in an Inch breadth is 14 or 15."

CHAPTER XIV

THE SIGNIFICANCE OF NAMES

In that incomparable history, *The Decline and Fall of the Roman Empire*, we read that Augustus was sensible that mankind is governed by names. In the pursuit of oriental rugs the free people of the Mighty West defer to rug names as to the names of monarchs, unless perchance discovery has been made that they are only partial equivalents of the things which they represent, or altogether meaningless, like other proper names. Augustus was not always august. Similarly, Mahal rugs are Arak, Muskabad, Sultanabad, Savalan, Buluk, Mumtaz and Extra Modern Persian in a market that disregards the extraneous and concerns itself exclusively with substance, which is value.

To the ancient Greeks and Romans all oriental rugs were Babylonian. To Venetians and Genoese, trading with Turks, and to Americans of the Revolutionary War period, they were "Turkey carpets." Not until the nineteenth century were the rugs of Persia and the Caucasus semi-accurately designated as such in Europe and America. Trade revealed modern rug sources, and scholarship in art ancient sources. Trade and scholarship combined probably know to-day twenty-five per cent of the essential facts which twenty-five centuries of time, five million square miles of territory, and untold millions of weavers might reveal.

ORIENTAL RUGS AND CARPETS

Place of weaving is the desideratum in rug names because locality, no matter how it has been overrun and wholly altered, is the least transient of mental hitching-posts. In consequence a Persian rug may be designated as "Iran," which is Persia's other name, if nothing more of its source is known or believed. It may be assigned to the province of Azerbijan, if it is thought to come from northwestern Persia. More specifically it may be called Herez, after a district of Azerbijan; or Gorevan, after a village of the Herez district.

Locality names are used continually to designate both actual and theoretic rug grades. For example, Mehreban and Dargazin specify two of the better grades of Hamadan weavings; lesser qualities are Koumbat and Nobaran. But the rug-buyer who assumes that these names are as specific as Rolls Royce, Hudson and Ford should be placed under observation.

The true story of a reputable dealer, who did not know the specific name of the rug that he was endeavoring to sell, and who applied to it a spontaneous designation, because he considered the generic name too commonplace, is memorable, even unforgetable. He called the rug Dasgah, which gave delight because it was not to be found in rug books, and must therefore indicate a rare species. Nemesis, as usual, was fast on the heel of inadvertence. The customer returned indignant. "You gave me to understand that a Dasgah rug was a rare weaving. I find that all oriental rugs are Dasgah. A weaver tells me that the name means only, *loom!*"

Many honest but mistaken locality names are in every-day use. Most Kermanshah rugs do not originate in the important wool market of that name in western Persia. Lavher rugs do not come from Lavher, because there is no such place. Nor do Ispahan rugs come from Ispahan, Polonaise rugs from Poland, Damascus rugs from Damascus, Mosul rugs from Mosul, Bokhara rugs from Bokhara, Samarkand rugs from Samarkand, Kandahar rugs from Kandahar, or

Beluchistan rugs from Beluchistan, except rarely. In one way or another these names became rug burrs that no amount of beating and brooming would dislodge.

Sometimes physical phenomena of a locality become, directly or otherwise, the sources of rug names. "Elvand" rugs of Hamadan bear the name of the second largest mountain of Persia. Markets give name to vast miscellaneous assortments of rugs. Hamadan is an excellent illustration, because the varieties of Hamadan weaves are legion. In one instance a remote and unaccustomed place of export contributed a name to this interesting vocabulary. During the World War Persian rugs could not be sent Westward through Trebizond and Constantinople. In consequence the rugs of Kabutrahang were despatched through Karachi, an Indian port on the Arabian Sea, and subsequently were billed and sold as Karachi rugs.

Place of reputed use has conferred names on the most costly and the least expensive of rugs, antique Ispahans and modern Mosuls. Still, in present-day usage, Ispahan, as applied to rugs, need mean neither place of use nor that of weaving, but only style or type. For not many antique Ispahans were used in Ispahan; and modern Ispahans are woven at Meshed. Also Ispahan to-day is the market for the nomad rugs of the Bakhtiari tribes. Mosul rugs got their name from their purchase by Mosul merchants in Hamadan for use in trade at Mosul and Bagdad. Similar rugs of cheap quality are woven in quantities at Zenjan, a town midway between Tabriz and Teheran.

So much for rug names derived from cities, villages, districts and provinces. What now of the names of rugs that have no single birthplace, that are begun on lowlands, laboriously amplified on ever-ascending hills, and brought to completion in rich mountain pastures? Such rugs are named after Kurds, Bakhtiari, Yuruks, Kazaks, Tekkes and other nomads whose abiding place is "not the soil, but the camp." To this group belong the names of rugs woven by non-conforming

273

religionists, such as the Zoroastrians, whose remnants are scattered throughout Persia and India, and by the Bektash sect of Turkish Mohammedans.

When neither birthplace nor parents are known, rug children are named after the period of their advent. Antique Chinese rugs on this account are called Ming, K'ang H'si and Ch'ien L'ung, which are the names of dynasties and rulers. Antique Persian rugs of a certain type are designated as Shah Abbas. Certain antique Turkish rugs are called Holbein, and certain Spanish rugs of oriental technique are called Gothic and Renaissance.

The number of oriental rug names derived from design is legion. Garden and tree rugs, animal and hunting rugs, dragon and bird rugs, landscape and marine rugs, scholar's and traveller's rugs, triclinium and compartment rugs are names more descriptive than are the better-established names, Herati, Guli Hinnai and Mina Khani. One fascinating compound, Hispano-Moresque, was thought to designate both place and art, until discovery was made that the rugs were woven in Turkey.

The source and meaning of design names is frequently obscure. Herati is the possessive case of Herat. Mina Khani is a possessive case, meaning the beautiful object or jewel (Mina) of a Khan. Khan is both a title and a family name. Guli Hinnai is the flower of the henna plant, which is woven in rows, like stalks of planted corn. Sib or "apple" becomes Sibi, meaning apple-shape, when applied to pattern of apple resemblance; and Toranj, meaning orange, is the weaver's pet name for medallions.

Still more interesting are the names of designs that perpetuate the names of special patrons of the art. Common pattern was an aversion to kings and grandees, and special personal design, that the commonalty would not dare use, an enhancement of self-esteem and reputation. Hence the Sardar pattern of rectilinear arabesques called "lightning," created for the Sardar, Marshal or General of the district of Azerbijan; the Zellé-Sultan pattern of vases and nightingales, created for the Shadow of the Sultan, namely the son of Nasir-u-Din Shah, Governor of Ispahan; and the Mustafi pattern of graceful arabesques and garlanded rose-clusters, probably inspired by the design of an Aubusson carpet, woven for the Grand Mustafi or Secretary of State under Nasir-u-Din Shah. As no useful purpose would be served by translating the special names of the various parts of each design, the same are herewith mercifully omitted. Nevertheless, each portion of pattern has a name.

The color, soul and spirit of rugs play strangely no part in rug nomenclature. Arcadius, Emperor of the East, clothed in robes of silk embroidered with the figures of golden dragons, "had a chariot whose purple curtains, snowy carpet and precious stones glittered to the motion of the carriage." The only snowy carpets that have gained recognition are the antique "Ivory Rugs" of Asia Minor.

The materials of oriental rugs, on the other hand, supply names that teem with suggestion and instruction. Silk and metal rugs, tokens of wealth, are the pride of owners from Constantinople to Pekin. India rugs of especially fine goat-wool are "Pashmina," which strictly means only wooly or shaggy, for *pashm* is wool. Persian rugs woven on machine-twisted cotton thread obtained from Manchester, England, are called in Sultanabad, their principal market, "nakh-farang," which means "thread [warp] European," in contrast to "nakh-irani" or "thread Persian." We call nakh-farang rugs Saruk, a designation which the Persian would fail to understand, for only a small quantity of rugs come from the insignificant village of that name. The centre of "Saruk" weaving is the district of Sultanabad or Arak.

The most interesting of many names indicating quality is Turkbaff, meaning "Turk weave," applied to one of the best products of the looms of Meshed, Persia. The natural inference would be that the rugs

275

are woven by Turks. Instead, they are woven by Turkish-speaking Persians who came to Meshed from Tabriz. Other common "baffs" are Armenibaffs, "weavings of the Armenians," and Makhmarbaffs, meaning "velvet weaves."

Actual use, as distinguished from locality of use, supplies such intriguing names as Palace and Court rugs, Mosque and Temple rugs. It provides also Namazlik, or Namazi, meaning prayer rug; Odjaklik, meaning hearth rug; Hammamlik, meaning bath rug; and Yesteklik, or Poshti, meaning pillow rug. Of these varieties, only Mosque carpets and prayer rugs are distinguished by invariable design.

Size and shape rank after locality and design as the source of rug names. Dozars, sold everywhere, are rugs two zars long. A zar is a Persian "yard," varying in different localities but theoretically equivalent to three feet five inches. Dozars, therefore, are rugs six feet ten inches. A Zaronim, meaning one and one-half zars, is a rug five feet in length. A Kharak, meaning donkey-cover, is a rug approximately four feet long, and a Sedjadeh, meaning to bow or kneel, a rug approximately four by six to seven feet. Kazakjeh means a small Kazak.

Sarandaz means head-cover and specifies the rug which is laid at the head of the room that serves both as living- and dining-room. The Turkish name for head rug is Khali, which we convert into an Hibernian Kelley and mistakenly apply to the "Mian-farsh" or centre floor-covering. Kenareh (Kinari), meaning border, are the long, narrow rugs which we use for passages and stairs, and which the Persians lay on either side of the Mian-farsh. In combination, Sarandaz, Mian-farsh and Kenareh, sometimes woven together, constitute a triclinium, which is a Greek word meaning three couches. At meals the oriental host and chief guests sit at the head of the room on the Sarandaz, the lesser persons along the sides, on the Kenareh. This became a Roman custom. In the period of Commodus the triclinium consisted of a square-topped table and three square sofas about it.

THE SIGNIFICANCE OF NAMES

Trade names number somewhat more than a corporal's guard, but command only a corporal's authority. This latter circumstance, due to limited capital and negligible certification, is unfortunate, because trade-named rugs represent a laudable attempt to produce and market thoroughly good rugs.

Trade names are largely old names, contractions and compounded syllables, adapted to new purposes. Laristan, a province of southern Persia, which produced a scanty fringe of Shiraz weaving, is the trade name of a fine quality India rug woven in the city of Amritsar. Seljuk, lifted out of Turkish history, and Dinar, famous gold coin of the caliphs of Damascus, are the names of oriental rugs produced in Greece. Zarif, a contraction of Zarifali, meaning refinement, is the name of a modern Asia Minor rug. Shahristan, land of the Shah, is the designation for well-known rugs of fine Persian character woven by Persian-trained weavers in Bulgaria. The first modern Chinese rug to deploy its own banner bears the name Ta Shansi—Ta meaning great and Shansi a province—the source of its wool.

Trade names, like other rug names, suffer continuous substitution. Laristan rugs of India, in other hands than the producers, are sometimes sold as Shahristan, Iranshah and Bharistan, the names of competing weaves. In one instance, the name Astrakan, district of Southern Russia, was used to cover a wholesale transaction in this merchandise. Objection elicits the inquiry: "What's the difference?" The theory is that these rugs are all good or of a general character of excellence.

The trade vernacular is replete with substitute names that probably mean something to the man who uses them, but little to any one else. In place of Karabagh we hear Houdja, Georgian and Jabraeel; Kabistan becomes Hila and Magun; Baku is Souraghan; Kazak is Akstava; Bijar is Mellakhir. Gulistan, common name for flower-garden, is applied to rugs woven near Kashan, "at a place where roses bloom profusely." When, finally, special manner of handling rugs creates a rug name, the topic is near an end. Luleh in Persian means tube or cylinder. Rugs so heavy in construction as to require to be rolled, because folding in the usual manner is impossible or injurious, became known as Luleh. Bijar weavings are Luleh.

Oriental rug names are derived, therefore, from people and period, from design, material and workmanship, from use, size and shape, and from trade and special circumstance. Comparison of their number and accuracy with the paucity of similar designation for the hand-made hook rugs of New England will enhance appreciation of whatever truth there is in them, and disarm criticism.

A venerable dealer in hook rugs, derived from an area of Maine that would serve only as a foot-stool to the continent of the oriental rug weaver, confessed that the only advantage his long experience gave him in the matter of names was that he could distinguish the product of a single town! "As for the rest, I couldn't tell where they come from, unless I saw them carried out of the houses."

CONCLUSION

CAPITULATION of the position and influence of oriental rugs among people of culture in the Occident discloses a well-earned victory for Asia in one of the noblest arts of peace.

In the sixteenth and the seventeenth centuries, the people of Europe, particularly of Russia, Italy, Spain and the Netherlands, discovered in the rugs upon which the Oriental had lavished centuries of talent and effort an art of floor-covering adequate to the requirements of courts, churches, palaces and residences upon which they, in similar creative mood, had lavished countless lives and substance. Prior to this period, which instituted another era of culture, European floors were bare or covered with homespun fabric which the Oriental had surpassed even in the days of Babylon.

Subsequently, every effort of the European to equal the foreign art of rugs, whether by hand or machine process, was abortive of attainment even remotely approaching a competitive result. The default lay in promiscuous effort. Rugs, like every form of art, exact a blood-sworn allegiance from their subjects, generation after generation, even to the day of judgment. Such dedication, which Asia had made in the cradle, Europe could not make, so full was its world of a million other things.

As for America, the colonists at Jamestown were making cabins out of forests when the last of the great patrons of rugs, Shah Abbas, received the embassies of the kings of Europe upon the court carpets of Ispahan. America's contribution to the art has been patronage, without which, possibly, this particular expression of creative talent would have perished.

INDEX

INDEX

Cæsar, 128
Cairo, carpet industry in, 25, 153
Caliphate, Western, 228
Camel, wool and hair of, 244
Camel-foot, gul, 197
Cappadocia, 4
Careri, Doctor Gemelli, 138
Carthage, rugs of, 4
Cartouche rugs, *see* Compartment rugs
Caucasus, rugs of, 95, 174 ff.; description and historical sketch of, 170 ff.; Persian influence in, 175
Ceramics, Spanish, 230-231
Chaldiran, battle of, 150
Chardin, Sir John, 93; quoted, 81, 270
Chewsurs, tribe of, 173
Chichi rugs, 179
Ch'ien L'ung rugs, 216
Chinchilla, 232
Chin-chou Fu, 216
China, Arabs settle in, 18; influence of, in Persia, 30; palmette design from, 62; religions of, 205-207; list of dynasties, 221
Chinese art, in Persia, 73, 75; in ancient rugs of Asia Minor, 146; in Turkish rugs, 156; in Caucasian rugs, 176, 177
Chinese rugs, 203 ff.; age of art, 204; designs, 62, 73, 204, 206 ff., 210-212, 219-221; effect of religion on, 204 ff.; deities, portrayed in, 207; ceremonial and kong, 214; uses of, 214; travel, 214; variety in, 215; source of, 216; modern, 216, 217; weaving of, identical with that of Central Asia, 218; significance of names, 274
Chosroes I, 7, 13
Chosroes II, 14
Chwang, Yuan, 143, 144
Clavijo, Ruy Gonzalez de, 30; quoted, 156
Coal-tar, used in making dyes, 252
Coleridge, his *Kubla Kahn*, 146
Color, Turanian red, 193; Tekke, 197; natural black, 244; fastness of, 250
Compartment rugs, 74, 80
Confucius, 205
Constable, John, 75
Constantinople, 148-150; imperial looms in, 154; mosque and fountains built in, 157; modern rugs of, 168
Contarini, M. Ambrogio, 36
Coptic rugs, 26, 233
Cordova, 228, 229
Coronation rug, 47
Cotton, importance of, in rugs, 244, 245
Crane, in Chinese symbols, 209
Crusades, the, 27, 144
Ctesiphon, palace at, 84
Cuenca, 236
"Current Events" rug, 140
Cyrus the Great, 2, 7, 10, 11, 120
Czartoryski, Prince, 83

Daghestan, rugs, 171, 178; tribes of, 173
Dai, Kurban, 105
Damascus, imperial rugs ascribed to, 154
Darabdscherd rugs, 40
Dass, Amar, 142
Date-tree, 72

David, Gerard, 146
d'Honnicort, Vilard, 88
de Keyser, Thomas, 157
de Vos, Cornelius, 157
Delhi, 49; throne, 129, 130
Demirdji, rugs of, 165
Derbend rugs, 178; principal source of Soumak rugs, 179
Dergesin rugs, 40
Designs, Greek and Romans, 6; floral, 6, 18, 57, 58, 72, 93, 140, 179, 181, 212-216; animal, 18, 72; mosaic pavement, 25; garden rug, 58; Chinese, 62, 73, 206 ff., 219-221; cross-current, 62; stream of, 62; star, 63, 64, 147, 148; curved and lobed, 64; law against figural, 69-71; prismatic, 79; inspired by mural decorations, 85, 86, largest Persian, 97; Bijar and Kerman ompared, 101; Sehna, 103; Herati, 103, 110, 119, 124, 126, 127, 181; Mina Khani, 111; all-over, 124; pear, 125; "Shah Abbas," 126; Rawar, 127; geometric, 6, 146, 147, 177, 194-199, 202, 210; Egyptian, in Turkish weavings, 152, 154; arabesque, 147; diamond, 194, 195, 199, 202; tree of life, 194, 201, 202; dog, 198; "bird" and "cloud-globe," 156; Katchli, 201; Punjdeh, 201; method of translation, 265, 266; rug names derived from, 274, 275; Sardar, 274, 275; Mustafi, 275
Dido, tribe of, 173
Dimand, M. S., 84
Dinar rugs, 267
Djangur, 108
Dorosch rugs, 112, 118
Dozars, 276
Dragon rugs, Armenian, 175; controversy about origin of, 177
Du Mans, Raphael, 77
Dyes, introduction of Western, 109; of ancient times, 248, 249; value of Tyrian purple, 249; process of making, 249-252; durability of, 250; sources of, 250; synthetic, 252, 253; pile of rugs cut by, 268

East India Company first, 135, 141
Ecbatana, 120
Edwards, A. Cecil, 103
Egypt, weavers of, 5; rug art of, 25, 26, 151; becomes Turkish province, 151
Elephant rug, Widener's, 140
Elizabeth, Queen, 46, 157
Elizabethpol, 95
Ersari rugs, 198, 199, 201
Ertoghrul, 144

Fars, 24
Farsbaff rugs, 112-114
Fath Ali Shah, 51
Fathpur, 132, 133
Feraghan rugs, 118, 123, 124; copied, 105; sold as Khorassans, 117; attributed to Joshaghan, 126
Festival, court, for weighing of monarch, 134
Fethy Bey, 45
Fiber, cotton, 245; mineral, 247
Fil-Pa octagon, the, 199
Floral-stem carpets, 62

284

INDEX

INDEX

286

INDEX

Ninghsiafu, 215
Nomad rugs, 95
North Africa, Egyptian art in rugs of, 26
Numaniyah, 24

Obdolowean, King, 180
Octagon design, 194-199, 202
Odjaklik, hearth rug, 276
Olearius, Adam, quoted, 46, 64-67, 77, 86, 241
Omar, 16, 19, 20
Oriental Carpet Manufacturers, Ltd., 142
Oriental Carpets Merchants, Ltd., 108
Ornamentation, elaborate, of Shiraz rugs, 96
Othman, 20, 145
Ovid, quoted, 4

Pahlavi, Riza Shah, 51
Palestrina, mosaic floor of, 6
Palmette, the, in Ispahans, 61, 75, 76; chief ornament of Herat rugs, 62; Chinese, 64, 75; in Caucasian rugs, 176
Pamir Kirghiz tribes, mats used by, 1
Parvis, 14
Pashm, 193
Pashmina rugs, 265
Paterna, 230
Peacock rug, in Vienna Collection, 139
Peacock Throne, the, 139
Pekin, 216
Peony, Chinese symbol, 75, 212
Pergamum, see Bergama
Perkin, Sir W. H., 252
Persepolis, architecture of, 84
Persia, Babylonian arts appropriated by 2, 3, 7, 11; the centre of life of weaving, 9; religion of, 9, 10; increment of Greek art with that of, 12, 13, 18; Arab conquest of, 16-19; passion play in, 21; Tartar conquest of, 26, 27; Chinese art in, 30; period most productive of great rugs, 39, 40; first ambassadors to courts of Europe, 44, 45; loss of status as a nation, 51; hunting in, 64, 68; art of, 84; law against Western dyes, 109; Meshed religious centre of, 115; heights and depths of rug art of, 116; cession of Caucasus provinces to Russia, 172; influence of, on Caucasian rug art, 175, 176, 179
Persian rugs, connecting link between early and late, 18; gardens source of, 53 ff.; medallion, 63, 150; summary of, 88-90; comparison of designs of Indian and, 140, 141; Indian imitations of, 142; called Turkish, 153; Caucasian copies of, 175; both Sehna and Ghiordes knotting used in, 262; sold as Karachis, 273
Petag, 106
Peter the Great, 48, 68, 172
Phœnic, or love-pheasant, emblem, 209
Philadelphus, Ptolemy, 3
Phrygia, rugs of, 4
Phutchaghtchi, the, 95
Po Chu-I, 203
Poetry, in Persian rugs, 87
Polish silk rugs, 83
Polonaise rugs, 44, 79-83; silk-and-metal, 61; three groups of, 82; specimens of, 83; silk, 126; Khotan silk compared to, 226
Pontus, 4

Portuguese carpets, 61
Potteries, of Sultanabad, 73
Prayer rugs, Persian, 61, 84; Ghiordes, 106, 165; of Moguls, 141; Turkish, 158 ff.; characterization of, 160; Melas, Kir-Shehr, Mujur, Konia, and Anatolian, 165; Western Turkestan, 201, 202; Chinese, 208; Chinese Turkestan, 224; with gold and silver thread, 260
Pushkin, quoted, 171

Quyundjik, wall reliefs found at, 1

Rameses II, rugs depicted in palace of, 2
Rawar, rug fame of, 94
Reliefs, wall, found at Quyundjik, and Khorsabad, 1, 2
Religion, influence of, on rugs, 10, 11, 201, 204 ff.; Persia's centre of, 115
Resht, 123
Reyes de Taifas, 229
Riegl, 177
Riza Shah, rugs being made for, 113
Roe, Sir Thomas, 134
Rome, weaving brought from Greece, 5, 6
Roxalana, 153
"Royal Bakharas," 196
Ruby, of Aurung-Zeb, 50
Rugs, beginning of, 1 ff.; plain, 4; method of early weaving depicted on vases, 4; of ancient rules, 9 ff., 130, 137 ff., 146 ff.; "Spring of Chosroes," 13, 17; sources of, 32, 33, 59 ff., 77, 78, 82, 83, 104, 123, 139, 176, 216; gifts of Persians, 44-47, 79, 80; chronology of, 52; most marvellous of existing, 68; nomad, 95; finest single collection, 139; used as tablecloths, 147; wall, 192; pillow, 192; chemical washing of, 254, 255; future of art of, 256; streaks in, 256; variations of tint and shade in, 264; alteration of size, 266; mending of, 266, 267; uneven surface, 268; destruction of, 268, 269; significance of names, 271 ff.; trade names, 277
Rugs, silk, Kashan, 64; masterpiece in Austrian State, 68; and metal, 80, 81; Polish, 83; India, 141; cheap, 169; Khotan, 225, 226
Rukh, Shah, 31, 32, 50, 60, 62
Russia, sovereignty in Caucasus, 170, 172; Western Turkestan territory of, 190, 191; wool purchased annually by, 242

Saddle rugs, of Sehna, 103
Saduch, Mahomed, 121
Safavi dynasty, the, 37; Chinese art in rugs of, 73
Safi, Shah, 46, 47, 64, 81
Safi, Sheik, 105
Sahib, Sheik, 142
Sakkara, discoveries in tombs at, 2
Saladin, 25
Salonika, 272
Salors, the, 188, 195, 197
Saman carpets, 25
Samarkand rugs, lost art of, 222; Chinese Turkestans called, 222; Chinese art in, 223
Saraband rugs, 119, 123, 125
Sarandaz, meaning of name, 276
Sardar pattern, 274, 275

INDEX

INDEX

DATE DUE

#47-0108 Peel Off Pressure Sensitive